IMAGES
of America

HISTORIC EAGLE LAKE

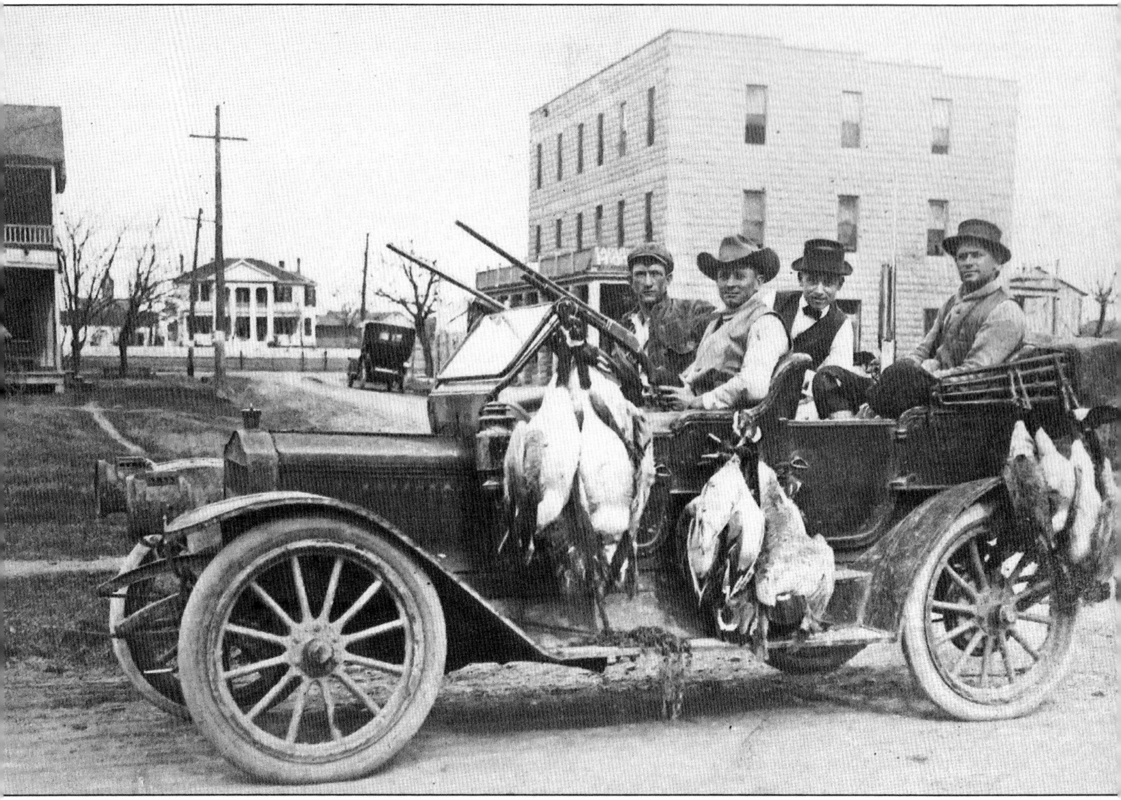

On the Cover: Duck and goose hunting around Eagle Lake has been popular since the late 1800s. The successful hunters in this c. 1920 image show their trophies across from the train station near the Brown/Heiney/Eagle Hotel. They are (front seat) Jim Douglas (left) and driver W.T. "Duke" Eggers; (standing) Ray Munn Fitzgerald; and (backseat) Howard Strahan. The J.W. McCarty home is in the background, with Belle Nail's rooming house on the left. (Courtesy of the Eula and David Wintermann Library and the Nesbitt Memorial Library.)

IMAGES
of America

HISTORIC EAGLE LAKE

Sandra C. Thomas, PhD
for the Prairie Edge Museum

ARCADIA
PUBLISHING

ISBN 978-0-7385-9512-2

Published by Arcadia Publishing
Charleston, South Carolina

Printed in the United States of America

Library of Congress Control Number: 2012936589

For all general information, please contact Arcadia Publishing:
Telephone 843-853-2070
Fax 843-853-0044
E-mail sales@arcadiapublishing.com
For customer service and orders:
Toll-Free 1-888-313-2665

Visit us on the Internet at www.arcadiapublishing.com

The Historic Eagle Lake *photographic history book is dedicated to the citizens of Eagle Lake, to those who have grown up here, to those who have returned, and to all who remember the richness of this small town in Texas. The tireless men and women who came here as pioneers left their legacies by establishing a successful farming, ranching, and business community at the edge of the great coastal prairie. This book is also dedicated to their pioneering spirit.* Historic Eagle Lake *was written to benefit the Prairie Edge Museum. The museum's role in the collection and safekeeping of local history—and in the education and enjoyment of its visitors as they take a walk through history—is a community treasure to be preserved.*

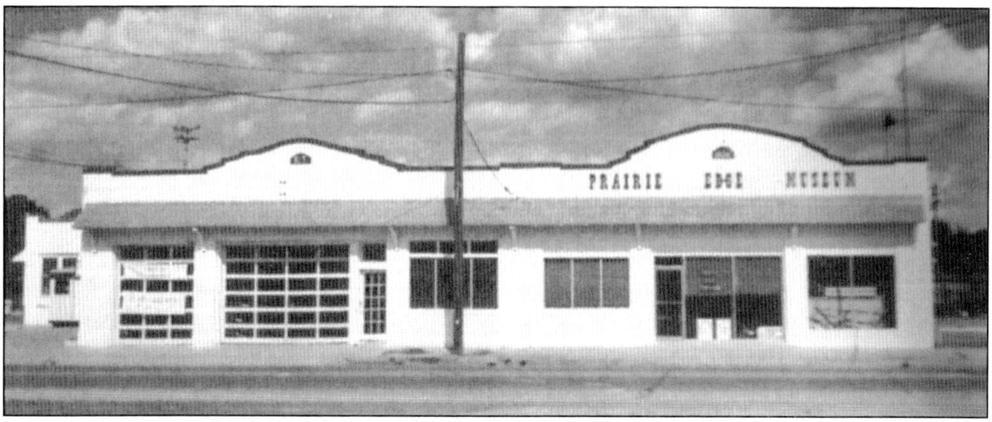

Contents

ACKNOWLEDGMENTS

Historic Eagle Lake has been made possible through the contributions and assistance of many who have preserved historic documents and photographs for study and research purposes. The Eula and David Wintermann Library and the assistance of librarian Vicki Powers, the library staff, and archivists Harry and Nancy Anderson have been invaluable to the conducting of research. With the longstanding and valuable support of the Wintermann Foundation, the Eagle Lake Study Club is commended for its continued leadership and community support to secure the outreach and contents of the library. Appreciation goes to the Nesbitt Memorial Library Archives for its sustained support of the growing collections of Colorado County documents and historical data that provide an excellent county resource. Thanks go to the *Eagle Lake Headlight*, whose staffers' reporting and archives are necessary to researching Eagle Lake history. The work of the Colorado County Historical Commission and the Eagle Lake Preservation Alliance, their contributions to preserving town treasures and historic buildings, and their work to create markers for the town's historic sites are essential to the community.

Special appreciation goes to all who contribute time and effort to preserving local history and supporting our museums and libraries through volunteerism, donations, stories, oral histories, family papers, artifacts, and photographs. Recognition goes to the Prairie Edge Museum, its volunteers and supporters, and to Christine Owen, Martin Herman, and Morris Howland for their dedication. Thanks go to Ken Stavinoha for his preservation of railroad history and his excellent Eagle Lake Depot museum, which has brought credit to the community. To all the teachers and students who will create the next generation of people to keep our local history in trust for the future, we acknowledge your importance. Special thanks go to Ernest Mae Seaholm.

Finally, a personal tribute goes to William H. Harrison Sr. and his wife, Roseanne, whose pioneering spirits and work in the research and preservation of local history are unparalleled. William Harrison's books, writing, research, and photography have given us countless resources for study, which have opened the doors to our understanding and appreciation of our rich past. The Harrisons' leadership and efforts in the establishment and continuation of the Prairie Edge Museum, and in compiling and publishing *A History of Eagle Lake, Texas*, have provided invaluable resources to the community.

Unless otherwise indicated, all photographs are courtesy of the Eula and David Wintermann Library and the Nesbitt Memorial Library. *A History of Eagle Lake, Texas* and *Colorado County Chronicles* (Volumes I and II) have also been invaluable resources, as was the Prairie Edge Museum.

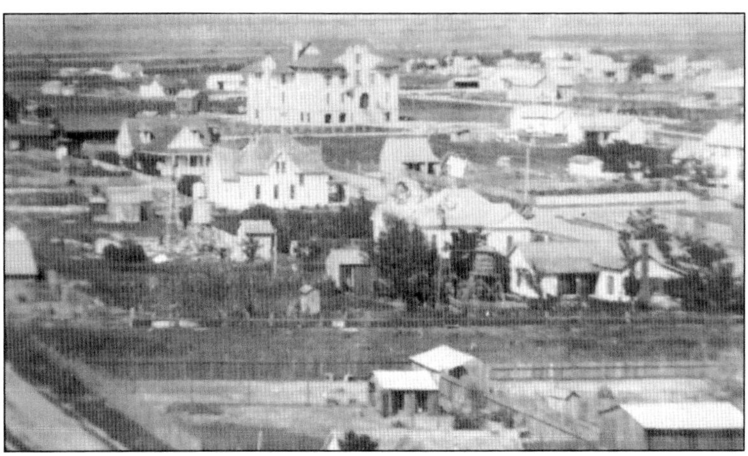

The third Eagle Lake Public School, on Prairie Street, is an imposing structure in this c. 1911 aerial view of the town of Eagle Lake. The school and grounds provided a center for community activity.

INTRODUCTION

Pioneer and "Father of Texas" Stephen F. Austin brought the first 300 settlers to the area under an agreement with Mexico to promote the colonization of these vast lands, soon to become the Republic of Texas. He sought an area rich with rivers and fertile soil amenable to the cultivation of crops and the raising of livestock. He and two scouts, James Beard and William Little, set out to explore the land around the Colorado River to see if the area was suitable for the livelihoods of the colonizing families. The scouts set up camp on the shores of Eagle Lake, which they named for a fallen eagle, and deemed the area acceptable for settlement. Thus, Eagle Lake and Colorado County were part of Austin's first colony.

The lake area was once inhabited by the Karankawa Indians, who fished for subsistence. While Austin himself settled some 20 miles away, near the Brazos River in San Felipe, pioneer families soon began to come to the Eagle Lake area. Among the early families were the Matthewses, who came in 1828, and later the Thatchers and Montgomerys, who settled in 1836 just below Eagle Lake in the fertile bottomlands of the Colorado River on the Nelson and Cartwright Leagues.

The original grant to Austin was approved on April 23, 1823; other adventurous pioneers, mostly from Virginia and Tennessee, began to move in and build log cabins south of the lake between 1827 and 1836. Lands on the east side of the Colorado were claimed by such daring pioneers as Rawson Alley, Thomas Cartwright, John Nelson, and Patrick Reels. In 1831, Reels was granted the land surrounding the lake.

Pioneer Gamaliel Good built a log home on the shores of Eagle Lake in 1855, and it became a stagecoach stop between Matagorda and San Felipe. Good helped to plat the town of Eagle Lake around the third stop on the Buffalo Bayou, Brazos, and Colorado Railway, the first operating railroad in Texas. Eagle Lake's history as a settlement began when the railway's first locomotive, the *General Sherman*, arrived in 1859. The town was officially incorporated in 1888.

Since that time, Eagle Lake has been the center of a rich agricultural and cattle-farming area. After the Civil War, Capt. William Dunovant began growing sugarcane and cotton and built a large sugar mill called the Lakeside Sugar Refinery; it was among the largest and finest in the South. Dunovant founded a town called Lakeside near the shores of Eagle Lake. There, he operated a cotton gin and the first rice mill west of Beaumont, with large plantations of cotton and sugarcane in the Matthews and Bonus areas. In 1898, he was the first to grow rice in the area, and he had the first electric pumping plant in Eagle Lake. Dunovant partnered with William T. Eldridge, another entrepreneur, to establish—with other farming interests—the Cane Belt Railroad, which eventually went from Sealy to Matagorda. Eldridge later became a founding partner in the Imperial Sugar Company.

Through the years, Eagle Lake has had many leaders in business and agriculture. To lure settlers, land developers partnered with railroads in the Midwest to bring potential farmers and pioneers to the area. The prairie farmlands were enticing; but until rice was under cultivation with successful irrigation systems, many farmers endured financial hardship and returned to the Midwest. Cotton and corn have also been leading crops in the Eagle Lake area. The rich bottomland and the vast prairie have proved to be excellent farmlands. The cattle and gravel industries also helped make Eagle Lake a railroad shipping center.

The lake provided water for cultivation and was also a popular recreational spot for visitors during the early 1900s. A large lake pavilion was the center of social activity, and trains from Houston would bring weekend guests to enjoy boating, fishing, sailing, picnics, and dancing. In the 1920s, the lake was leased as a private hunting club (with primarily Houston-based members) called the Eagle Lake Rod & Gun Club.

Because it is along the waterfowl flyway from Canada to Mexico and South America, Eagle Lake has continued to be a popular area for goose and duck hunting. It has earned its nickname as the "Goose Hunting Capital of the World."

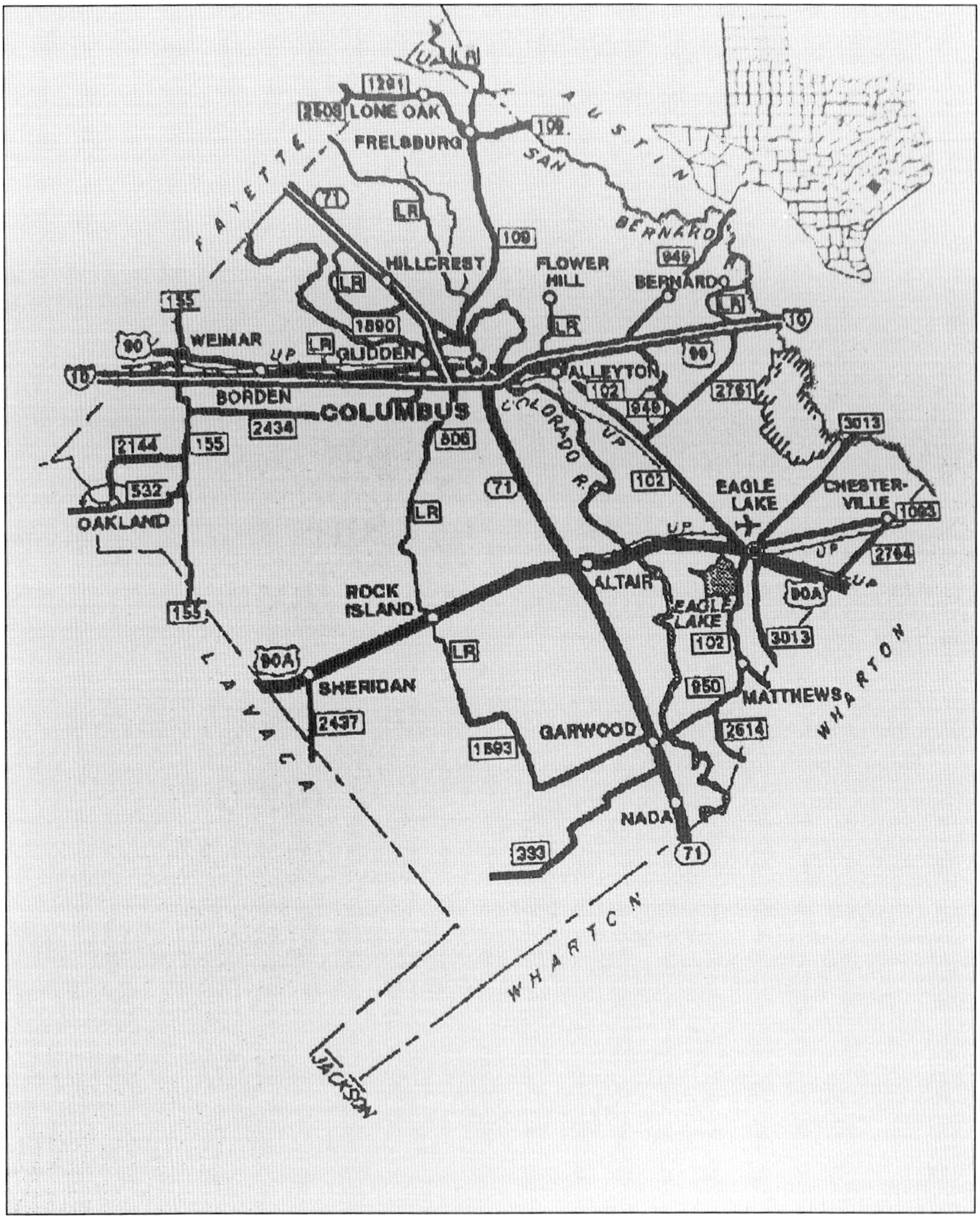

Colorado County is located in South Central Texas, about 60 miles from the Gulf of Mexico. The county was named for the Colorado River, with neighboring Columbus, 16 miles away, as the county seat. Eagle Lake is only six miles from the Colorado River and lies at the edge of a vast prairie. The county was settled by Stephen F. Austin and members of his "Old Three Hundred," who were among the original colonists in 1821. Among the earliest families to settle in the area were the Matthewses, who claimed land in the Nelson League in 1828; the Thatchers and the Montgomerys, who settled on the Cartwright League in 1836; the Angus McNeils, who were in the Ross survey in 1844; and the C.C. Herberts, who bought land in the McNair survey in 1845. The county, one of the original Texas counties, was organized in 1837.

One

Pioneers and Early History

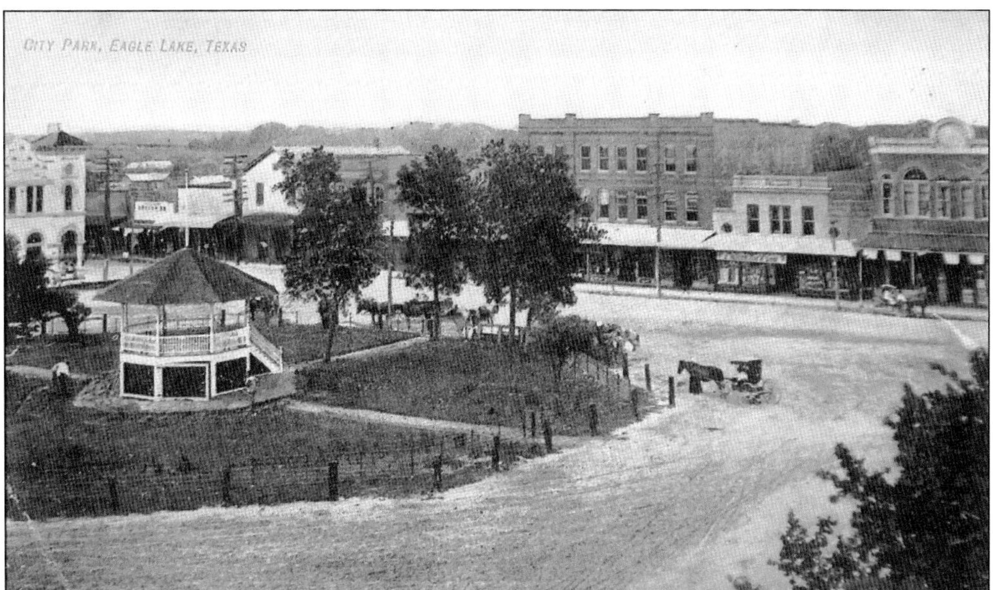

Located in the heart of the main square and across from the train station, the Eagle Lake Bandstand became the symbol of the town. It was the centralized locale for concerts, trade days, entertainment, and social activities. In the early days, livestock—which roamed freely—would bed down on the sand near the water trough in the city square.

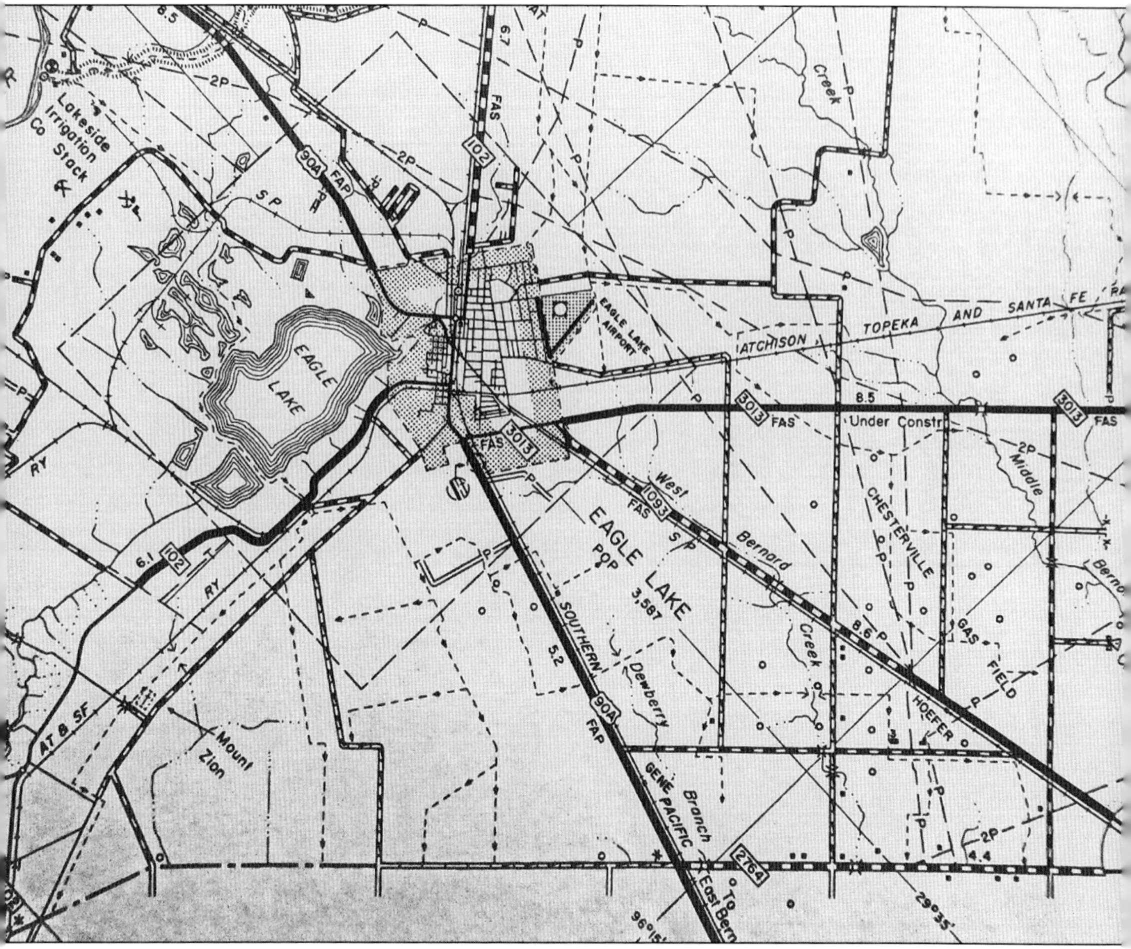

This map of Eagle Lake and adjoining farmlands shows the railroads, the lake, the city plat, the airport, the irrigation plant, and highways and farm roads coming into the city. The town was first platted in 1857 as a stop for the Buffalo Bayou, Brazos, and Colorado (BBB&C) Railway; it became the third stop on the railroad in 1859. Early roads were primitive and almost impassible in rain. As an early railroad stop, it soon became an active shipping center for gravel, livestock, and farm produce. Surrounded by rich farmlands, Eagle Lake has been an agricultural center, ranching area, and a notable producer of oil, gas, sand, and gravel.

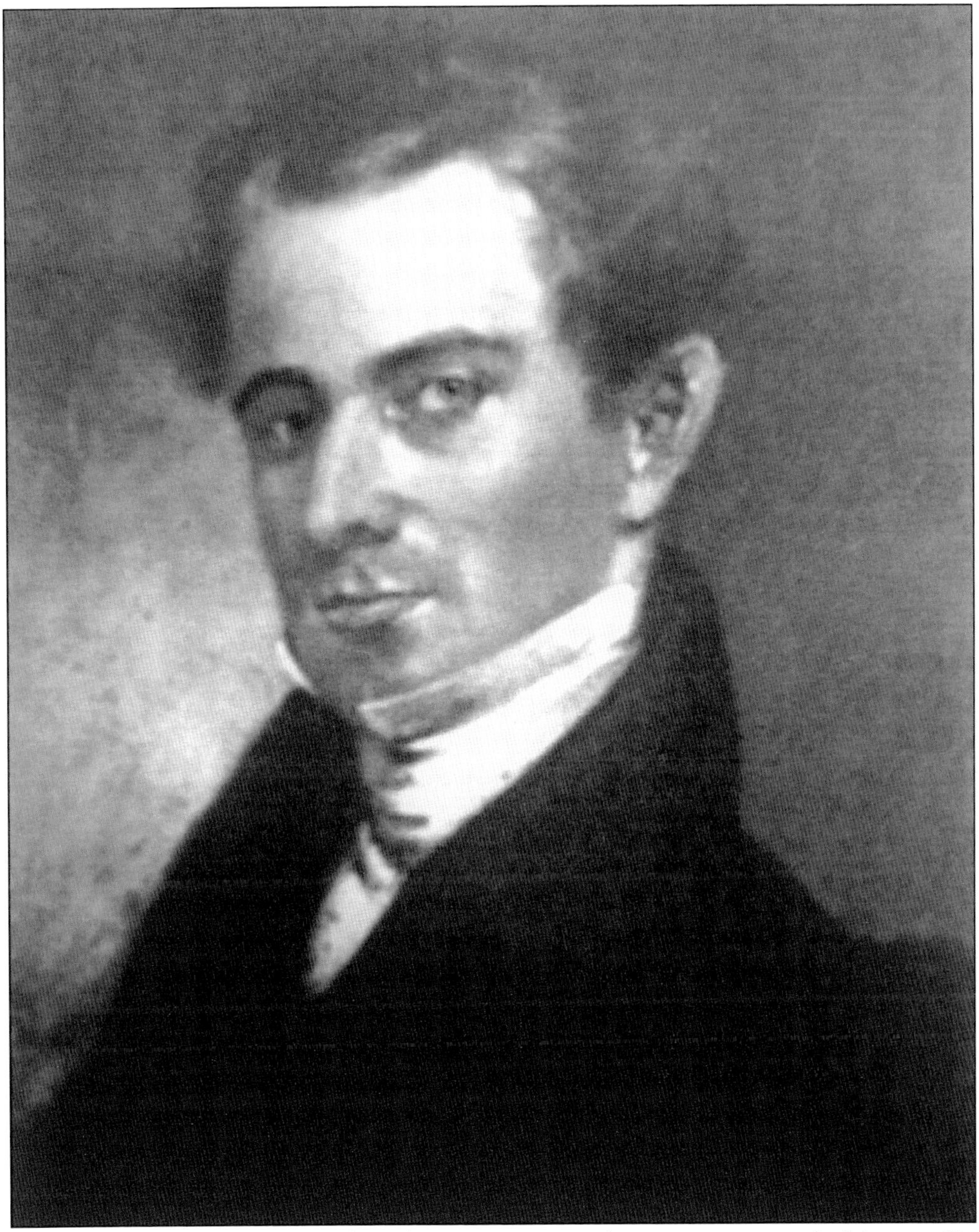

Stephen Fuller Austin (1793–1836) was born in Virginia and grew up in present-day Missouri. His father, Moses Austin, had received a grant from the Spanish government to bring 300 families to colonize Texas. Upon his father's death, Stephen brought the families to Texas, arriving in 1821, just after Mexico became independent from Spain. Austin chose land near the Gulf Coast and the Brazos and Colorado Rivers, with fertile soil, rich river bottoms, and abundant prairie grass for cattle and game; food was plentiful. Austin, who settled just 20 miles from Eagle Lake, became a military leader during the Texas Revolution (the fight for independence from Mexico). He led the first successful United States colonization of Mexico and is known as the "Father of Texas." The Eagle Lake area was located in the Austins' original land grant, which was approved on April 23, 1823.

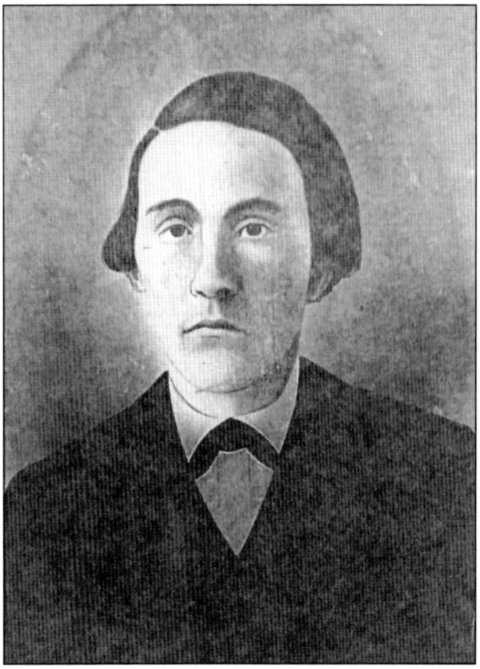

Edward Good (1839–1871), the son of Gamaliel Good (1800–1888), was born in Tennessee. He and his family came to live on the shores of Eagle Lake in the early 1850s. Edward and his brothers and their father, Gamaliel, were pioneers in settling the area. In 1855, Gamaliel, his wife, Julia, and their sons were the first to build a log cabin on the eastern shore of Eagle Lake. The Good home was a stagecoach stop between Matagorda and San Felipe. Edward served as the postmaster for Eagle Lake from 1857 to 1859 and again in 1866. Between 1856 and 1857, Gamaliel, along with D.W.C. Harris, platted the town of Eagle Lake along the proposed Buffalo Bayou, Brazos and Colorado (BBB&C) Railway track. In 1856, Edward's brother William and his father built the Good Hotel, which was run by William and his wife, Phoebe, and operated for 50 years near the railroad tracks and depot. It was replaced by the Dallas Hotel in 1912.

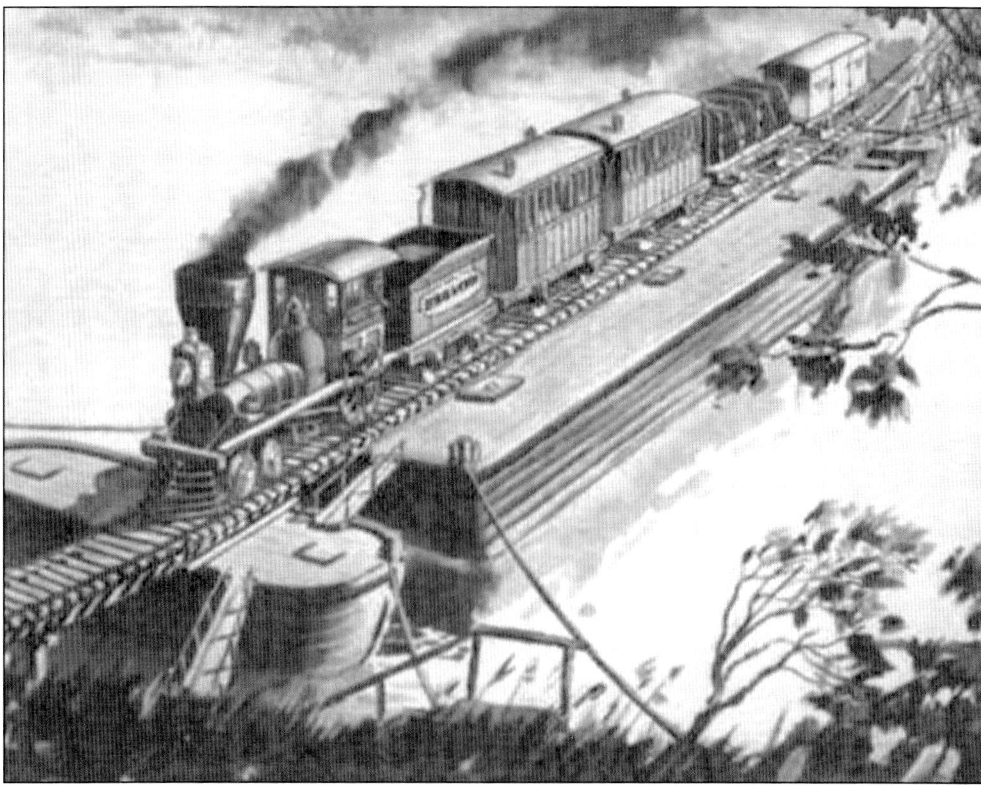

In 1859, the locomotive *General Sherman* came through Eagle Lake, making the town the third stop on the BBB&C Railway, Texas's first operating railroad. The Town of Eagle Lake was incorporated in 1888. Here, the *General Sherman* is depicted crossing the Brazos River on a floating bridge.

George W. Thatcher was born in Frederick County, Virginia, in 1808 and came to Texas in 1835. He and his wife, Sarah, moved to be near her family, the Montgomerys. Thatcher had a cotton plantation, and he oversaw a stagecoach stop between Eagle Lake and Wharton. In 1849, he was the town's first postmaster. He emigrated to Texas at the time of the Texas Revolution and was known for his social graces and hospitality. He died at 59 and is interred at the Montgomery-Thatcher Cemetery near Matthews. Thatcher and his family participated in the Runaway Scrape brought about by Antonio López de Santa Anna of Mexico.

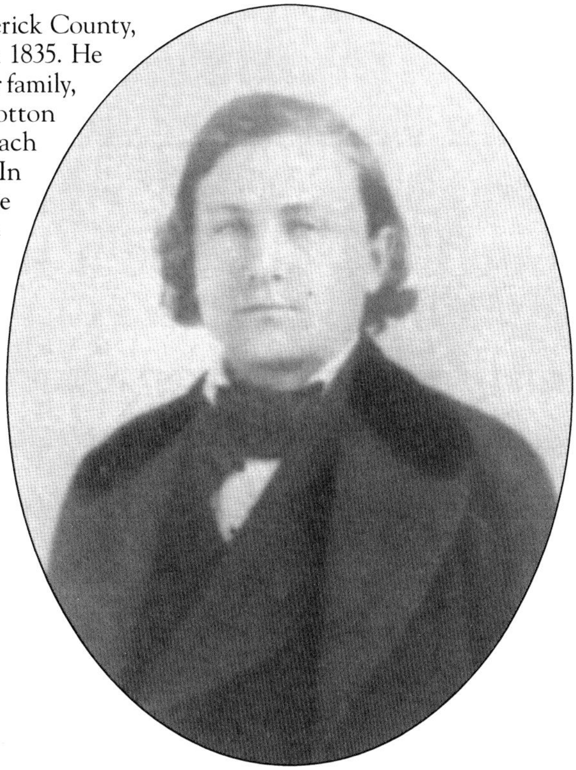

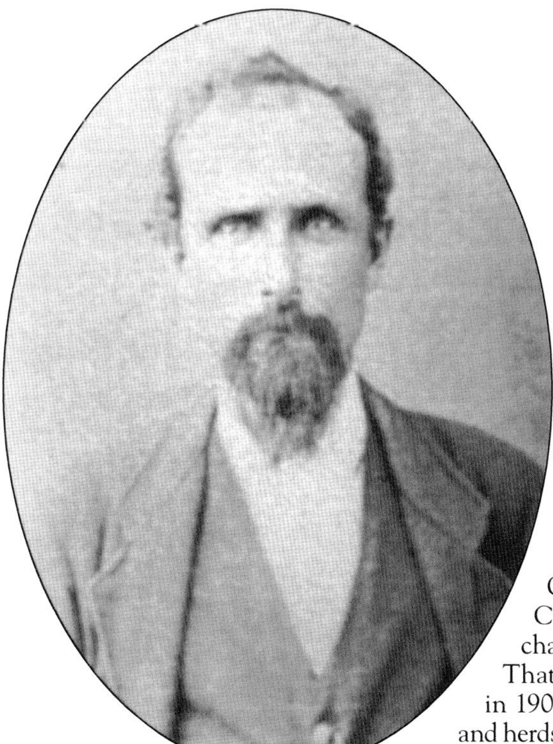

John Ward Thatcher was born on the Thatcher plantation in Texas in 1840 and later became a farmer and cattleman. He was appointed postmaster in April 1856, at age 16, and held the post for four months; he was succeeded as postmaster by Gamaliel Good. He served in the 35th Texas Cavalry (Brown's) and also participated in the charter of the Cane Belt Railroad Company. Thatcher moved to town from his plantation in 1900. He later remembered bears, mustangs, and herds of buffalo in the area. (Courtesy of Prairie Edge Museum.)

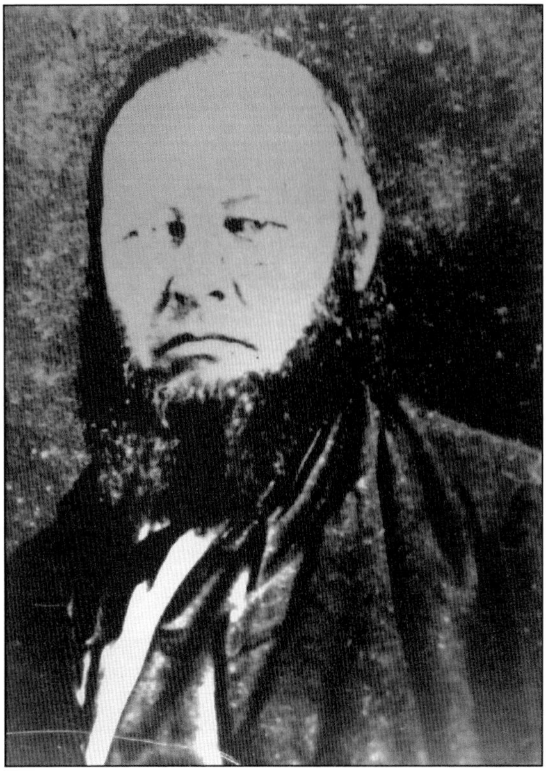

Caleb Claiborne (C.C.) Herbert was born in Virginia in 1814. He had a plantation near Eagle Lake and served in the Texas Senate from 1857 to 1860. During the Civil War, Herbert was captain of a Home Guard Company in Eagle Lake. He served in the house of representatives of both the First and Second Congresses of the Confederate States of America. He was a strong supporter of states' rights. The prominent planter and legislator was killed in 1867 and was buried on his land near the Colorado River at Reel's Bend.

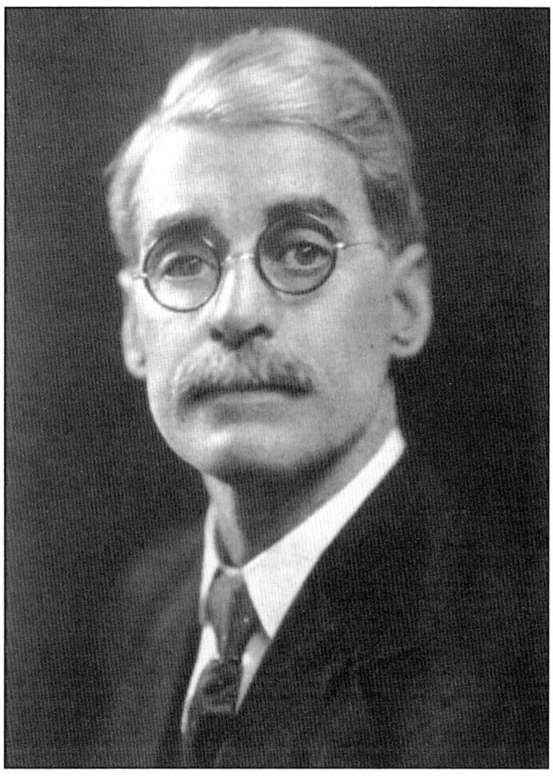

Joseph Jefferson (J.J.) Mansfield (1861–1947) was a lawyer, city attorney, mayor, county attorney (Colorado County), county judge, and a US congressman from 1916 to 1947. The Mansfield Dam at Lake Travis—formerly the Marshall Ford Dam—was named for him. He helped raise funds for the Lower Colorado River Authority and served in Congress until his death. He was Grand Master of the Masonic Lodge of Texas in 1912 and 1913. He also served as editor of Eagle Lake's first recognized newspaper, *The Canoe*. He was married to Annie Scott Bruce, daughter of Dr. Jaquelin Bruce, an early Eagle Lake resident and physician. The community of Port Mansfield, Texas, and the Mansfield Memorial Library (now part of the Nesbitt Memorial Library) in Columbus were also named for him. He died in 1947 and is buried at Masonic Cemetery.

Capt. William Dunovant (1845–1902) came from South Carolina to Eagle Lake. A leading farming entrepreneur, he was a planter of sugarcane, corn, and cotton and, in 1898, became the first farmer to grow rice in the area. Dunovant owned the Lakeside Sugar Refinery and built the town of Lakeside, Texas. A major shareholder of the Cane Belt Railroad Company, he also built a modern rice mill, cotton gin, and one of the area's first pumping plants. Dunovant fought in the Confederate army.

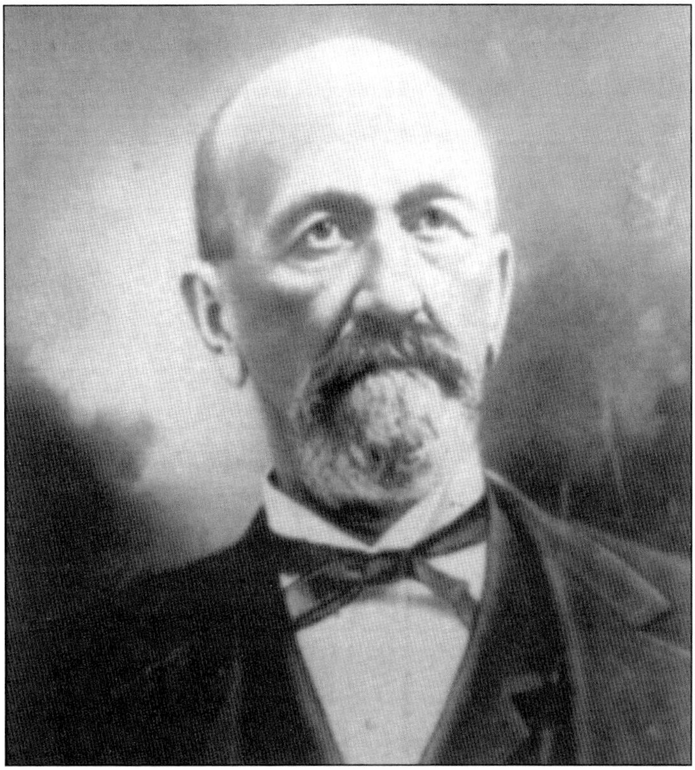

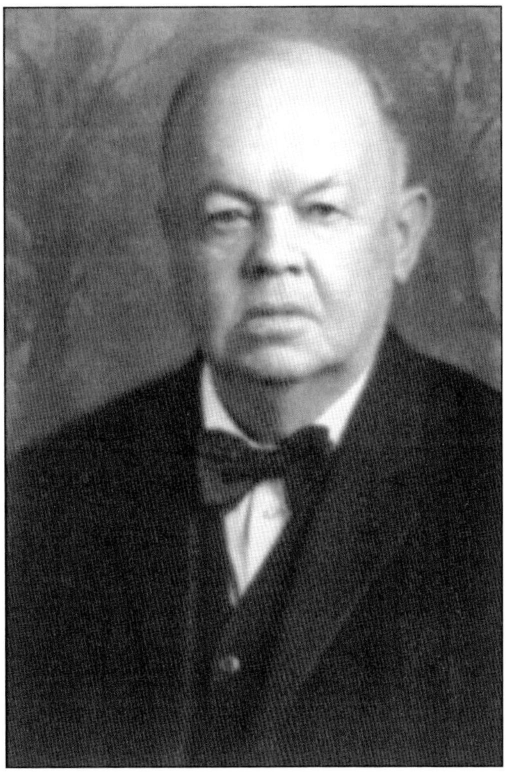

William Thomas (W.T.) Eldridge (1862–1932) came to Eagle Lake in January 1884, at age 22. He became the first city marshal of Eagle Lake. Eldridge partnered with prominent businessman William Dunovant, became involved in the sugar industry and land ownership, and chartered the Cane Belt Railroad Company. Eldridge later founded and managed Sugarland Industries and partnered with Isaac H. Kempner to lay the groundwork for the development of Imperial Sugar Company, which he also managed. Eldridge owned seven railroads in his career. He started the Sealy Mattress Factory, and helped create the company town of Sugar Land. He was a talented entrepreneur and namesake of the town of Eldridge. He built two Drummers' Home hotels and his personal home on Post Office Street. He was a founder of the First National Bank. He died in Sugar Land at age 69.

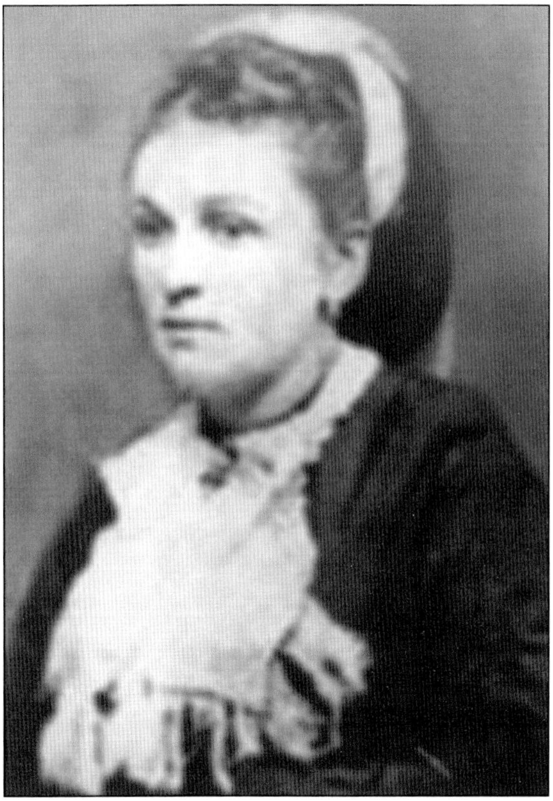

Mildred "Millie" Thatcher (1853–1914) was born on her father's plantation near Matthews. She was the youngest of nine children born to George and Sarah Montgomery Thatcher. The Thatchers came to Texas and were ordered by Gen. Sam Houston to join the Runaway Scrape. Millie's early education was on the plantation, and she was later formally educated at Ursuline Academy in Galveston. Her family later lived in Eagle Lake, and she farmed 500 acres her father gave her. She built her two-story home, one of the oldest houses in Eagle Lake, on the corner of McCarty and State Streets. Millie gave land for the Episcopal parsonage, and a stained-glass window in the church is dedicated to her. She was a member of the church for 30 years and was a widely known and popular citizen.

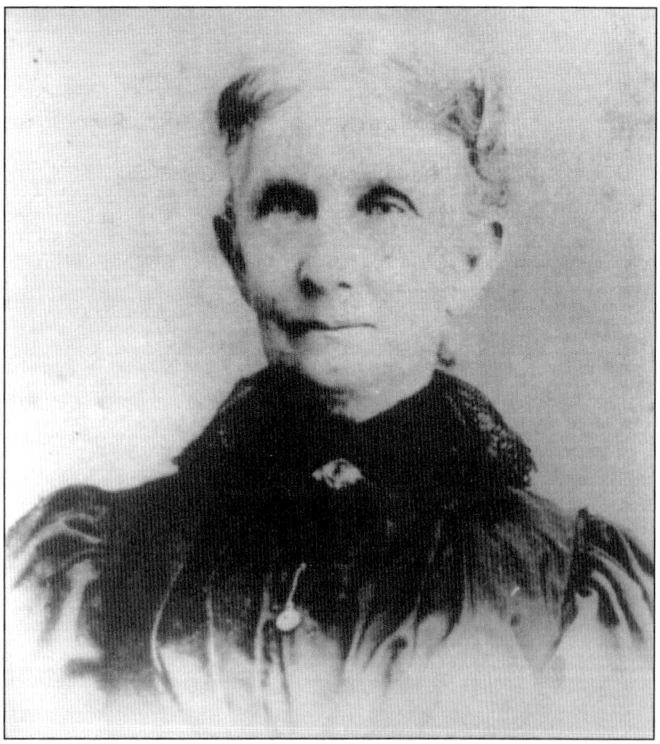

Dilue Rose Harris (1825–1914) was a pioneer and writer born in St. Louis, Missouri. After coming to Texas with her family at age eight, she took part in the Runaway Scrape and helped make bullets for men going to the Alamo. She wrote her memoirs at age 74, while living in Eagle Lake. Her reminiscences of pioneer life in Texas, assisted by her father's journal, include politics, economics, slavery, religion, and family life. Her writings about the period of the Texas Revolution have brought her acclaim. Harris lived in Columbus, and then in Eagle Lake, where she died in 1914. She was married to Ira Harris and had nine children.

Two

The Lake

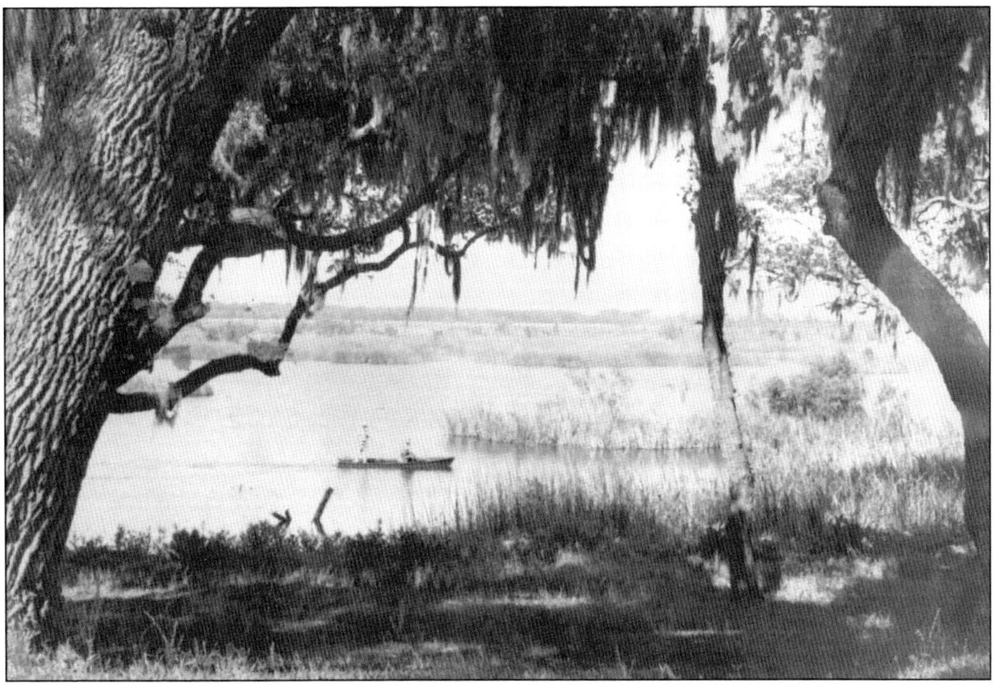

Eagle Lake was well known for its large, moss-covered oak trees and bullrushes, which helped to create the floating islands (which no longer exist) that moved about with currents and wind, creating pastoral scenes. It is home to the Eagle Lake Rod & Gun Club, and it has had a colorful history from the time of explorer René-Robert Cavelier, Sieur de La Salle, and the Karankawa Indian settlements.

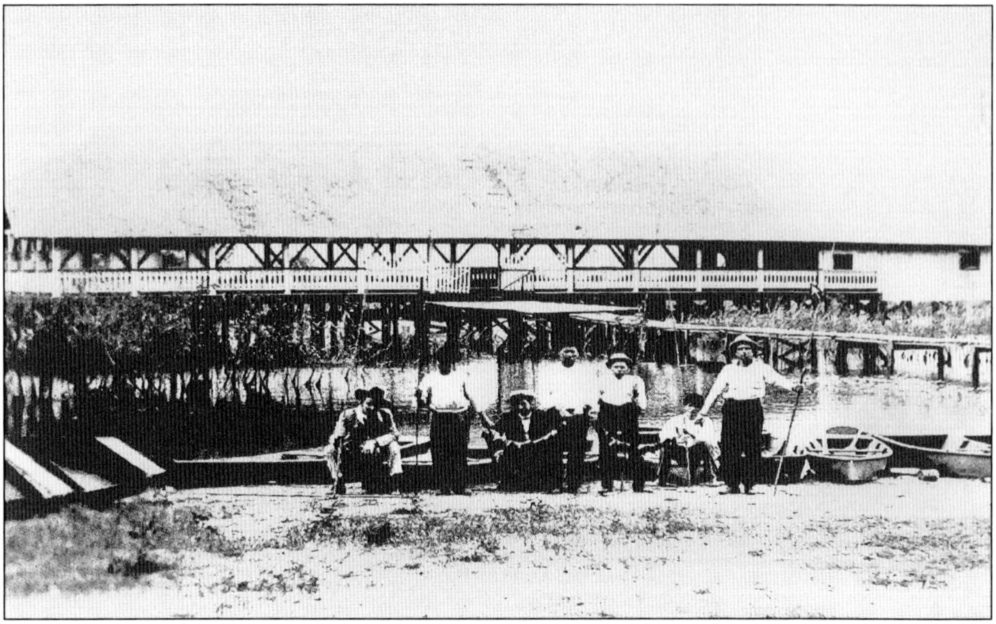

The Eagle Lake Pavilion, begun in 1893, was damaged heavily by the Great Storm of 1900. It was rebuilt, but damaged again by the Hurricane of 1909. A 1915 storm blew off the top of the pavilion. The rebuilt structure was destroyed in 1917 by a fire, which led to the end of the popular pavilion and the weekend visitors' revelry on the lake.

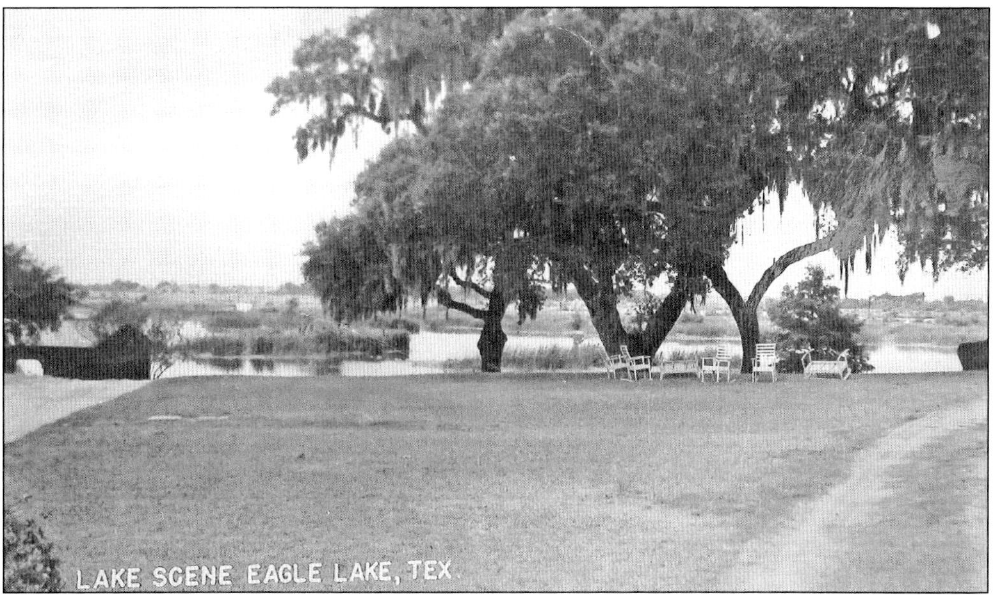

This popular postcard was sent by weekend visitors and vacationers who came to enjoy the beauty and serenity of the lake, with its lily pads, floating islands, and dance pavilion. Many came from around the county, while others arrived by train to the Lakeside depot.

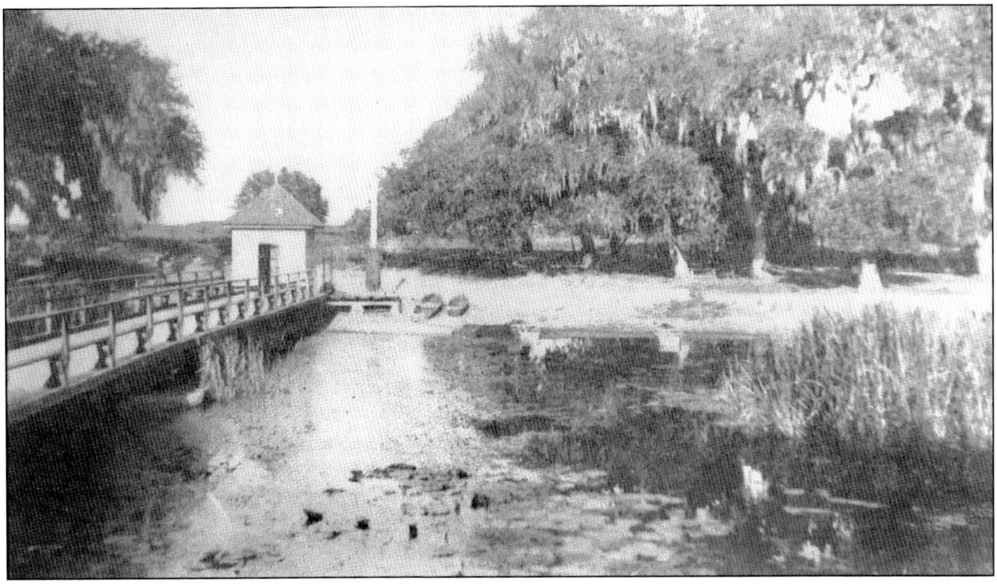

The moss-covered trees around the lake, along with the natural beauty of the shore and the flowering lily pads, provided a perfect setting for picnics, camp meetings, baptisms, fishing, and boating. This pier led out to the pavilion.

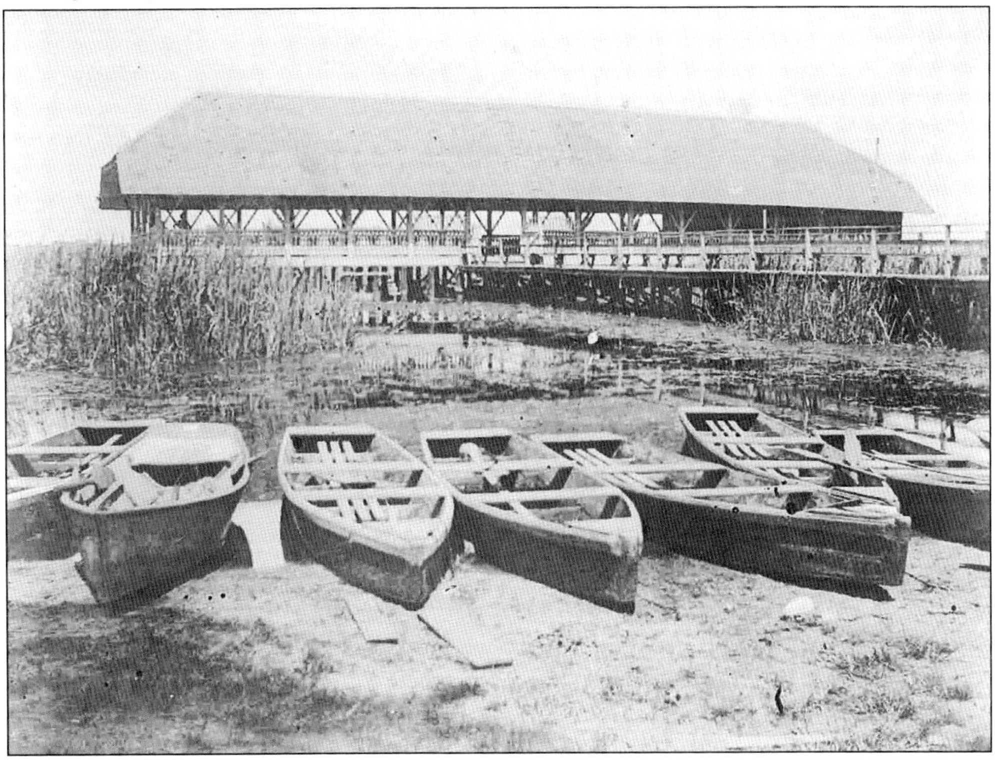

Boating and fishing were popular on Eagle Lake in the early 1900s. Sailing was also a favorite pastime. In 1898, Eagle Lake received a six-inch snowfall, and the lake froze over; fishing boats were converted to sleighs pulled over the ground by teams of horses. The lake also froze in 1899, creating a second season of rare winter activities.

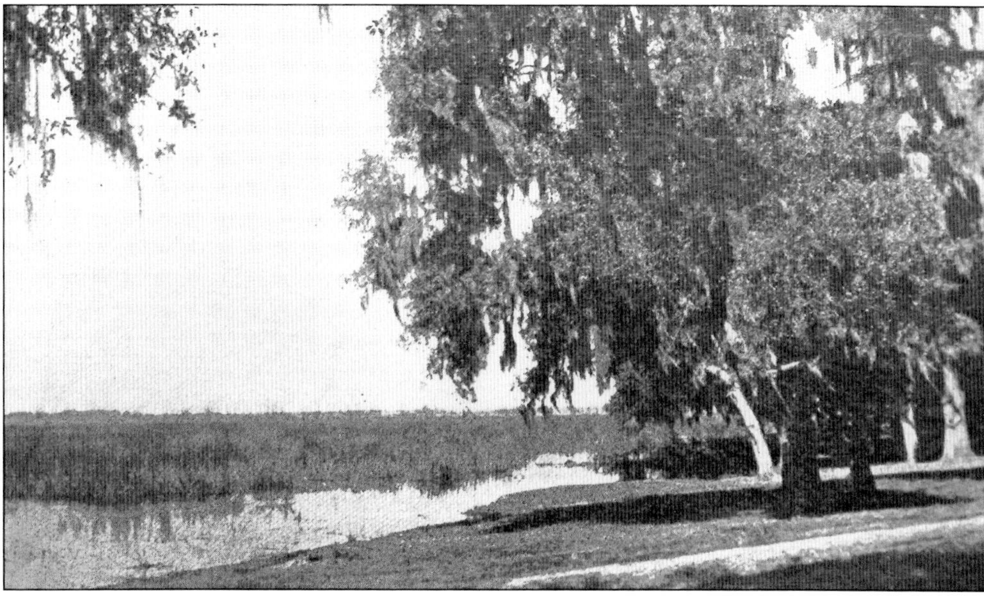

Before rice farming and irrigation began, Eagle Lake was a clear, serene lake with floating lily pads—as the Native Americans who first settled on the banks knew. It had an abundance of fish. With the fluctuation of the lake's water levels, reeds and rushes began to grow on the lake bottom when the water level was low. When the reeds and bullrushes broke loose in higher water and floated to the top, they created picturesque floating islands.

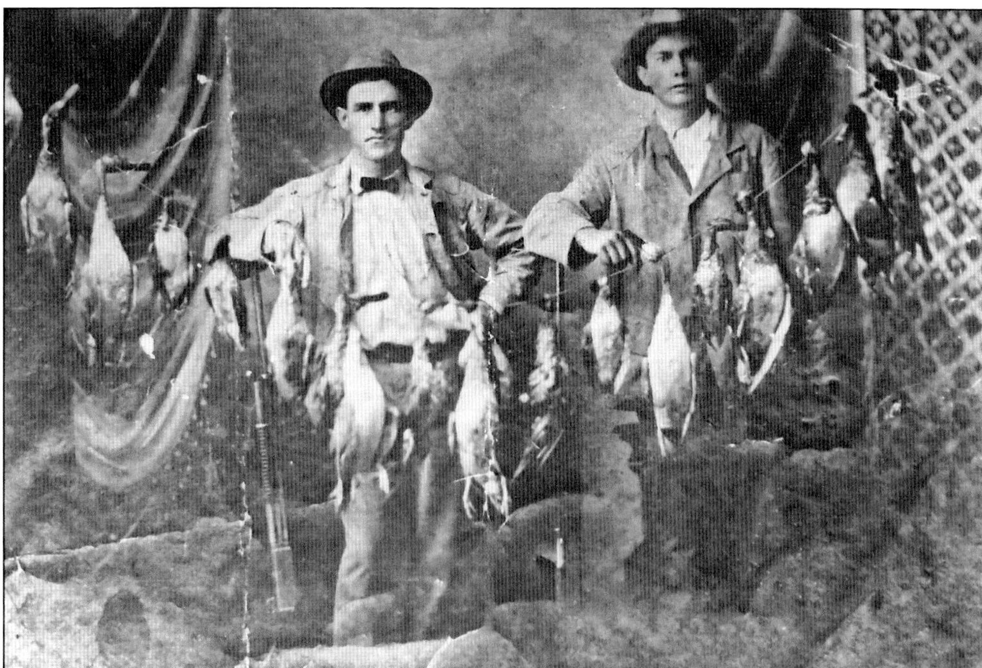

Eagle Lake has long been noted for its abundant waterfowl, and hunting and guiding have long been favorite pastimes. After an impressive hunt, W.C. Sanders (left) and Charles von Lengerke posed with the day's bounty.

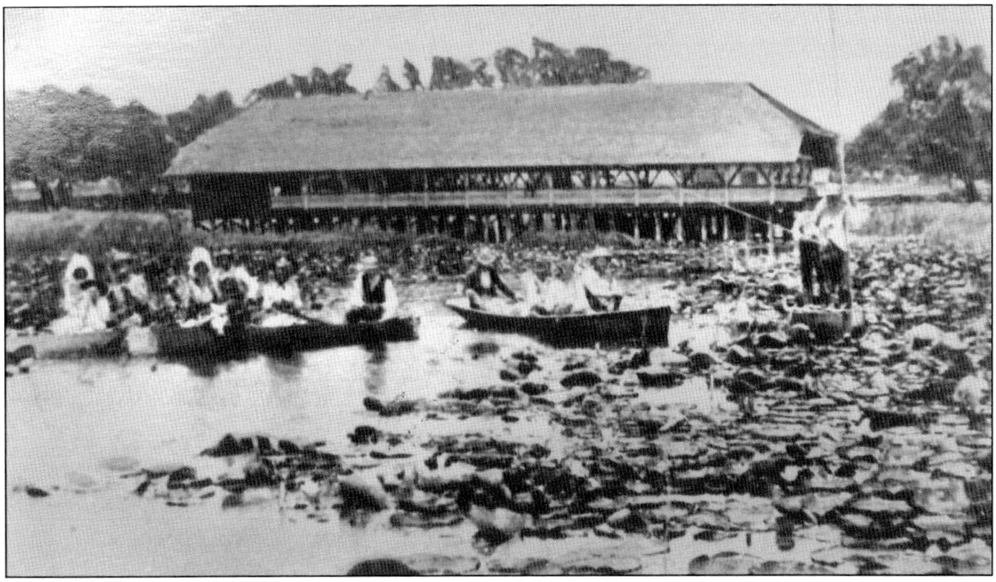

A large pavilion was built over Eagle Lake in 1893. The popular site attracted people from all over, who engaged in fishing, boating, dancing, skating, and picnicking. At times, the railroad ran three excursion trains per week, which brought families from Houston and other areas to enjoy the pavilion and lake activities.

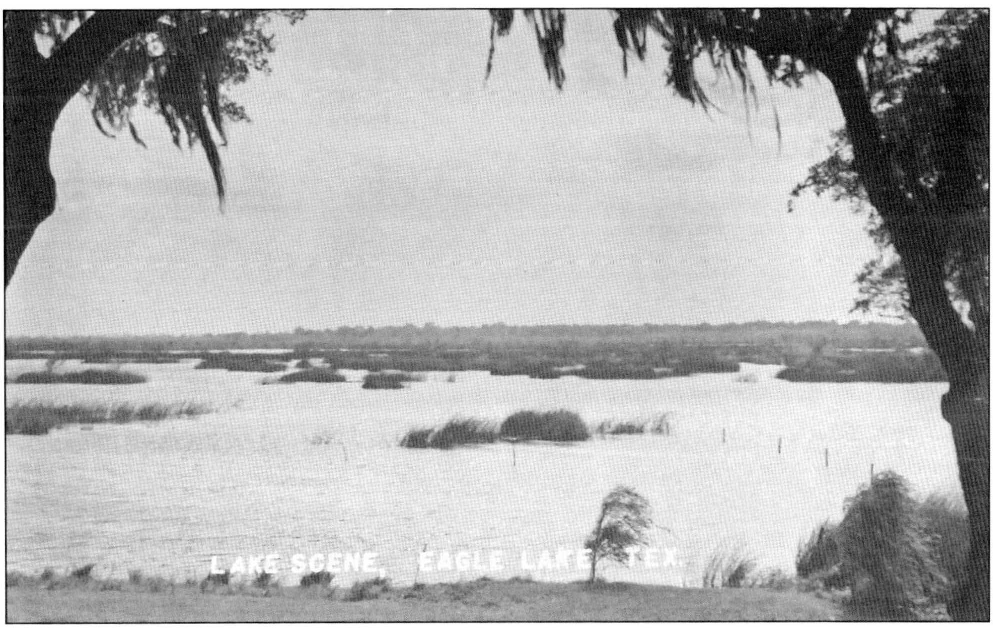

Eagle Lake had floating islands that, according to the *Eagle Lake Headlight*, "drifted and floated with the wind." Some were an acre in size, creating havens for fish and wildlife. The islands consisted of massive beds of roots and reeds, with trees and other vegetation created by the effects of irrigation from the lake.

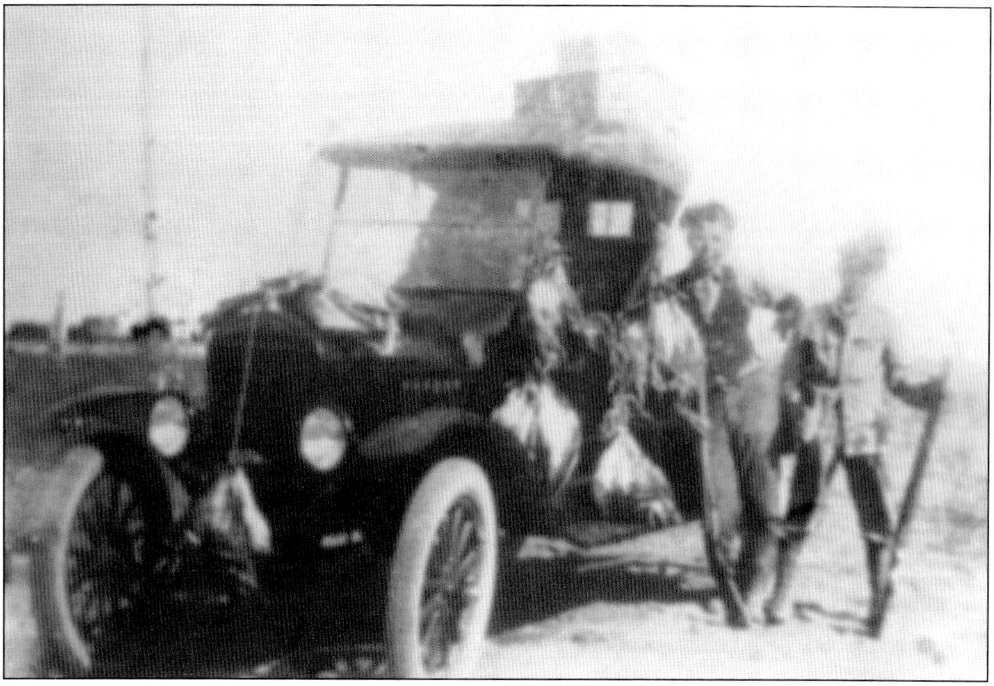

In 1929, an old car is laden with the spoils of a successful hunt at Eagle Lake. Hank Arnold (left) and an unidentified guide have brought in the day's waterfowl bounty from the thousands of duck and geese in the area. (Courtesy of Betsy Arnold Cates.)

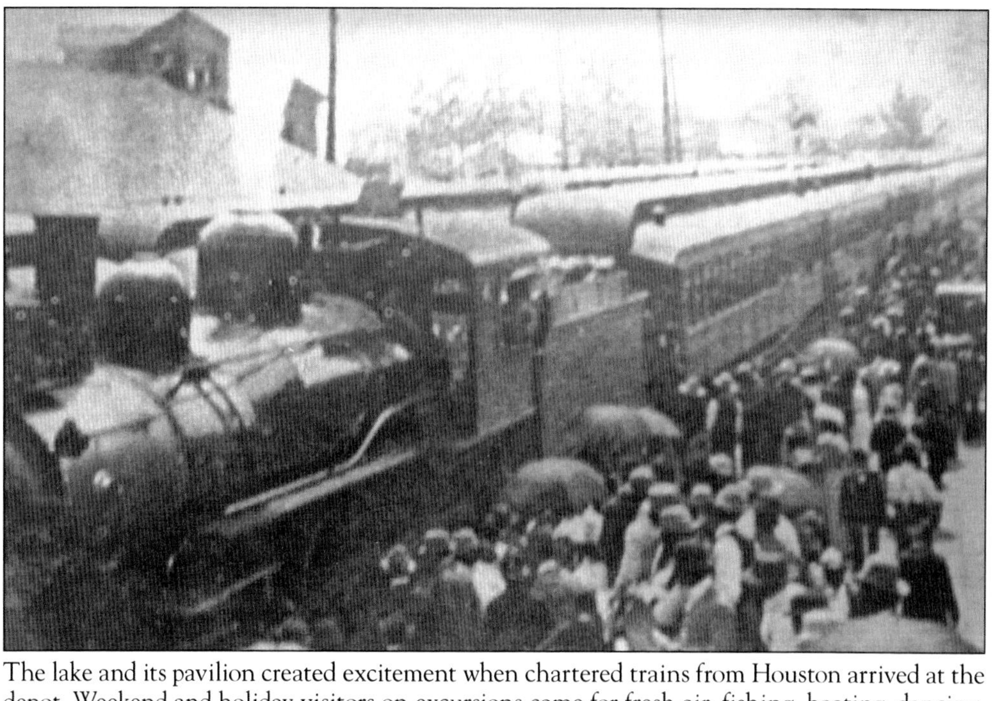

The lake and its pavilion created excitement when chartered trains from Houston arrived at the depot. Weekend and holiday visitors on excursions came for fresh air, fishing, boating, dancing, and socializing. Eagle Lake was a desirable destination because of its natural beauty. The train station took on a festive air with crowds of local onlookers and visitors.

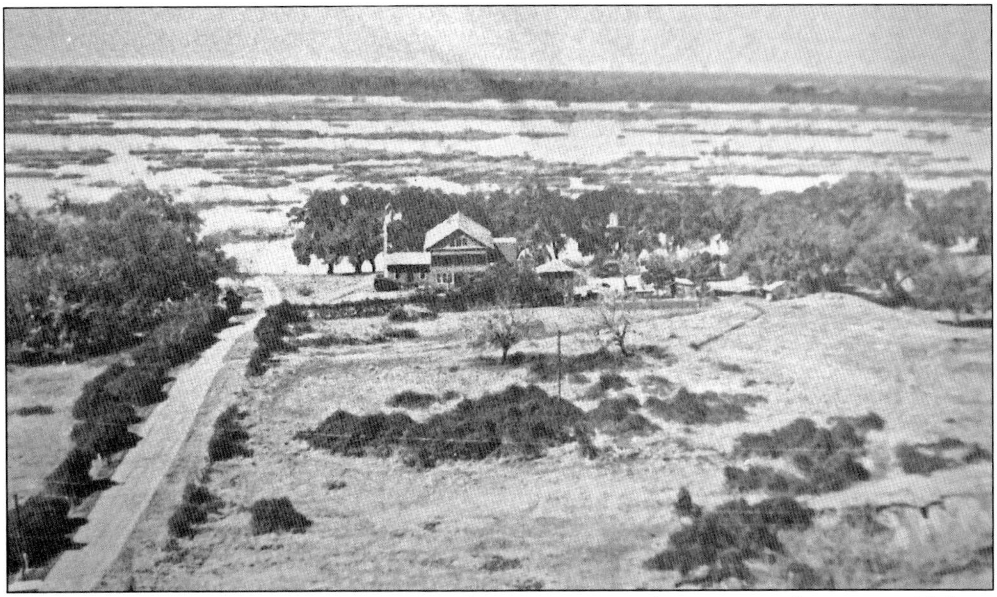

The Eagle Lake Rod & Gun Club was created in 1920 as an exclusive private hunting and fishing club. The large wood-frame, two-story clubhouse still stands by the lake. From its beginning, the club was managed by S.C. Smothers, a seasoned gamesman who hunted on the lake until his death in 1969. He hosted hunters from Houston and other areas who enjoyed the exclusive hunting, fishing, and lodging privileges of the Rod & Gun Club. While rustic, its sleeping and entertainment rooms complemented the main feature—the excellent family-style meal service overseen by S.C.'s wife, "Jakey" Smothers.

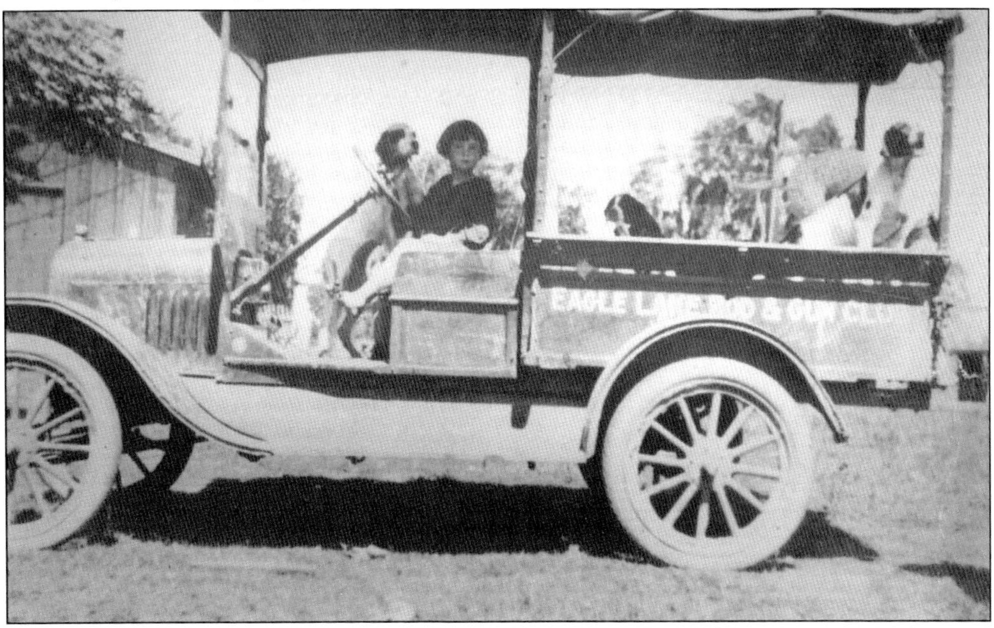

Caroline Smothers, daughter of Rod & Gun Club manager S.C. Smothers, sits in the Rod & Gun Club private courtesy vehicle with the hunting dogs. Guests were often transported to and from the train station or City Park (now called the square) via the country vehicle. Caroline's mother, "Jakey" Smothers, oversaw the lodge and prepared the excellent meals at the club.

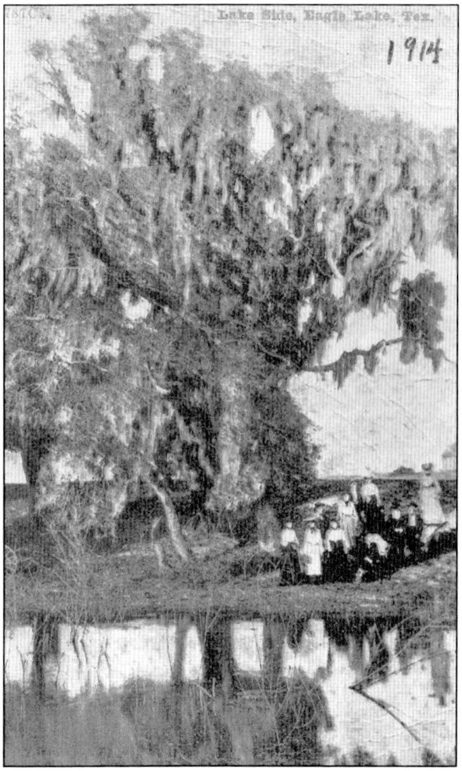

The lake was a spot for family and social gatherings, picnics, outings, camp meetings, and baptisms. On weekends, guests came from all over to enjoy the water, the cool breezes, and fellowship. In 1914, this group of family and friends was enjoying the water, the scenery, and the moss-covered live oak trees. Baptisms were also held in the lake. This early postcard was widely circulated to show the size of the famed trees along the lake and the groups that came to enjoy the lakeside's pleasant areas for social and church activity. Parades on May Day would process from the town to Lakeside. During World War I, the lake was used for bombing practice by the US Army Air Corps from Ellington Field in Houston, which had a satellite field in Eagle Lake called Griffin Aviation Field.

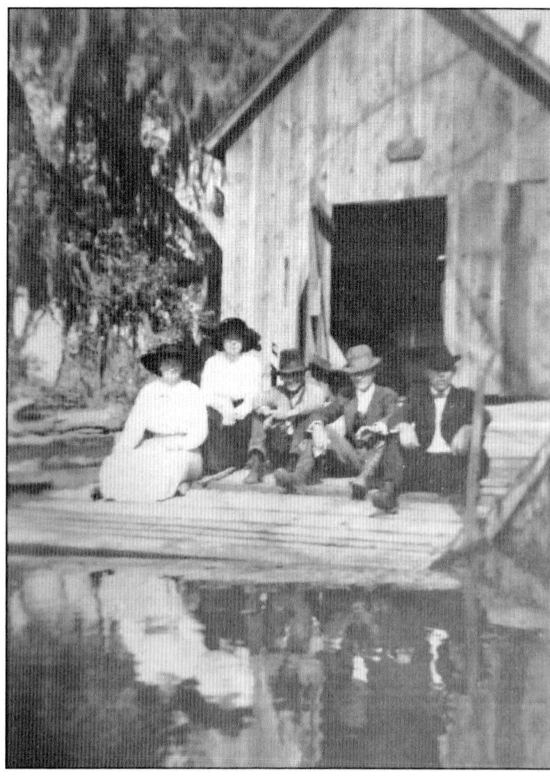

The old boat ramp was important to fishermen at the lake. This group is enjoying sunshine and fellowship at the Eagle Lake boathouse on a Sunday outing in the early 1900s. People brought picnics and enjoyed boating and socializing. A couple who lived at the lake rented boats and fishing poles and cleaned fish for the guests. Most boats had names painted on the sides. Boys picked lilies from the lake and sold them at the train station.

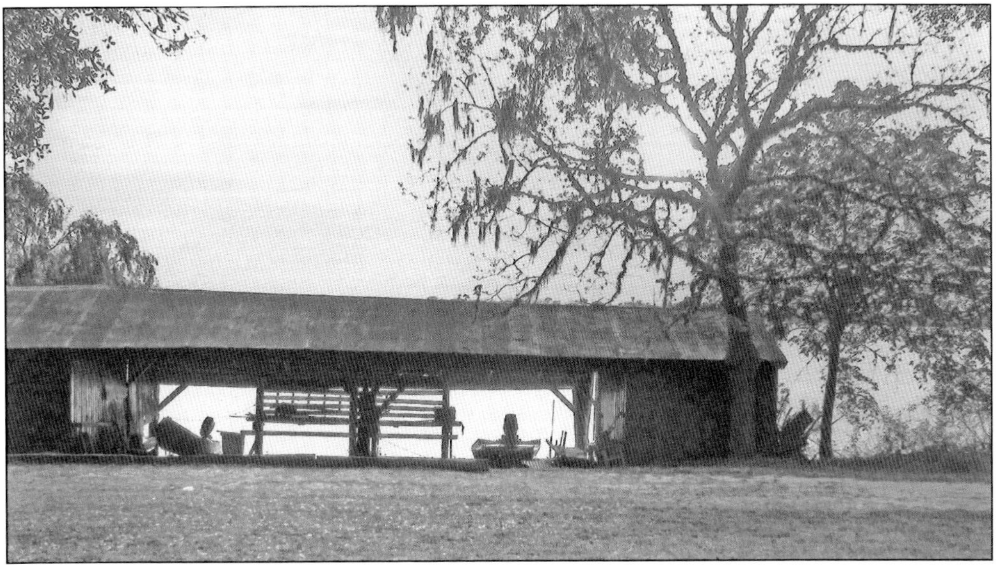

The Eagle Lake Rod & Gun Club boathouse held boats and equipment for fishing and hunting. In 1920, the lake was leased to the Eagle Lake Rod & Gun Club for hunting and fishing, thus making it a haven for private recreation. The depth of the 1,000-acre lake rarely exceeded eight feet.

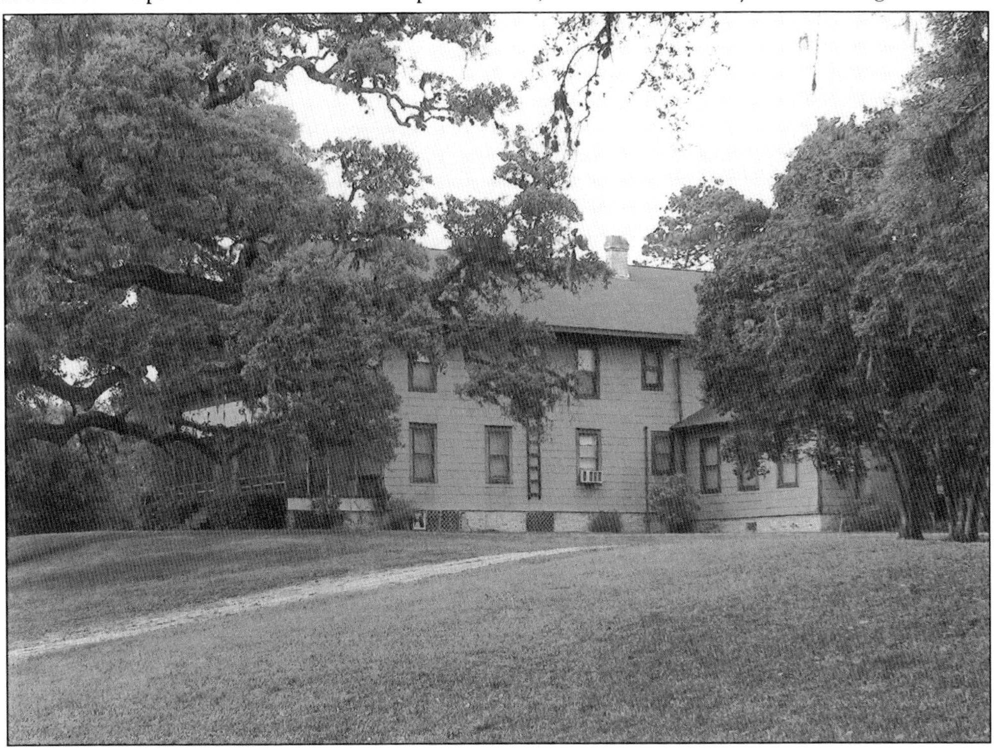

The Eagle Lake Rod & Gun Club was once considered the most exclusive private club in the area. Membership was passed down through eldest-son inheritance, and the club was one of considerable prestige and pride. Many guests arrived at the rail station at Lakeside for weekend activities. S.C. Smothers, the club manager, hosted hunters from Houston (and other areas) who enjoyed the exclusive club privileges.

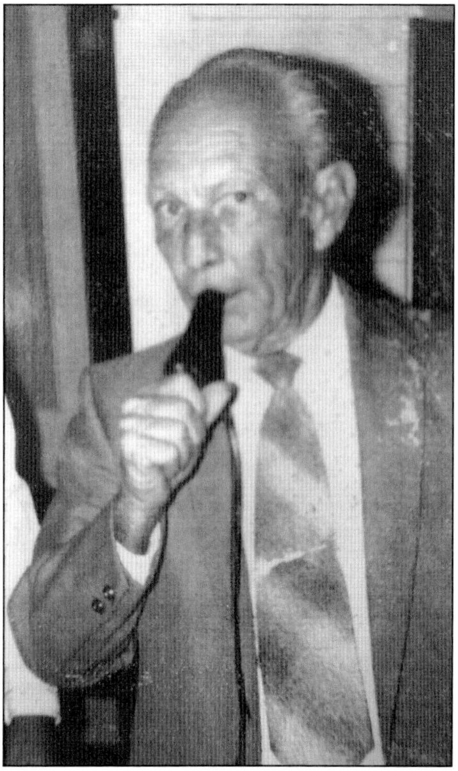

Jimmy Reel, a popular naturalist, shows his skills with a goose and duck caller. A well-known hunter and guide, Reel, along with Marvin Tyler, created a method of using decoys made from white rags or cloths and placed in the rice fields to attract snow geese. "The Texas rag spread," which helped to make Eagle Lake the "Goose Hunting Capital of the World," attracted hunters from all over the United States. In 1941, Reel leased hunting privileges and developed the Lower Lake Hunting and Fishing Club, which he opened in 1944. He won national acclaim in the art of duck calling, introduced hunting on a day or lease basis, and later ran the Silver Creek Fish Hatchery. The Texas rag spread is still used by hunters; it creates the illusion of nesting or feeding geese and attracts other birds along the southern flyway near Eagle Lake. Aided by the presence of large rice fields, it is a prolific hunting area.

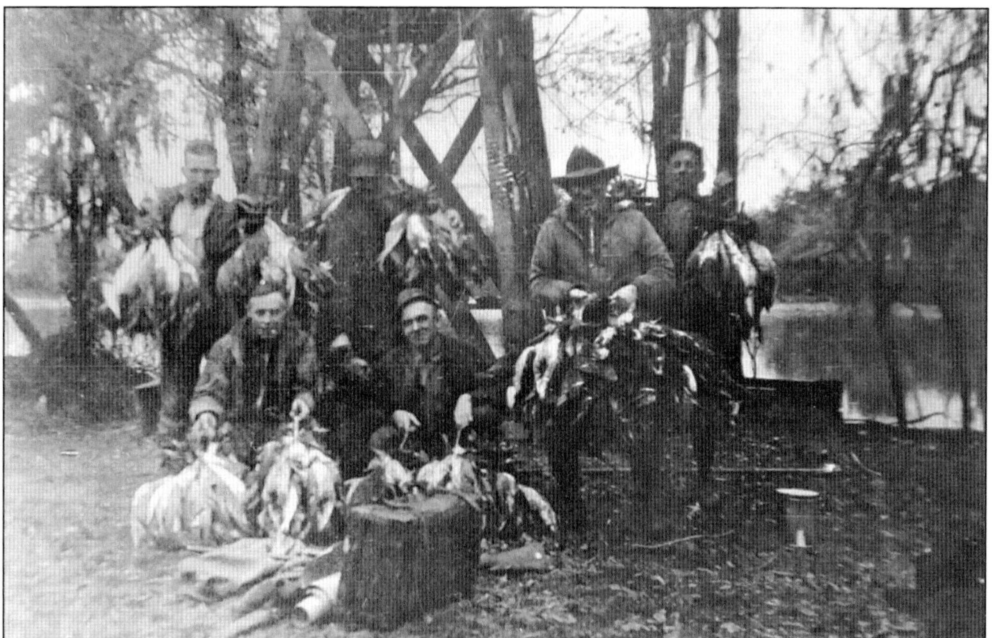

Hunters display their geese and ducks on a winter outing in the 1920s near Eagle Lake. Winter skies were darkened by thousands of geese and ducks flying in to nest on the nearby lake and rice fields. Guides and waterfowl "pickers" were kept busy during the season. Dogs were often used as retrievers. Blinds, decoys, and boats were also used in hunting.

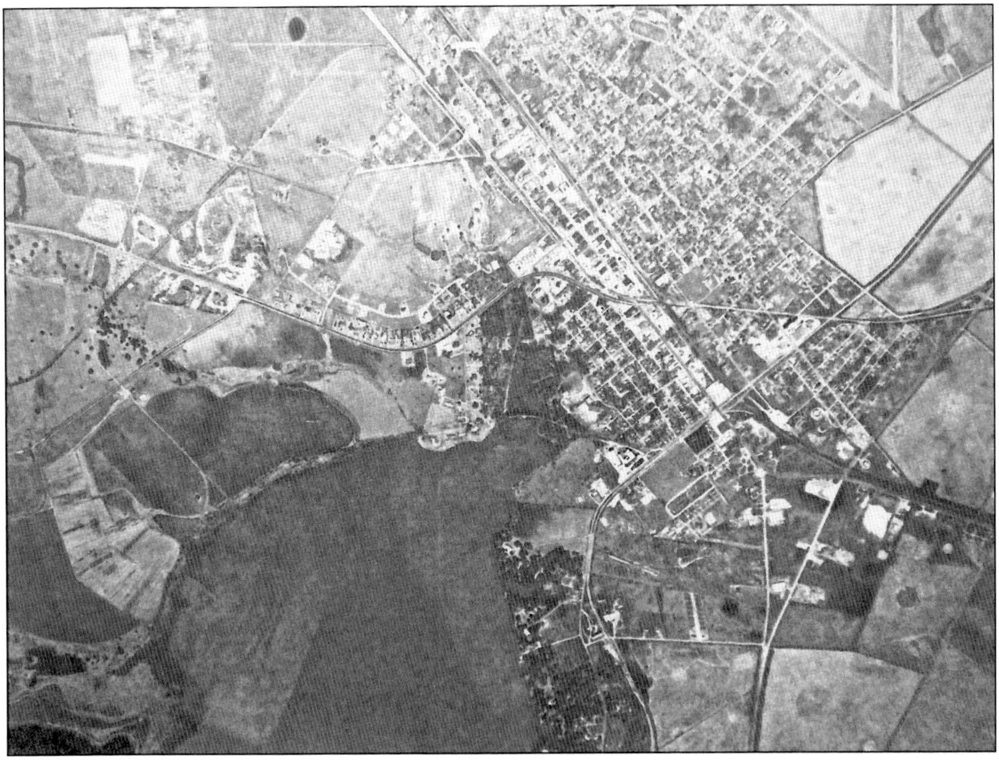

This 1977 aerial view shows downtown Eagle Lake and surrounding residential areas, along with the lake and nearby farms. The area's population has remained stable.

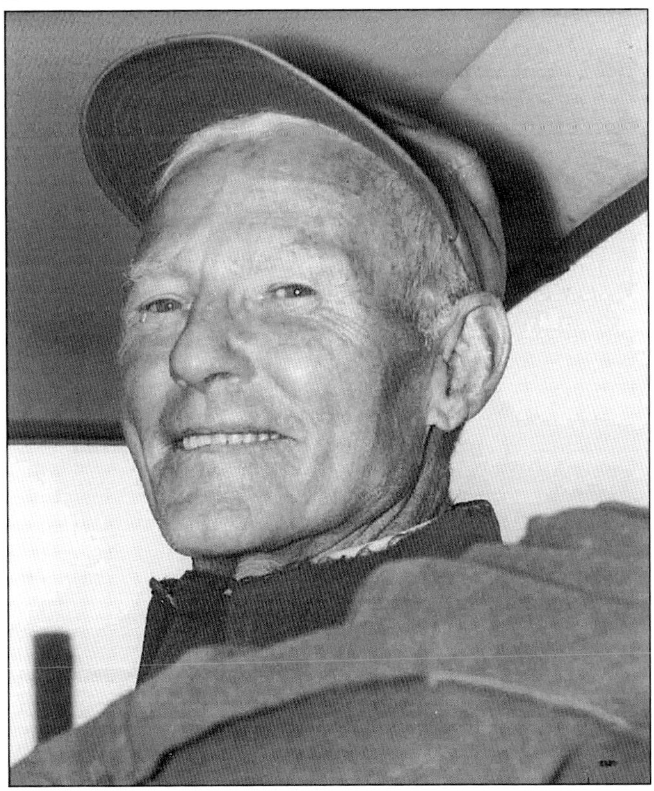

Tom Waddell, beloved game warden and farmer, was born in Scotland in 1899. He came to Eagle Lake in 1913 and retired in 1958 after 33 years as a state game warden with the Texas Parks & Wildlife Department. He was a leader in wildlife conservation, played professional baseball and football in Ohio, and was a protector of the Attwater's prairie chicken.

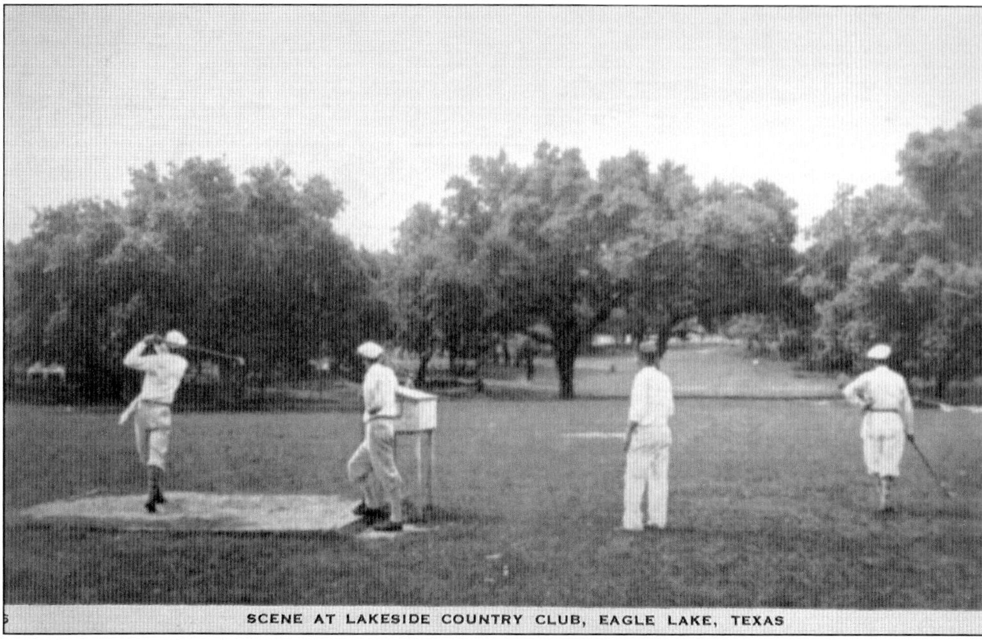

Golf began at Lakeside in 1925, when 30 men organized the Lakeside Country Club, which had a nine-hole course with sand greens. Located on FM 102, it was a popular club for golfing and outings. O.J. Wintermann was the first (and possibly the only) president. The first hole in one was made by S.C. "Jake" Smothers from 273 yards on hole seven in October 1926.

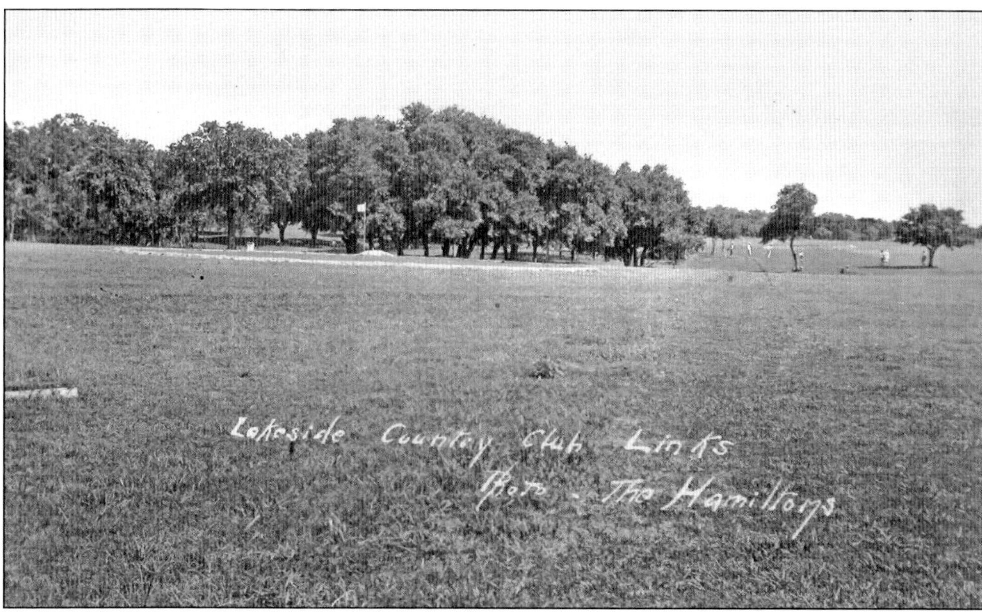

This Lakeside Country Club Golf Course real-photo postcard showing a panoramic view of the course was taken by Hamilton's, a local photography studio. Soon after the Lakeside club began, another golf club, with 48 younger men as members, was formed as the Eagle Lake Cavendale Golf Club.

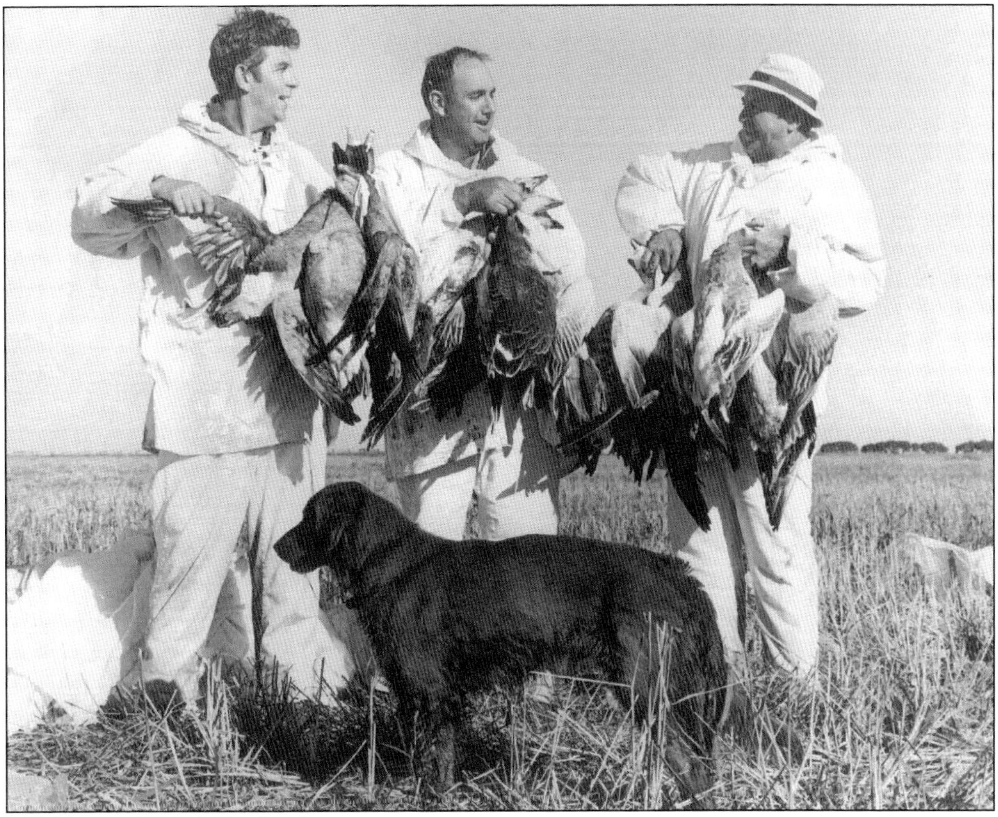

Television star Andy Griffith (left) and golfer Sam Snead (right) enjoy a hunt with guide Marvin Tyler while filming an outdoor sportsman television show in Eagle Lake. Tyler was a well-known hunting guide and fisherman and the owner of the popular Altair establishment Marvin's Restaurant, which was famous for its steaks, seafood, and game.

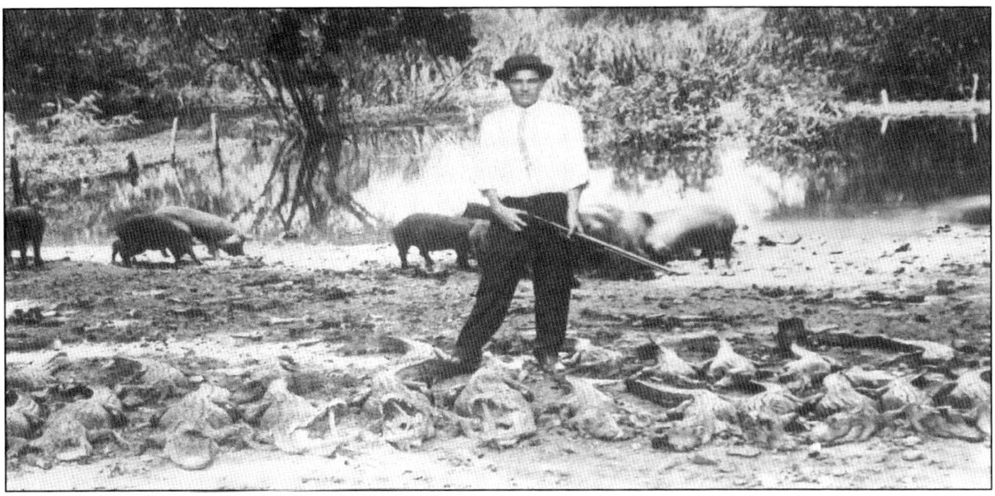

Alligators were abundant in the lake and, at times, could become nuisances and dangers. On occasion, hunters came in to hunt alligators for their skins. This 1910 image shows the bounty of one such hunter, with his array of alligators from the lake. As many as 70 alligators were killed at one time for their hides and to reduce the local alligator population.

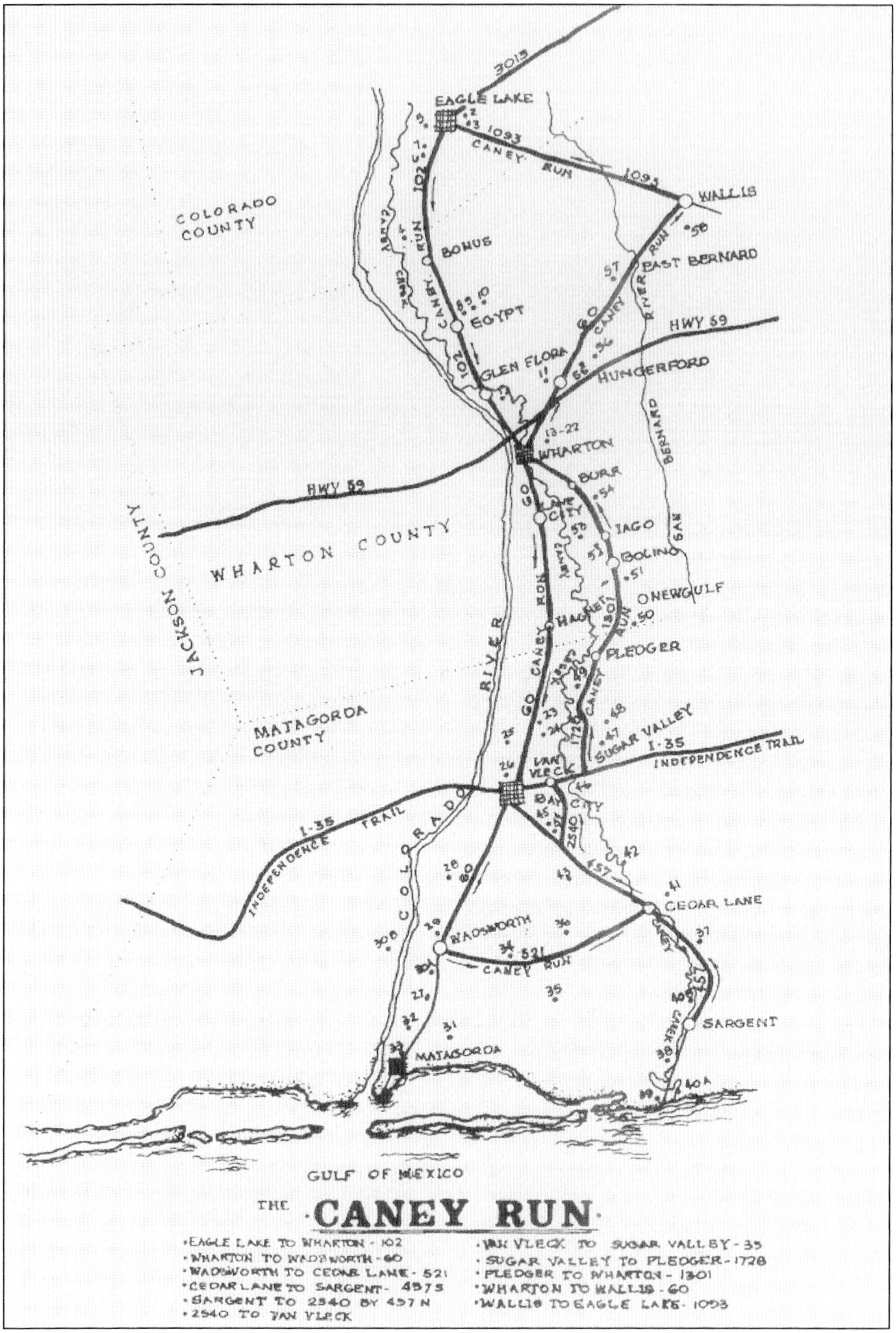

In the late 1800s, Caney Creek ran from near Eagle Lake to the Gulf of Mexico. Bamboo cane grew as high as 35 feet, and groves stretched 45 miles wide in some areas. Bamboo cane was used for seed, flooring, fencing, and mats. When it decayed, it made the soil fertile. This area of fertile soil was called the "Texas Sugar Bowl," and it ran between the Colorado and Brazos Rivers. Before railroads, Caney Run was the chief road for shipping goods to and from the gulf and inland.

Three

The Sugar Industry

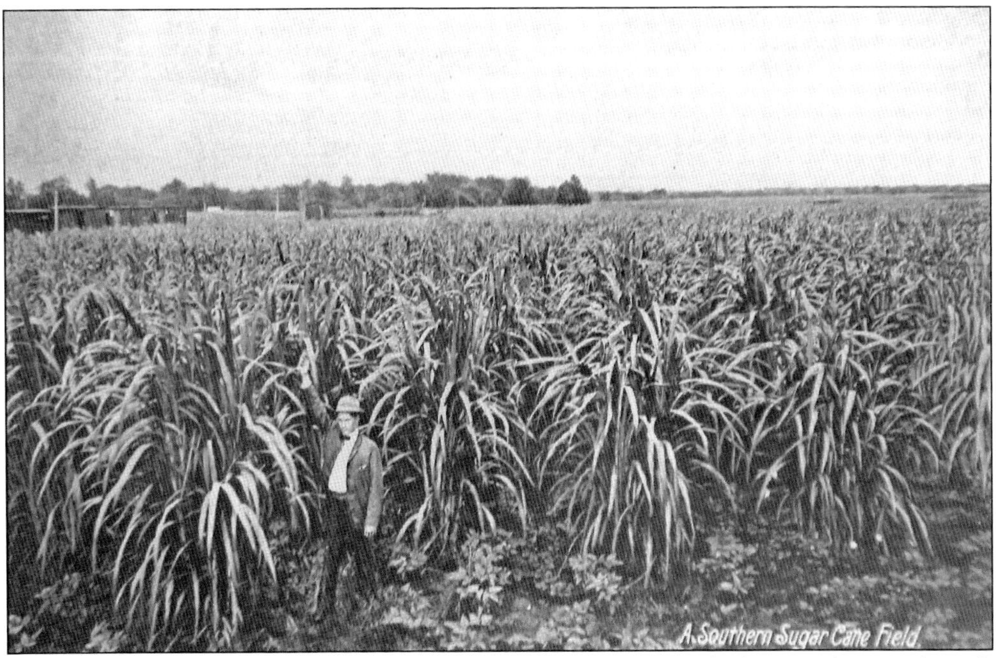

Early pioneers in Stephen F. Austin's colony brought sugarcane with them to plant in the rich soil of the Colorado River area. Sugarcane became a cash crop and an important industry in the Eagle Lake area after the Civil War. Thousands of acres of sugarcane were planted in the Matthews and Bonus areas. Harvests occurred from October to December, and harvested crops were transported by train to the Lakeside Sugar Refinery for processing.

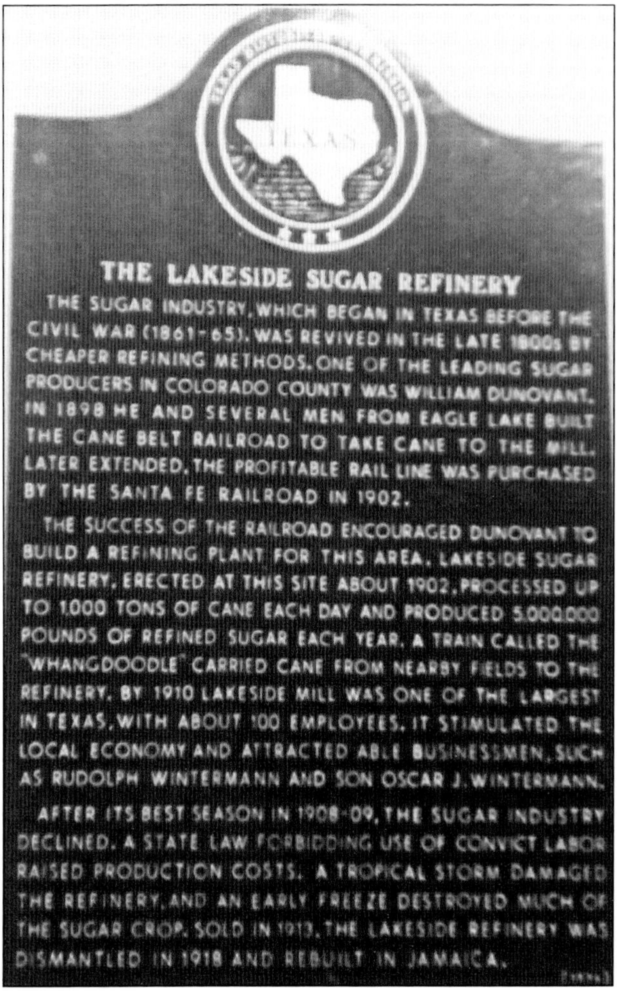

Today, all that remains of the Lakeside Sugar Refinery is a portion of its cement flooring and this historical marker at the site of the old mill on Lakeside Drive. After the refinery's most successful season—in 1908–1909—the area suffered weather setbacks, freezes, and substantial crop damages in 1909 and 1911, causing heavy financial losses. Ultimately, the refinery had to close in 1913. In 1918, it was rebuilt in Jamaica using the original materials.

This sugar exhibit at the 1909 Colorado County Fair was designed to represent the sugarcane and refining industry of Eagle Lake. Such exhibits reflected the agricultural richness of the county. This was one of numerous presentations of successful agrarian ventures throughout the county and was seen by hundreds of visitors and farmers during this festive occasion.

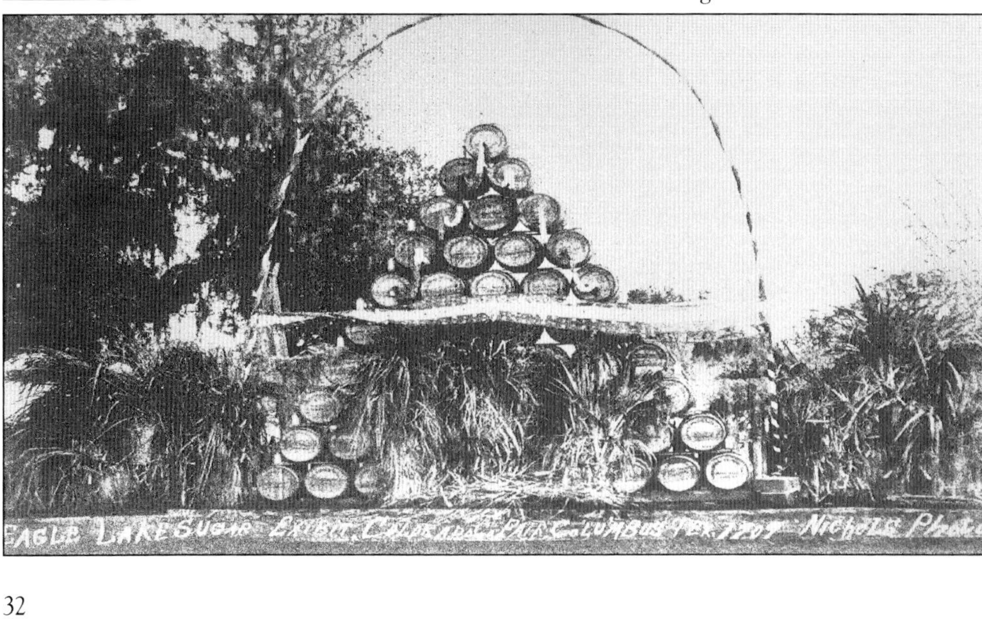

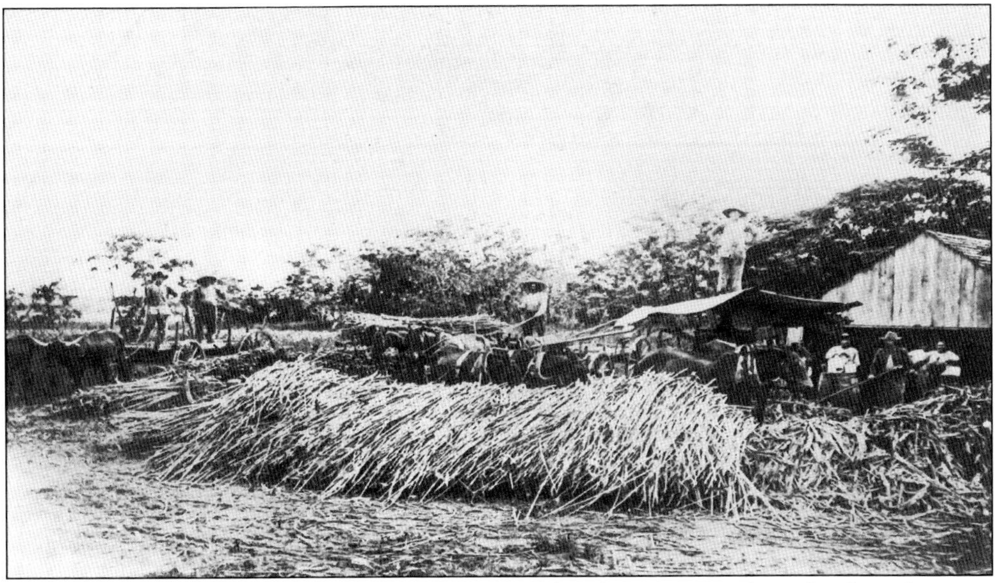

Sugarcane was also important to private farms in Colorado County, such as this farm that grew its own cane and processed it with crushers and presses powered by mules and oxen. Neighbors, friends, and family helped with the processing. The cane syrup was used by families as a food and was also sold for profit. Here, cane is being unloaded in the countryside near Mentz at the molasses press belonging to Rudolph Uhlig.

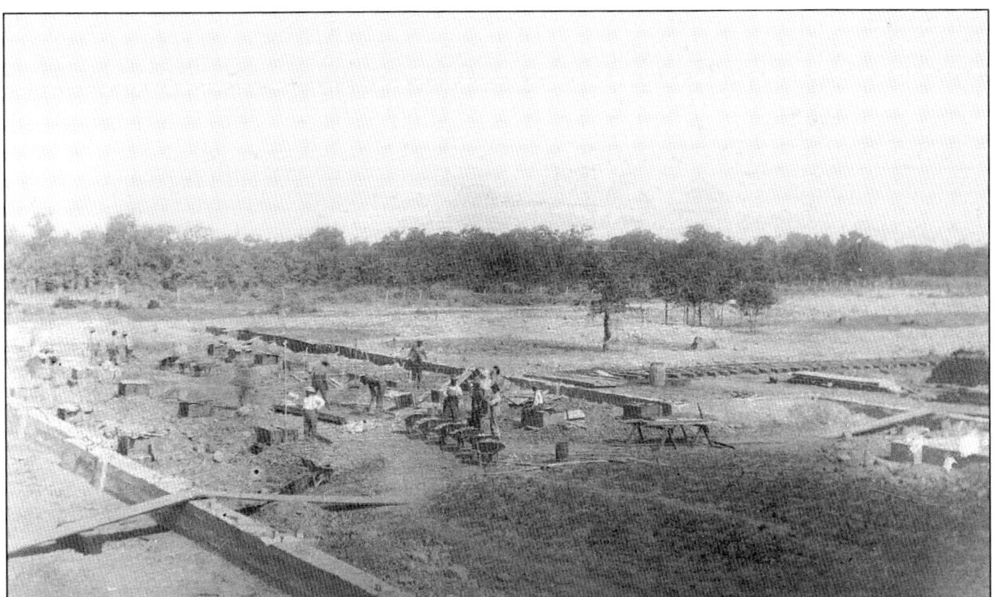

The Lakeside Sugar Refinery was owned by Capt. William Dunovant. Construction of the refinery began in 1902 in an area called Lakeside in the original Patrick Reels survey. It took many men and trainloads of materials to construct the large and impressive sugar refinery. This image shows workers in the first stages of the building process, setting up the foundation.

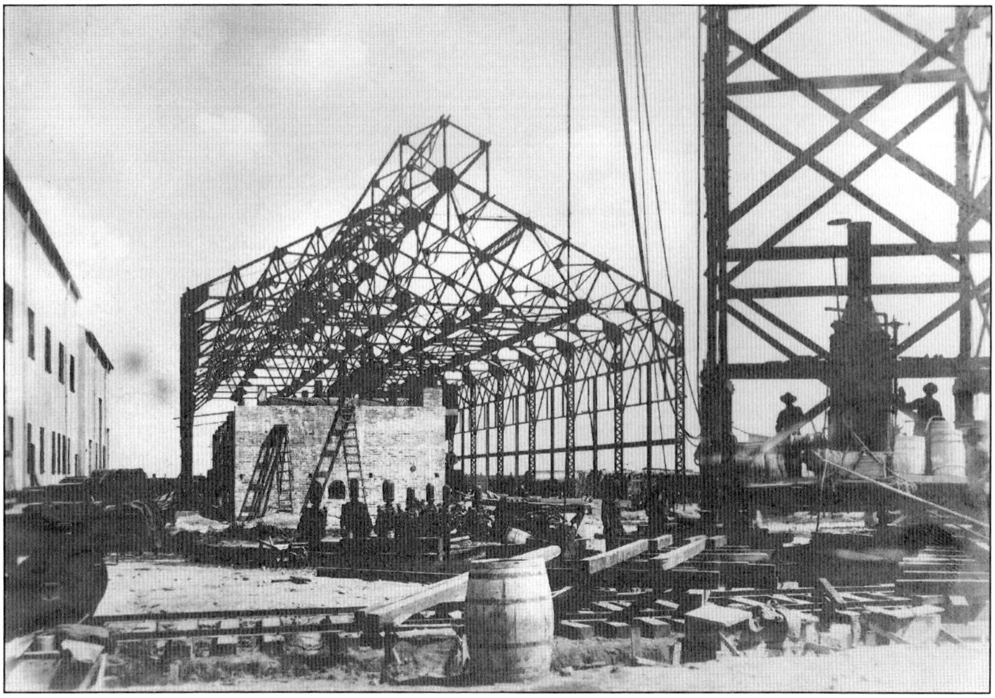

Large quantities of iron, steel, and tin were required for the buildings and framework of the refinery. It required the work of 100 men, which provided employment and a financial boost to the local economy. Refinery workers were important to the local shops, businesses, and restaurants in Eagle Lake, and many of the men resided in homes in the Lakeside area.

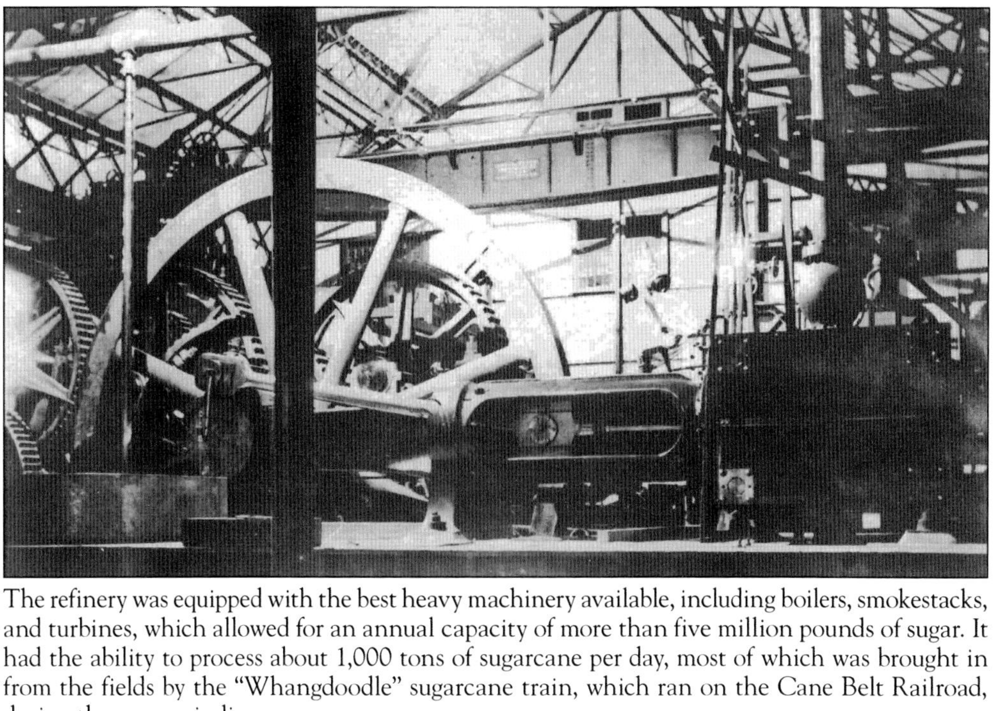

The refinery was equipped with the best heavy machinery available, including boilers, smokestacks, and turbines, which allowed for an annual capacity of more than five million pounds of sugar. It had the ability to process about 1,000 tons of sugarcane per day, most of which was brought in from the fields by the "Whangdoodle" sugarcane train, which ran on the Cane Belt Railroad, during the cane-grinding season.

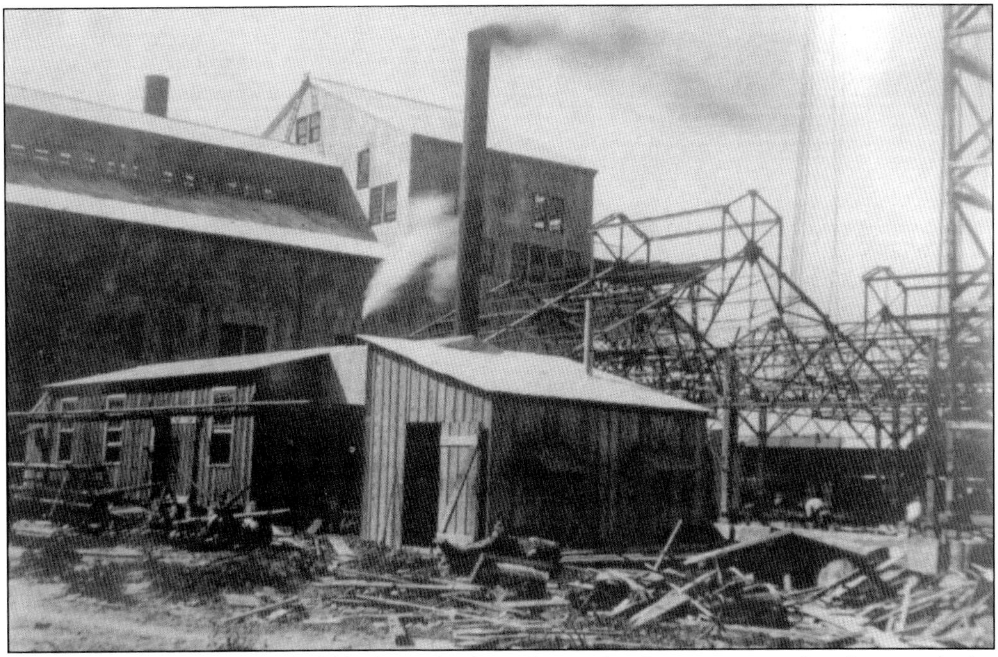

The working refinery expelled black smoke from the stacks. Sugarcane was hand-cut, with the leaves stripped or cut from the stalk before it was crushed or pressed for juice. Cane juice was boiled in iron kettles until it became dark sticky crystals. The residue that remained after crushing the cane, which is called bagasse, was burned as fuel to help generate power for the mill.

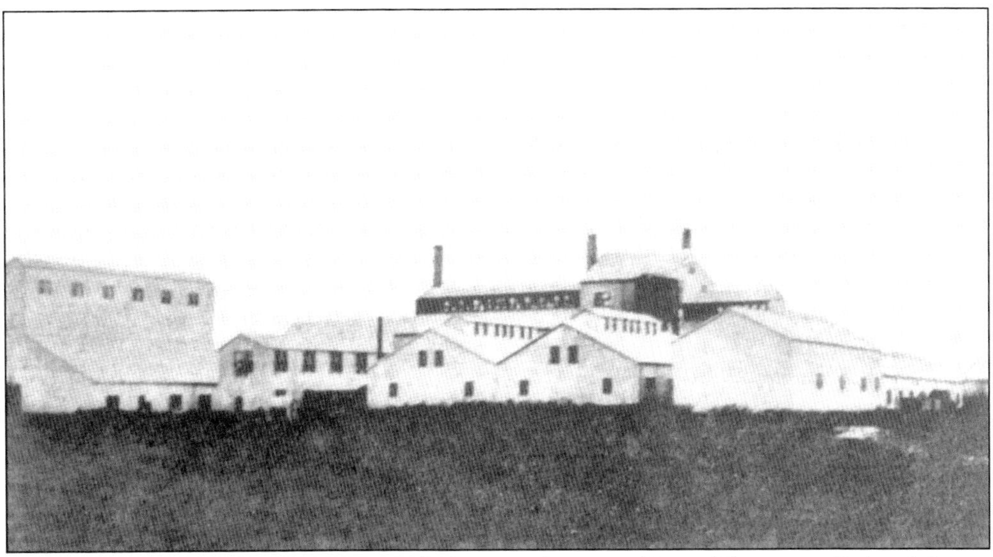

The Lakeside Sugar Refinery was among the largest refineries in Texas. The town of Lakeside began in 1898, when the Lakeside Depot was completed as a station on the Cane Belt Railroad. Capt. William Dunovant built a large warehouse by the depot, and Lakeside became the headquarters for his farming and business interests. It had a sugar mill, a rice mill, a cotton gin, houses, a store, a hotel, and, later, a recreation area.

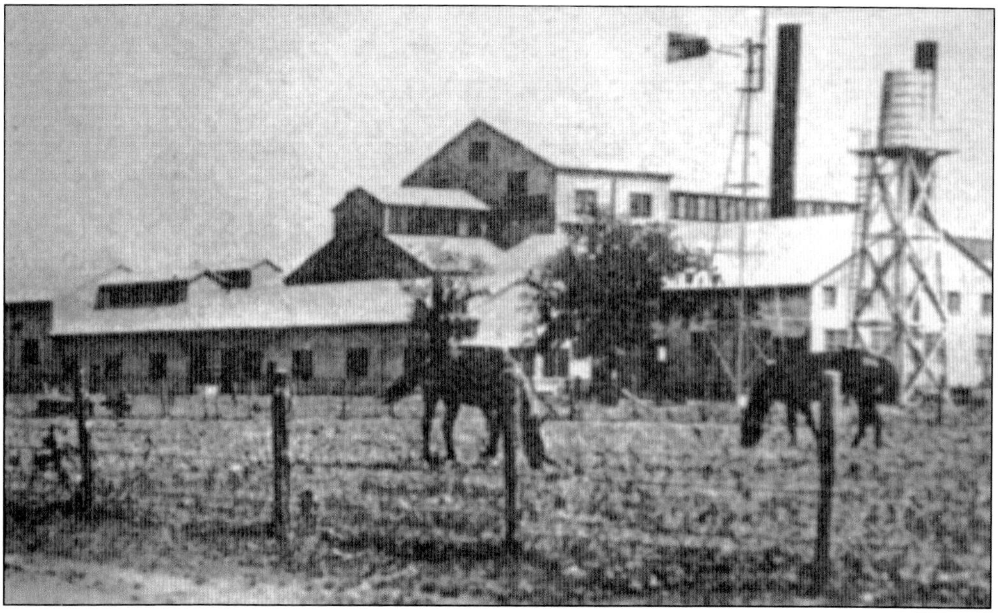

Capt. William Dunovant's horses graze at the refinery, unaware of the lively activity within involving fire, men, water, conveyors, and heavy machinery. The cane was lifted from the railcars with large hoists, and the stalks were usually processed within two to three days to retain high sugar content. Early railcars loaded with cane were pulled by horses and mules.

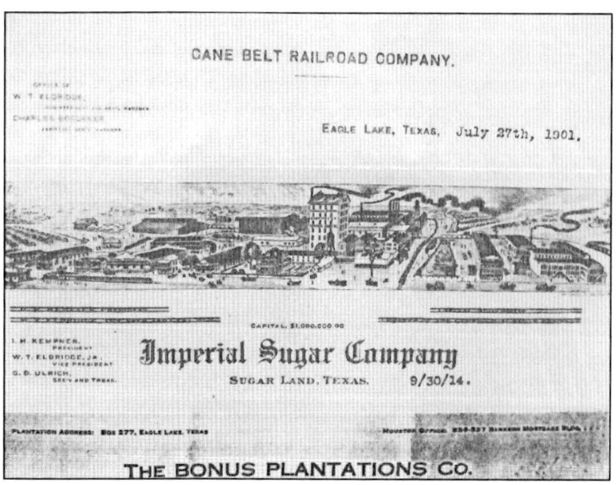

This document shows the later interests of W.T. Eldridge in the Imperial Sugar Company, Bonus plantations, and the refinery. Captain Dunovant often rode through the sugarcane fields in his buggy car with Eldridge, his business partner. During harvest, one fourth to one third of the sugarcane stalks were planted as seed cane, which was done by putting the stalks flat on the ground and covering them with the rich soil. This encouraged the growth of new cane, which could reach up to 13 feet in height.

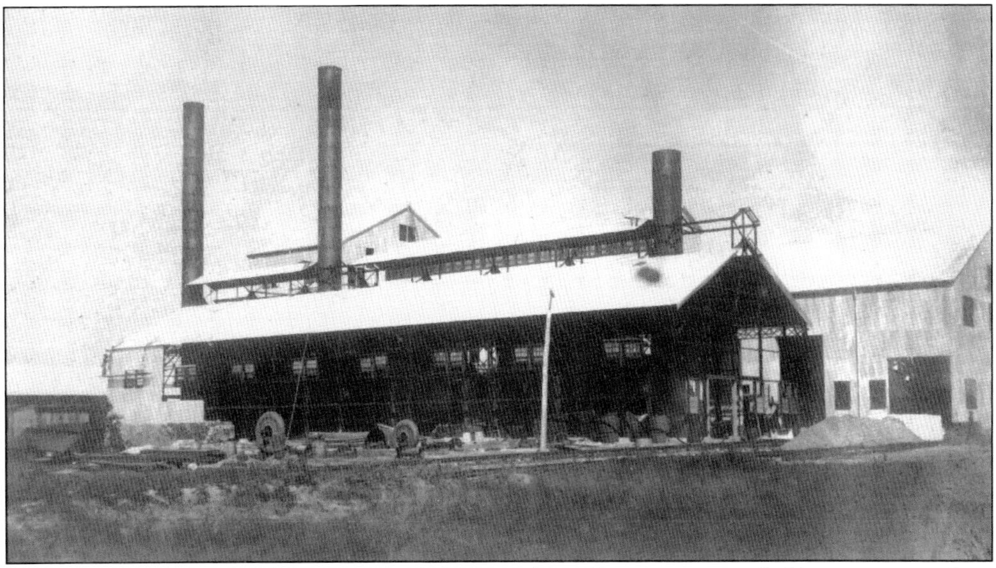

Much of the labor utilized in the cane fields and the refinery was provided by convict workers leased from the state to the refinery owners. In 1910, a state law was passed to prohibit the use of convict labor on privately owned plantations. Due to labor shortages, this created a blow to the sugar and other farming industries; the labor shortage was among the reasons the refinery closed in 1913.

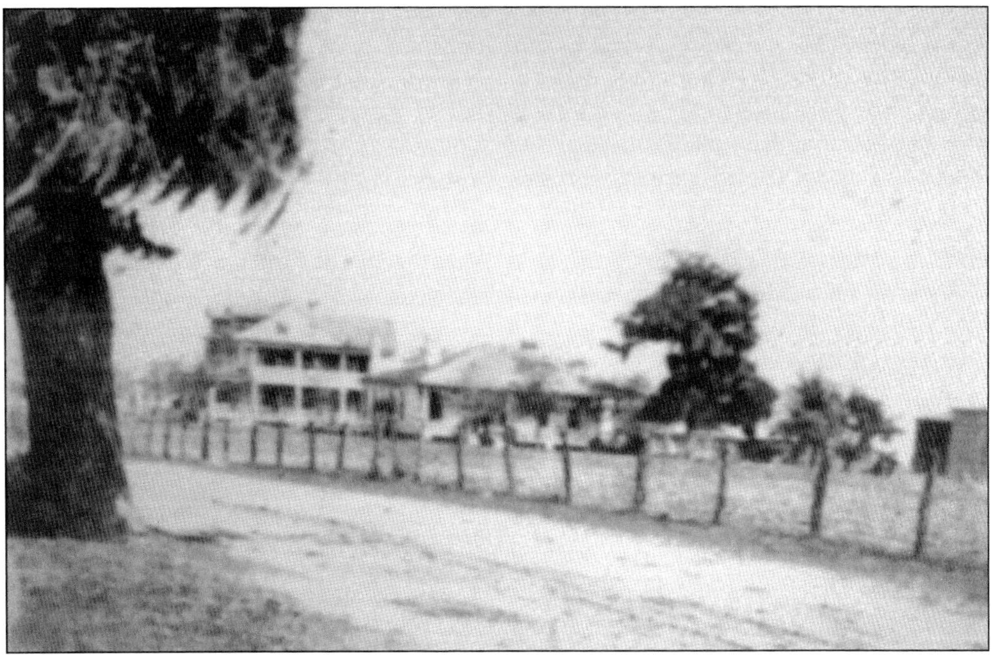

The moss-covered trees and sandy road leading to the Lakeside Sugar Refinery offices and buildings enhance a panoramic view of the refinery, its windmill, smokestacks, and water tower. Water was important for the refinery and its industrial output. Additional water was furnished from the lake through a permanent water-access agreement, which was sold to Capt. William Dunovant to satisfy the water needed for the sugarcane-refining process; the ingress is still visible along Lakeside Drive.

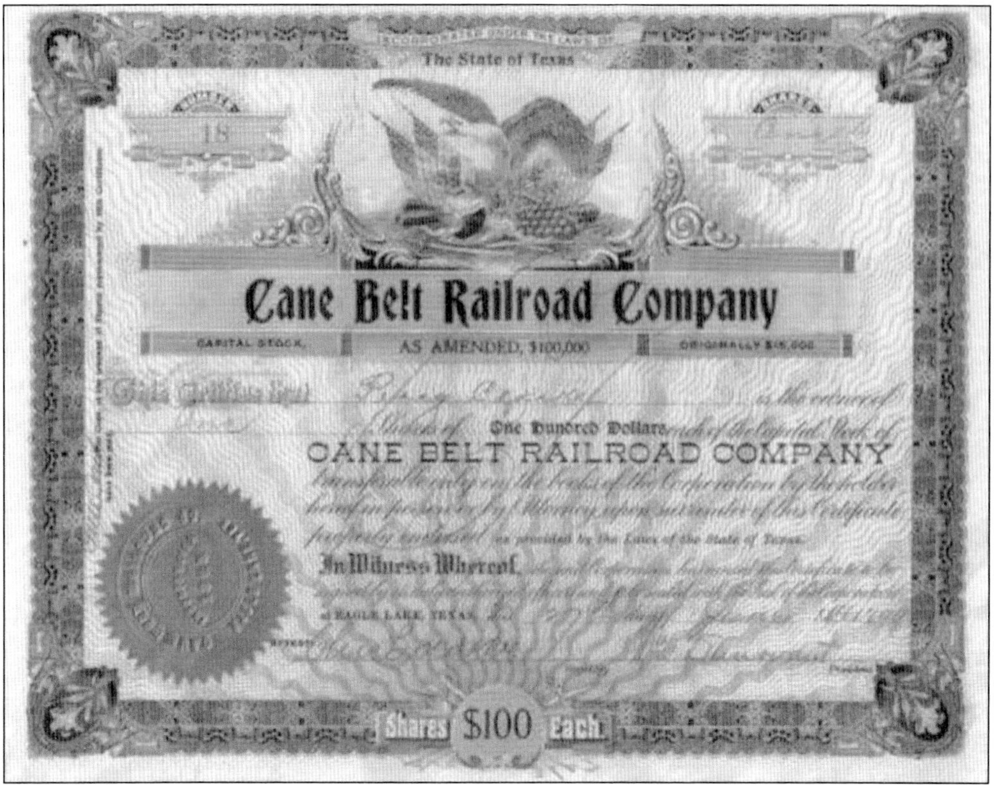

A Cane Belt Railroad Company stock certificate, issued in 1899, became an icon of the Cane Belt Railroad, which was formed and chartered by William Dunovant, William T. Eldridge, and several other Eagle Lake businessmen on March 10, 1898. The original goal of the railroad was to connect the Dunovant plantation at Bonus, Texas, to the Lakeside Sugar Refinery, which was 10 miles away. The refinery first transported the sugarcane from Dunovant's large plantation by mule-driven railcars and later used locomotive power. (Courtesy of Ken Stavinoha.)

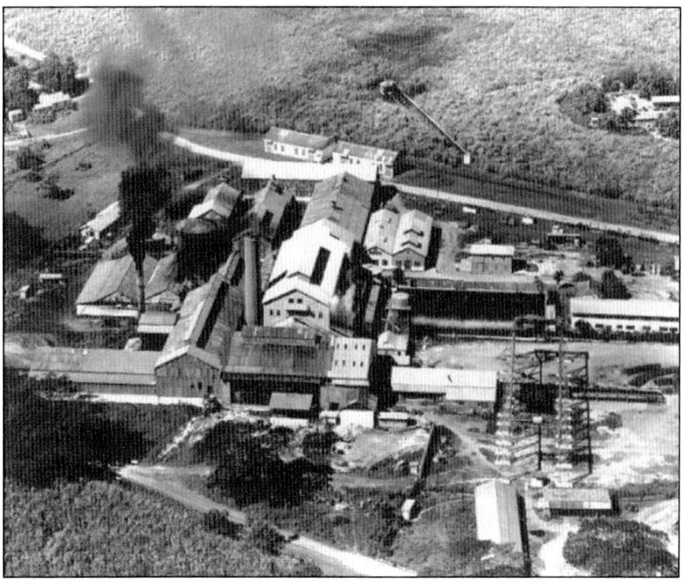

This aerial view of the Bernard Lodge Sugar Factory in Jamaica shows the rebuilt Lakeside Sugar Refinery, which was disassembled, shipped, and rebuilt using the original Lakeside materials in the cane fields outside Kingston, Jamaica, near Spanish Town. The sugar factory has been producing since 1919. It once had a railroad and is still surrounded by large sugar cane fields. (Courtesy of J.S. Tyndale-Biscoe.)

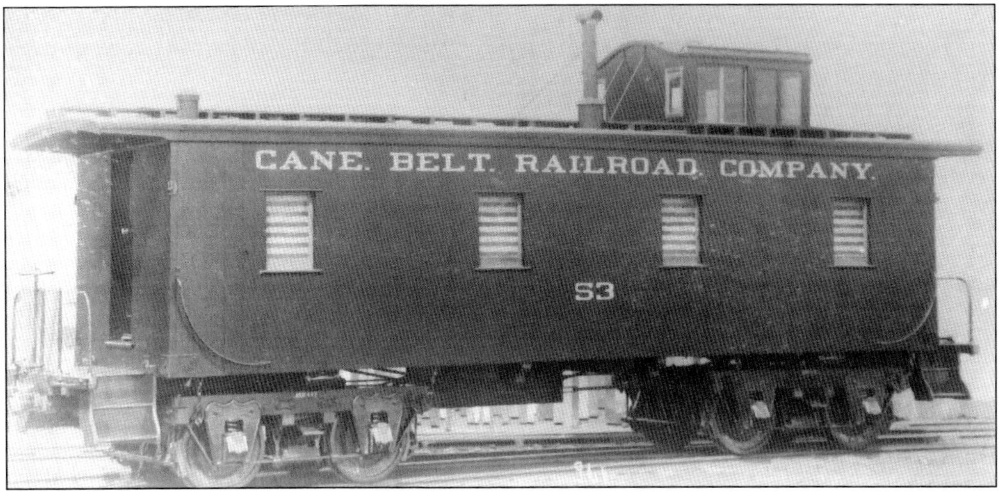

This caboose belonged to the Cane Belt Railroad Company. The railroad first extended 15 miles north to Sealy, and later 89 miles south to the Gulf Coast through Matagorda and Brazoria Counties, with the final line extending from Bay City to Matagorda. The Cane Belt Railroad was bought by the Atchison, Topeka & Santa Fe Railway on November 30, 1903. (Courtesy of Ken Stavinoha.)

CANE BELT RAILROAD.

WM. DUNOVANT, President. | CHAS. BOEDEKER, Gen. Fht. & Pas. Agent.
W. T. ELDRIDGE, Vice-Prest. & Gen. Mgr. | F. J. HUEY, Auditor.

General Offices—Eagle Lake, Tex.

No. 3	Mls.	*January* 27, 1901.	Mls.	No. 4
		LEAVE] [ARRIVE		
†8 40 A M	0	**Sealy**[1]	42.06	6 40 P M
9 14 "	9.47	Beard	32.59	6 00 "
9 29 "	13.35	Cantaloupe	28.71	5 30 "
9 53 "	17.80	arr. . **Eagle Lake**[2] lve.	24.26	5 01 "
10 35 "	17.80	lve. . **Eagle Lake** . arr.	24.26	4 37 "
10 42 "	18.00	Lakeside	24.06	4 30 "
11 01 "	19.21	Dunovant	22.85	4 20 "
11 19 "	22.18	Matthews	19.88	4 05 "
11 37 "	24.53	McDows	17.53	3 55 "
11 51 A M	27.53	Bonus	14.53	3 30 "
12 11 Noon	28.68	Quin	13.38	3 25 "
12 31 "	31.88	Egypt	10.18	3 10 "
12 51 Noon	36.48	Glen Flora	5.58	2 50 "
1 20 P M	42.06	**Wharton**[3]	0	†2 20 P M
		ARRIVE] [LEAVE		

† Daily, except Sunday. STANDARD—*Central time.*

This Cane Belt Railroad schedule for January 27, 1901, shows the stops between Sealy and Wharton, Texas, with connections. The railroad between Sealy and Wharton was completed in 1900, and the railroad reached Bay City by July 1, 1901. The final segment of the railroad was from Bay City to Matagorda, where oil exploration was occurring. This was an important shipping segment of the railroad. The Whangdoodle trains No. 111 and No. 112 brought sugarcane from the fields to the refinery. (Courtesy of Ken Stavinoha.)

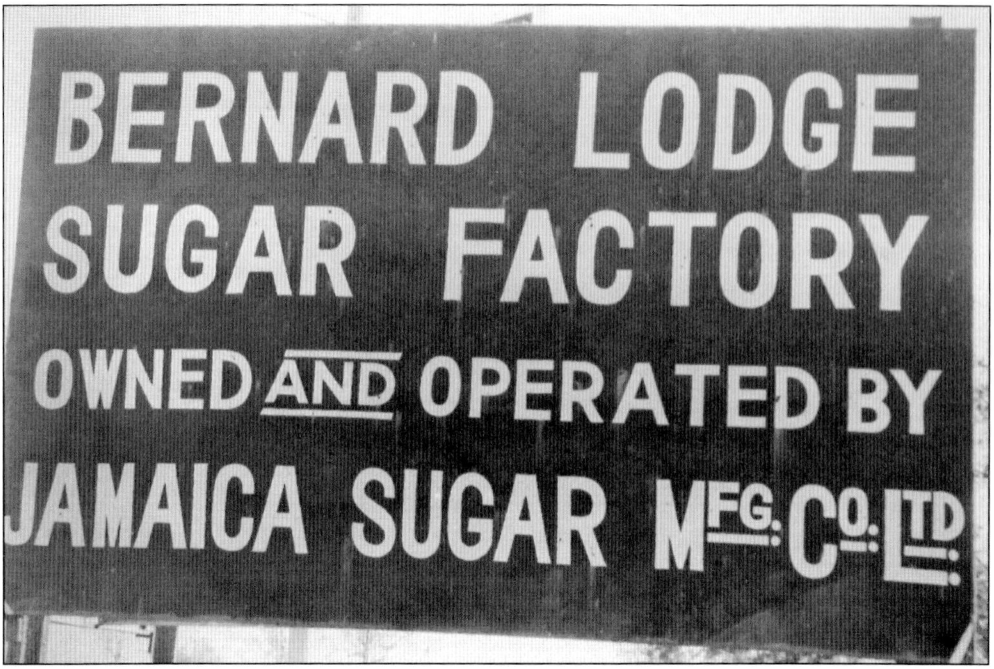

In 1918, engineer Maurice Miller of New York arrived in Eagle Lake and Lakeside and oversaw the dismantling of the refinery by 90 men. Miller supervised the loading of materials onto 100 railcars for transport to Galveston. From there, the cargo was sent by ship to Jamaica. Miller also oversaw the rebuilding of the Lakeside Sugar Refinery as the Bernard Lodge Sugar Factory—located near Kingston, Jamaica—for its first harvest in 1919.

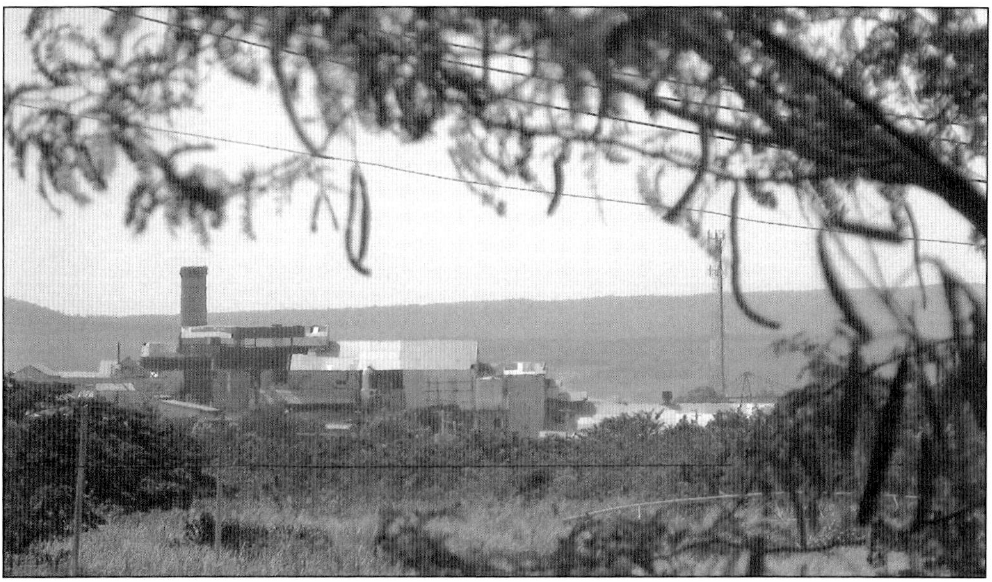

From its beginnings, the Bernard Lodge Sugar Factory was owned by several different private companies and by the government during its nearly 100 years of operation. In 2009, the factory was bought by a Chinese company interested in revitalizing and possibly rebuilding the last three remaining sugar mills in Jamaica with an infusion of $160 million and the idea of increased ethanol production.

Four

RICE, RANCHING, AND AGRICULTURE

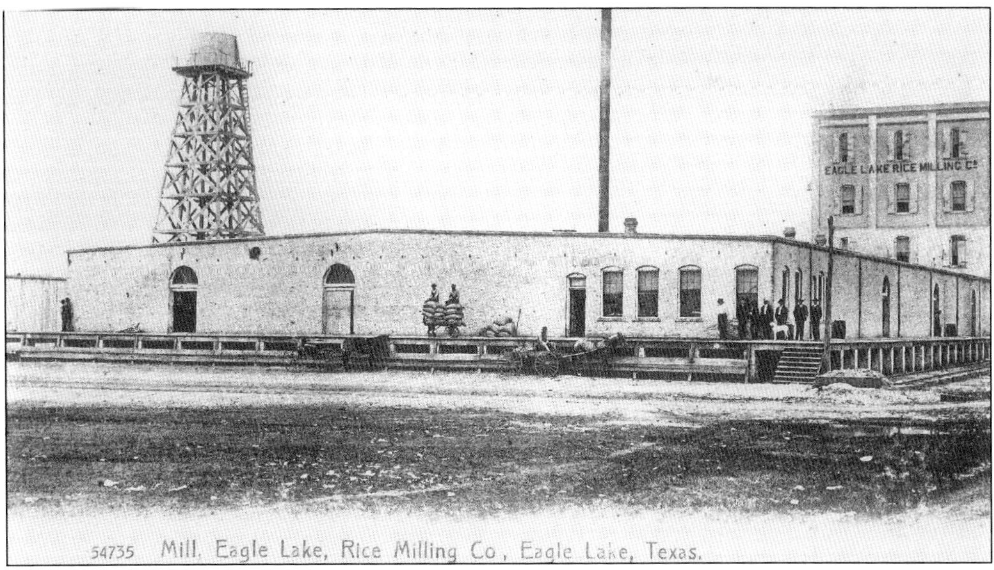

The Eagle Lake Rice Milling Company, which opened in 1902 with Paul Pritchard as the first manager, was a symbol of the rapidly growing rice industry in the coastal plains of Texas. Rice replaced cotton and sugarcane as the most important cash crop around Colorado County in the first decade of the 20th century. Rice brought about economic growth, the arrival of new families from the Midwest, and new uses of the flat prairie; it also fostered railroad expansion, the growth of related industries, and agricultural diversity in the area.

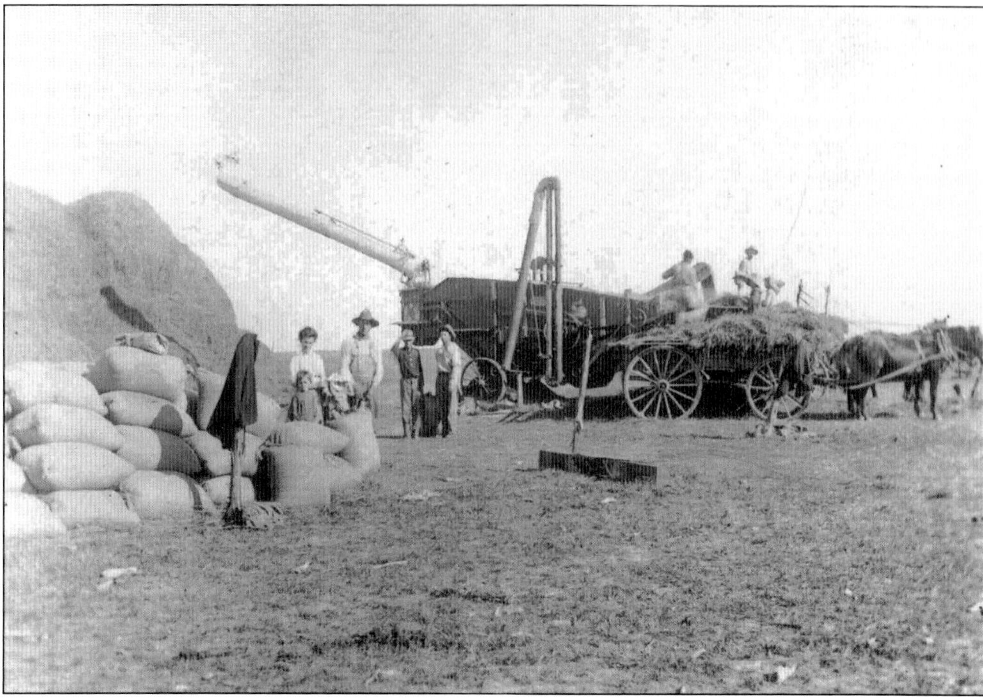

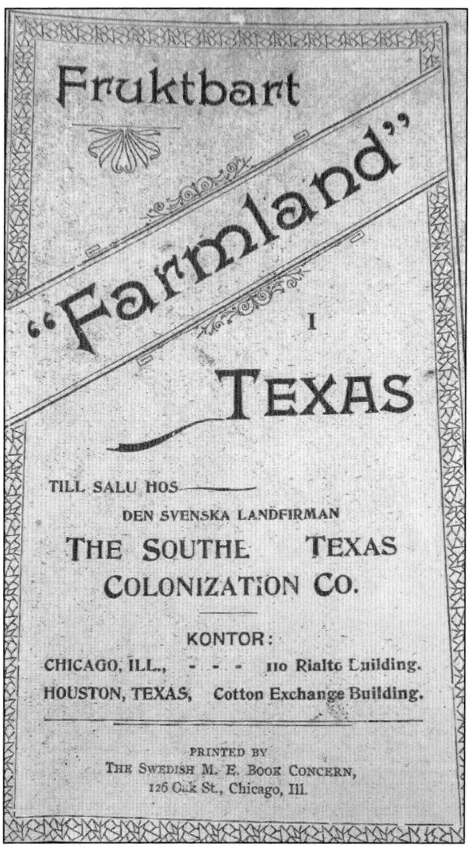

Rice was introduced to the Eagle Lake area in 1898 by Capt. William Dunovant, a leading agriculture and business entrepreneur. By 1901, the county had 13,500 acres under cultivation and has remained an important rice growing area. The towns of Garwood and Lakeside, Texas, were generated by rice interest, and the nearby farming towns of Lissie and Chesterville also became important rice cultivation areas.

The prairie surrounding Eagle Lake was largely settled by immigrants from the Midwest who were brought in by large land development companies, which partnered with the railroads to create real estate excursion trains to bring prospective buyers to Texas. Based in Chicago and Houston, the Southern Texas Colonization Company was one such enterprise. With this booklet printed in Swedish, the company was appealing to Swedish immigrants from the north to settle the farming lands around Eagle Lake. Many came with their families to contribute to the growth of area agriculture.

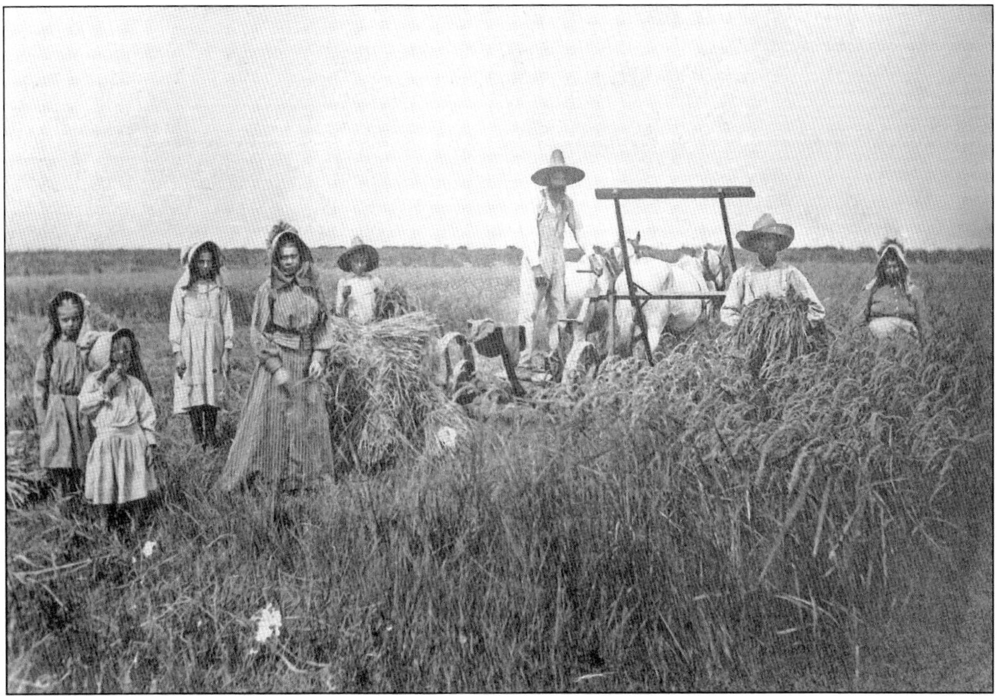

Local farmer Quinto Bottino was born in Milan, Italy, in 1865. He came to the Eagle Lake area from Illinois and settled with his family on the prairie near Chesterville, just outside Eagle Lake. This 1910 image shows Bottino driving a horse-drawn rice binder, with his wife, children, and neighbors standing nearby—an example of immigrant families working the fields as the rice industry was beginning.

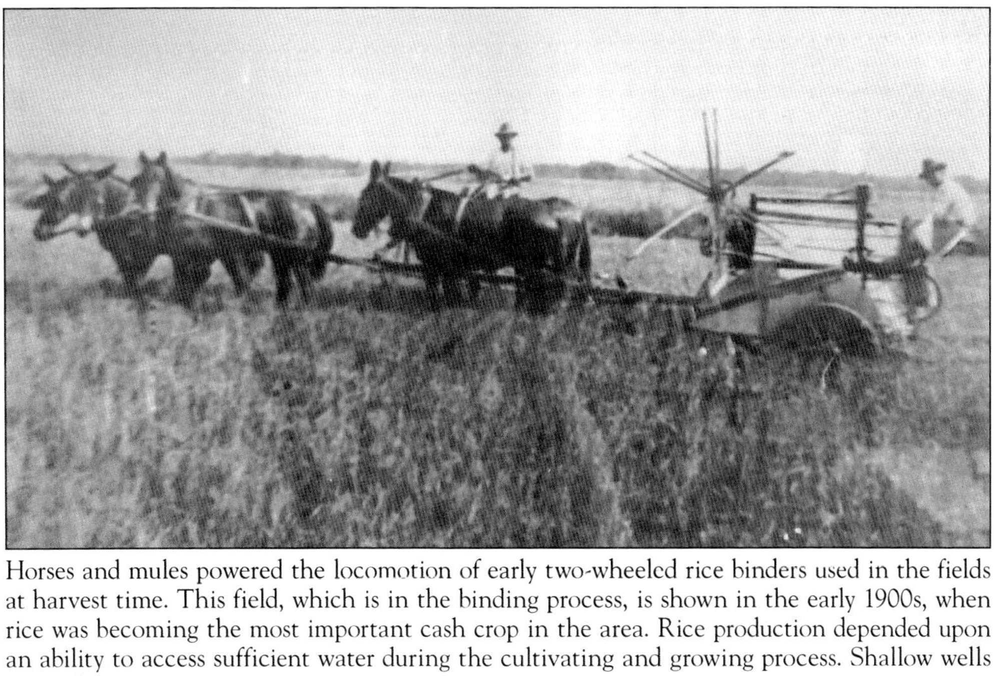

Horses and mules powered the locomotion of early two-wheeled rice binders used in the fields at harvest time. This field, which is in the binding process, is shown in the early 1900s, when rice was becoming the most important cash crop in the area. Rice production depended upon an ability to access sufficient water during the cultivating and growing process. Shallow wells assisted in crop irrigation.

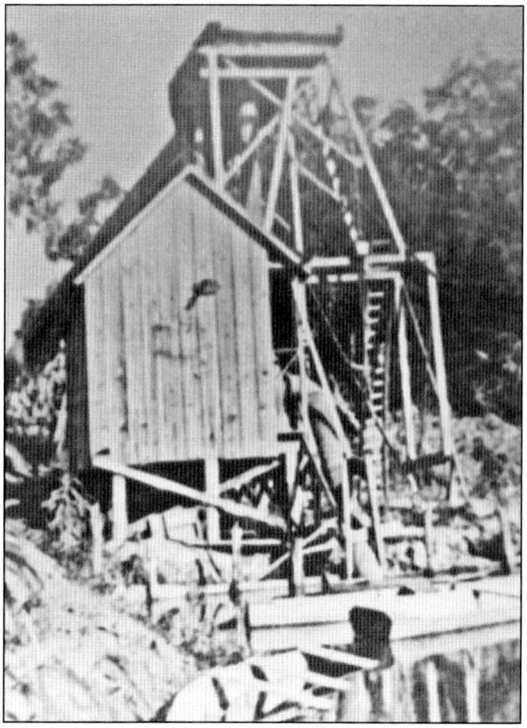

In July 1901, the Dunovant electric pump was one of a kind in the area. Powered by electricity that came from Capt. William Dunovant's Lakeside Cotton Gin and mill, the pump—in its process and with insufficient water coming in from the river—contributed to pumping the lake dry. This resulted in the loss of fish, lily pads, and natural life as farmers were unable to pump sufficient water to the lake from the Colorado River to keep the water level up. Dunovant put in two 18-inch pumps to flood his rice fields and to water 3,500 acres of sugarcane. Water was pumped directly from the river, which saved his crops. Dunovant planted his first successful crop in 1898 in the area called Lower Lake—for these first 40 acres of rice, he used a seven-inch walking plough and broadcast seed by hand. (Courtesy of Prairie Edge Museum.)

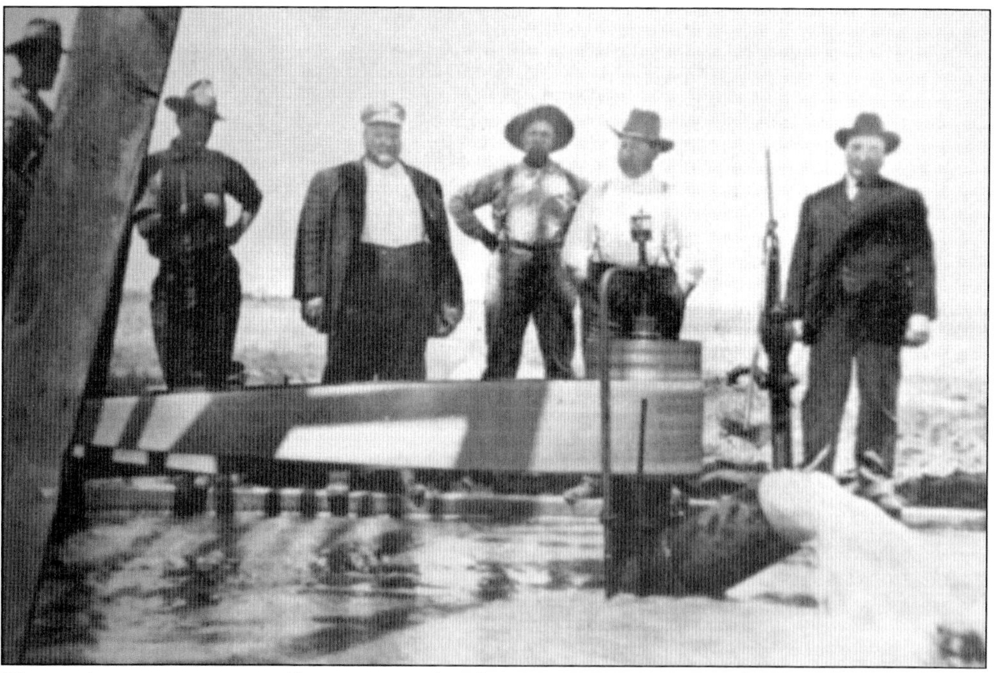

This early rice irrigation well is an example of ingenuity in extracting from wells, which could produce enough water to irrigate 40 to 80 acres of rice. In 1899, near Chesterville, John Linderholm dug the first irrigation well, which was completed by G.E. Thomas Sr. Standing at this well are, from left to right, Gus and Ernest Seaholm, Frank Stephens, Charles Banning, Hayes Stephens, and Fox Stephens. (Courtesy of Prairie Edge Museum.)

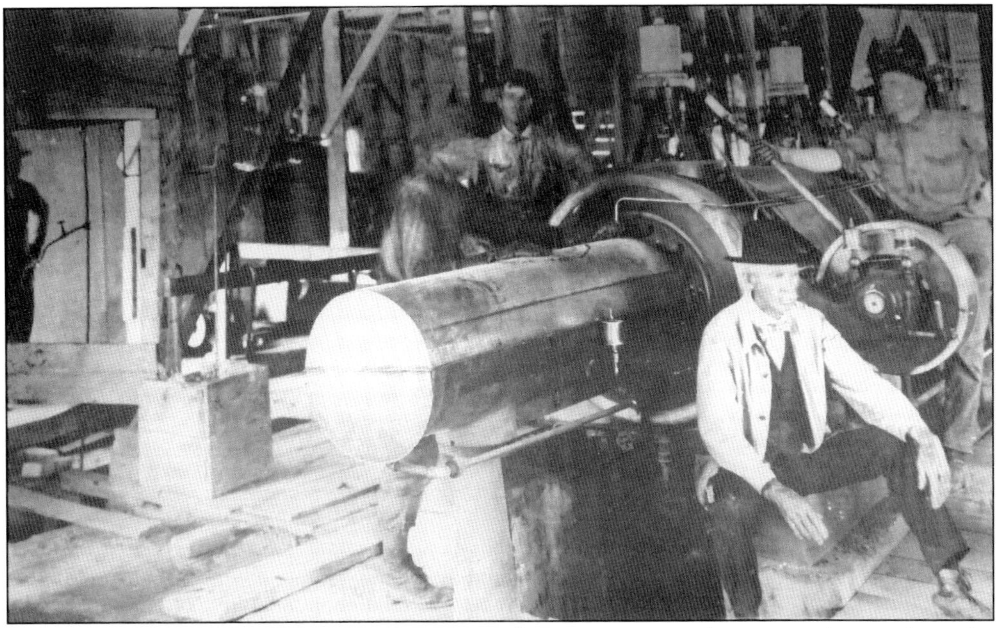

Early rice farming depended upon irrigation, with steam engines that pumped water from the river, as shown in this c. 1918 photograph of an early pump house. The Nordberg Cylinder High Pressure Steam Engines were installed by the Staffords—prominent landowners and farmers who lived in Columbus (the county seat)—at the Colorado River Plant, which was used for irrigation. Mr. Delaney, a supervisor, is seated; F.H. Porter is standing at right; the others are unidentified.

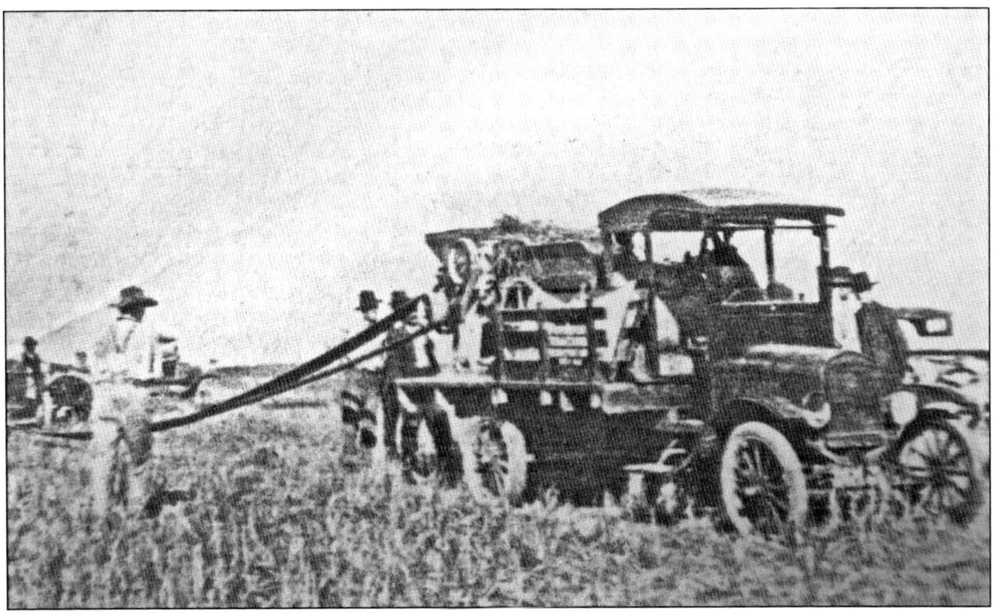

In the early 1900s, rice harvesting in the fields around Eagle Lake was normally done by mules. However, they could not always work as well when the ground was wet and muddy, and they were gradually replaced by more modern machinery and vehicles. This flatbed—one of the first on the local farms—holds the threshing machine and belt.

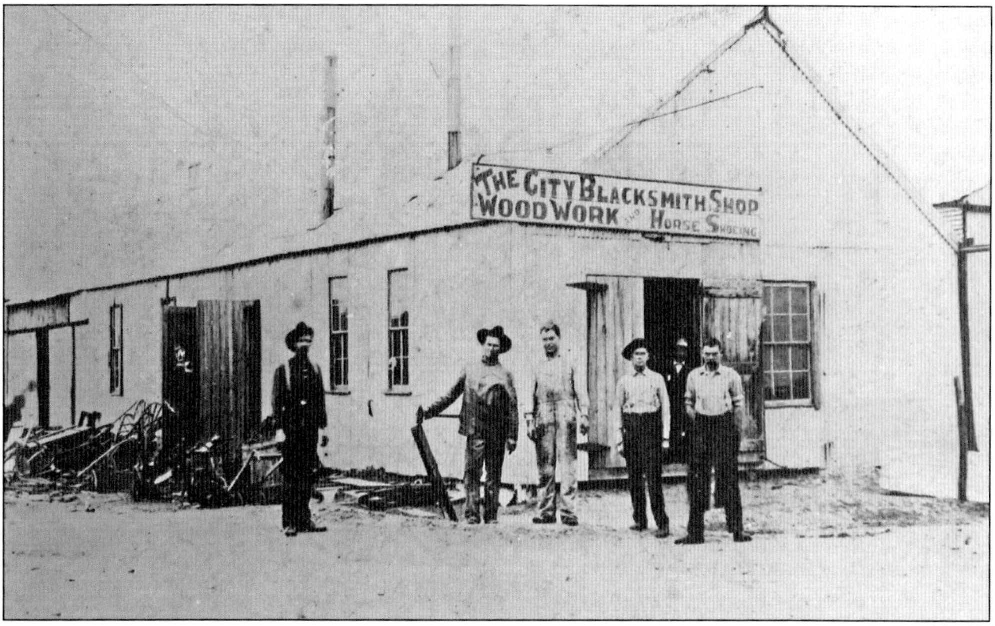

The city blacksmith and woodworking shops were important to early farmers, who depended heavily upon blacksmith shops, woodworking benches, harness shops, and skilled craftsmen. They could rebuild parts for machines—both metal and wood—and could come to the farmers' assistance in times of breakdowns of farming equipment, especially during harvest season. Many farmers had their own blacksmith shops. Pictured here are, from left to right, John Zemlisky, Frank Martin, Art Townley, unidentified, and unidentified.

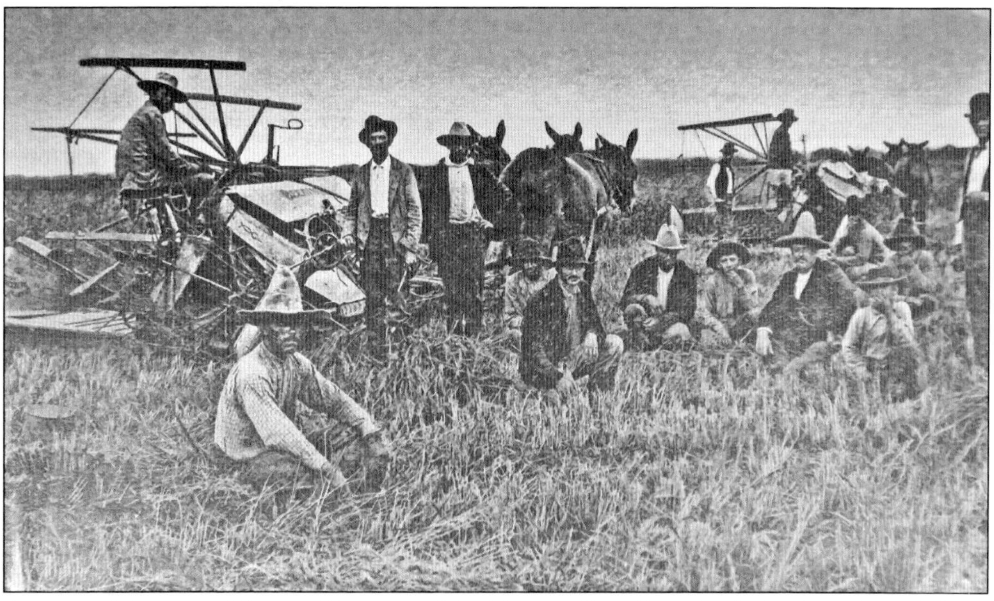

A postcard depicting "Harvest Time on a Rice Farm in Texas" in the 1920s shows farm helpers and members of the G.E. Thomas family at work in their field on the Lissie prairie. They have paused for a moment to pose for a photograph. Pictured here are, starting from third-left to right among the seated workers, Moses, Harold, G.E., and Ralph Thomas; the others are unidentified. (Courtesy of Prairie Edge Museum.)

The rice mill, elevator, and water tower at Lakeside, Texas, are pictured at right. The complex was built and owned by Capt. William Dunovant, who started the rice industry in the Eagle Lake area in 1898. His partner, W.T. Eldridge, was the manager. The area had been hit by strong winds in 1913, as evidenced by damage to the side of the rice elevator.

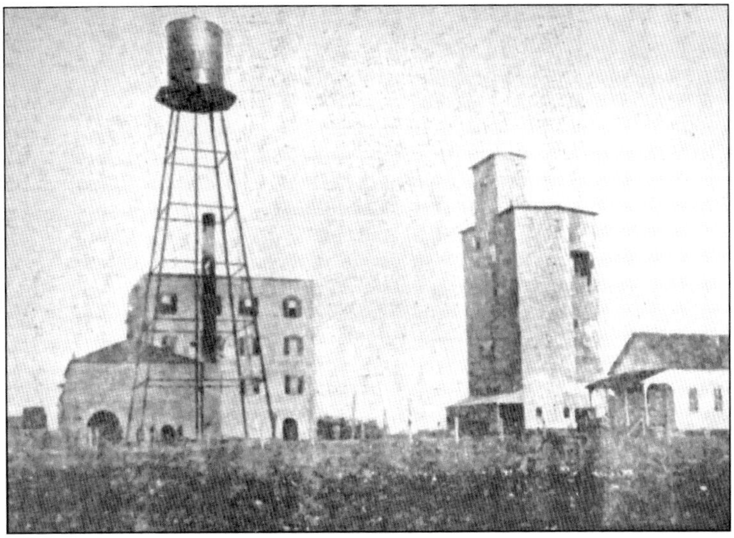

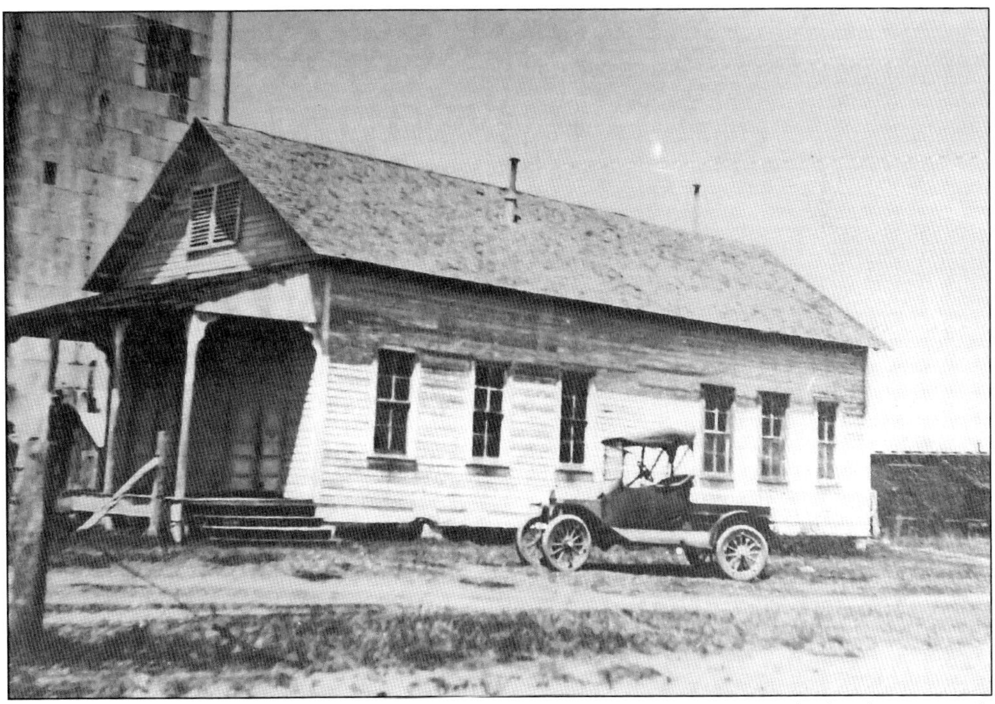

The Lakeside rice and cotton office of Capt. William Dunovant is pictured after heavy winds hit the area in 1913. The storm damaged buildings and equipment. This structure remained and was a second office for Dunovant and his partner, William T. Eldridge, where they conducted their rice and cotton business.

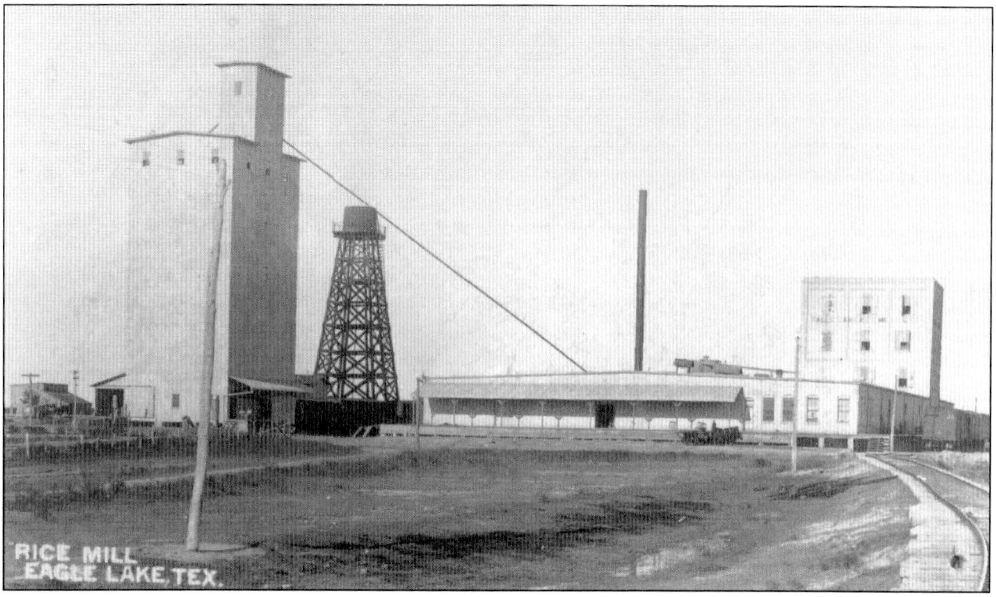

The Eagle Lake Rice Mill, the second rice mill in the area, was built in 1902. A.M. Waugh, Paul Pritchard, and John Chumney organized and managed the mill, which was acquired by Hibernia Bank and Trust during the Depression. After being partially destroyed in a 1932 storm, it was sold to O.J. and David Wintermann in 1935 for use as a farming warehouse.

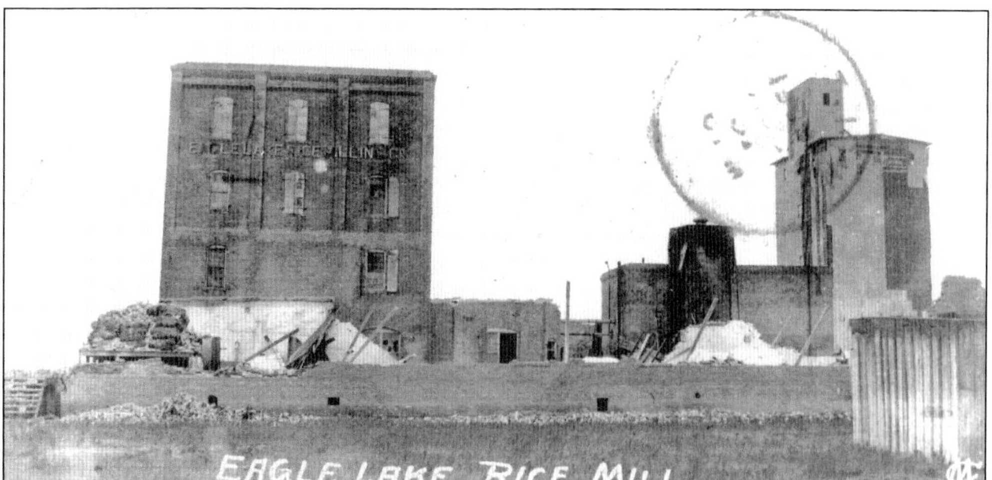

This image of the Eagle Lake Rice Mill shows the extent of the damage after the storm of 1913. Parts of the grain elevator and the buildings required reconstruction, as indicated by the storm debris, which landed on the cement platform. Many area farmers suffered economic hardship after the severe storms of 1900, 1909, and 1913.

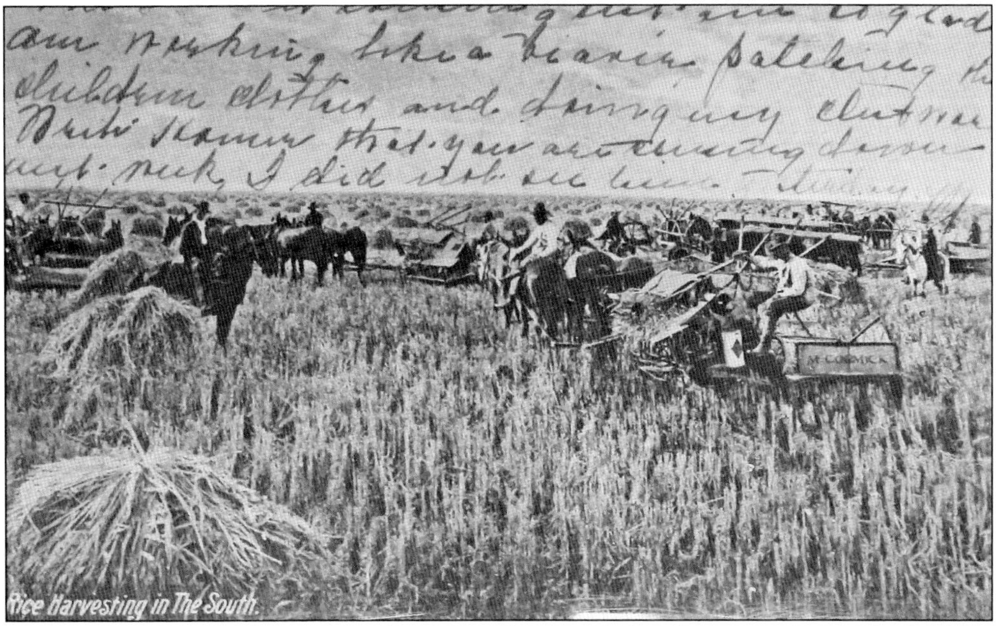

This postcard from the early 1900s shows a rice harvest and stacks of rice dotting the fields on the prairie near Eagle Lake. Rice harvest work was done with wagons, mules, horses, and rice binders. There was always a water boy on a wagon to assist the workers.

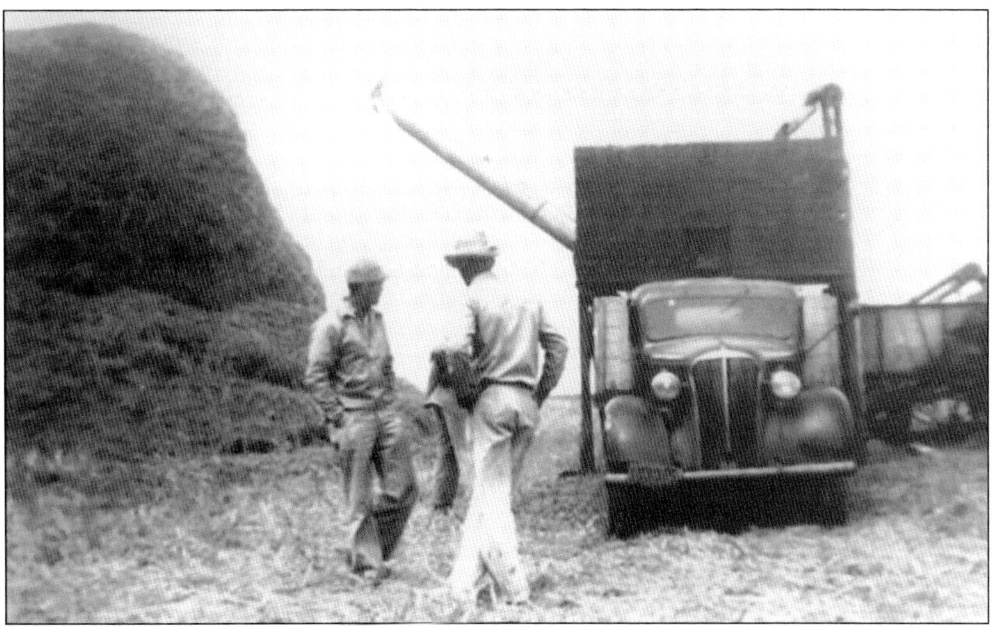

In this 1942 photograph, taken in a field owned by Mose Thomas, tractors and trucks have replaced mule-drawn binders and made harvest more efficient and faster. Farming became easier as planting and harvests were modernized by new and heavier equipment, requiring fewer workers and horse-drawn wagons.

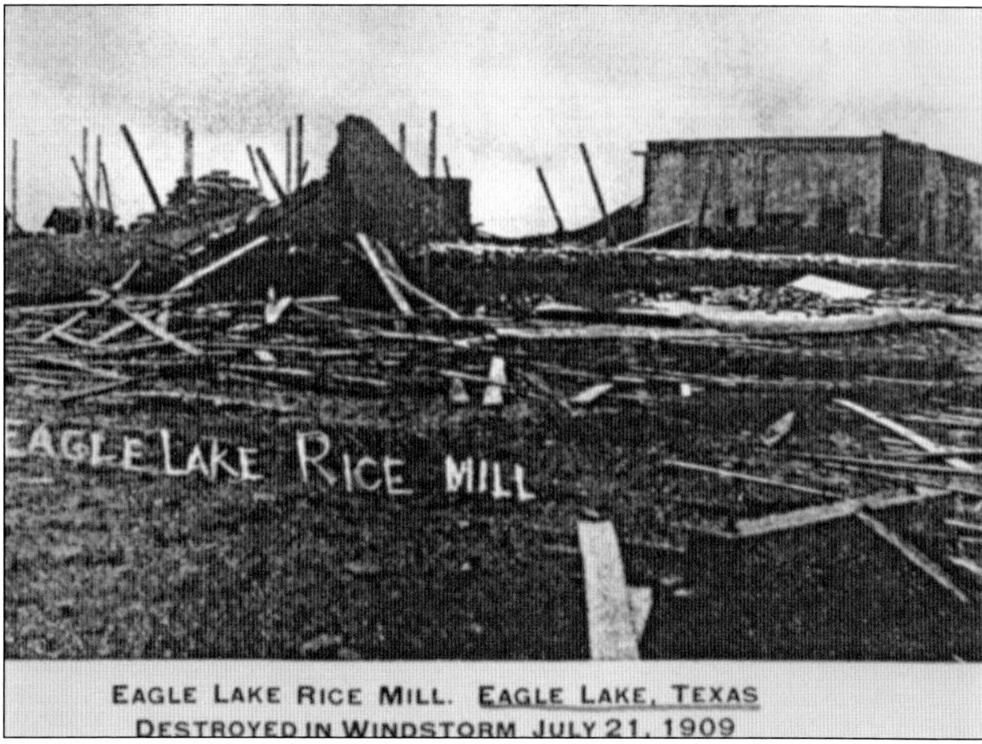

Storms, floods, and hurricanes played significant roles in early rice farming. The Eagle Lake Rice Mill was destroyed in a windstorm on July 21, 1909, making it necessary to suspend operations until the mill was reconstructed. (Courtesy of Prairie Edge Museum.)

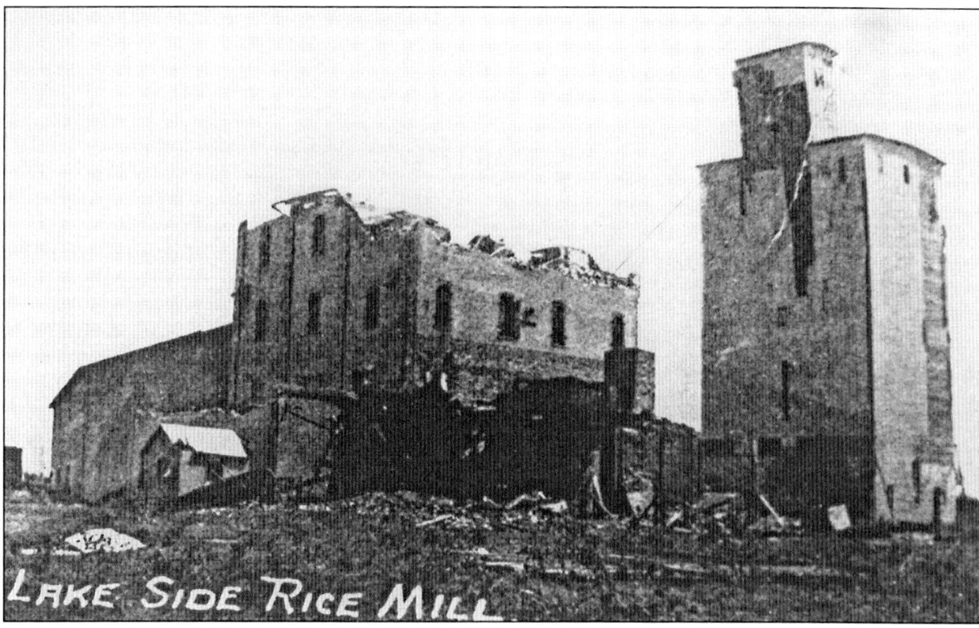

The Lakeside Rice Mill, owned by William Dunovant, suffered heavy damages in the 1909 storm. Almost half of the brick mill was destroyed due to a costly act of nature. Bricks and debris had to be cleared before reconstruction could begin. (Courtesy of Prairie Edge Museum.)

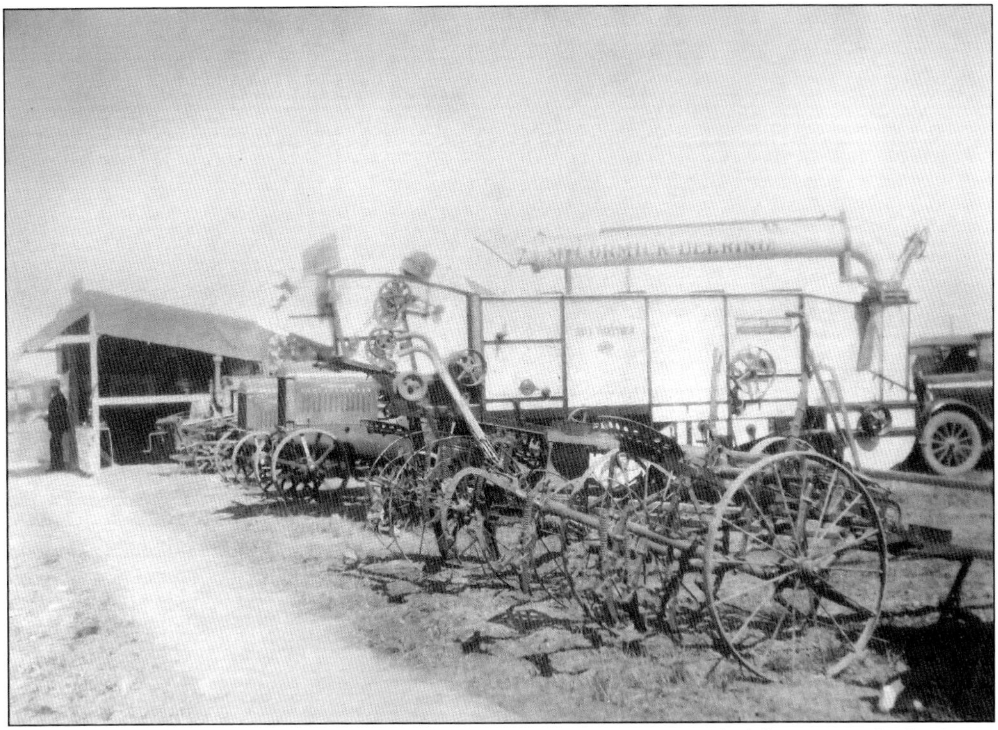

Early rice-farming equipment sold by the Stephens Company provided farmers with the latest technology for preparing the land and harvesting crops. The gasoline engine was an important assistant to farmers, and then modern tractors are visible at left. New equipment arrived by the railroad near the warehouse.

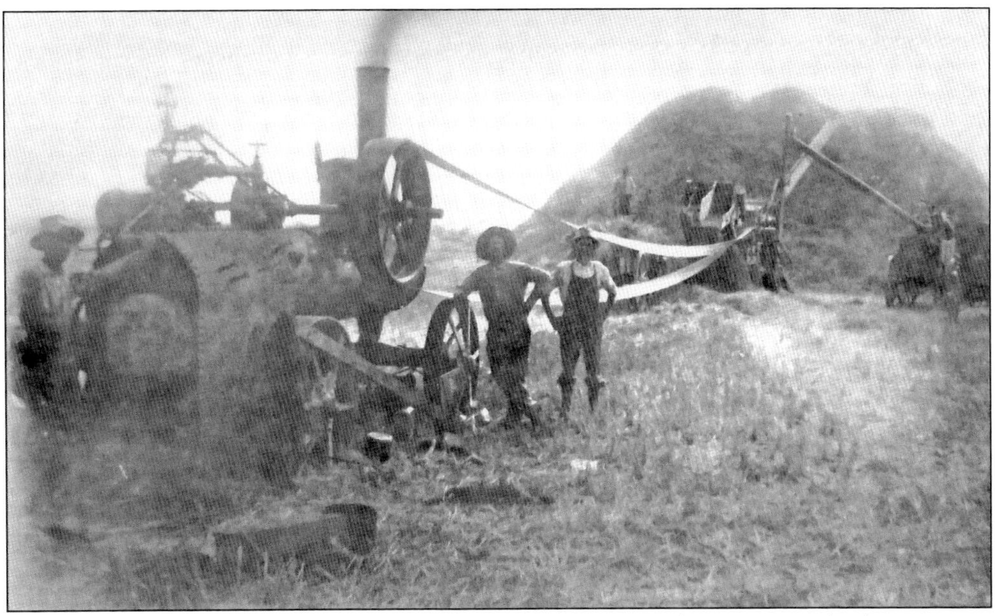

In this c. 1915 photograph, rice-threshing operation and rice stacks are pictured at harvest time in a field belonging to Ed Hodde. Rice stacks covered the countryside during harvest season. (Courtesy of Prairie Edge Museum.)

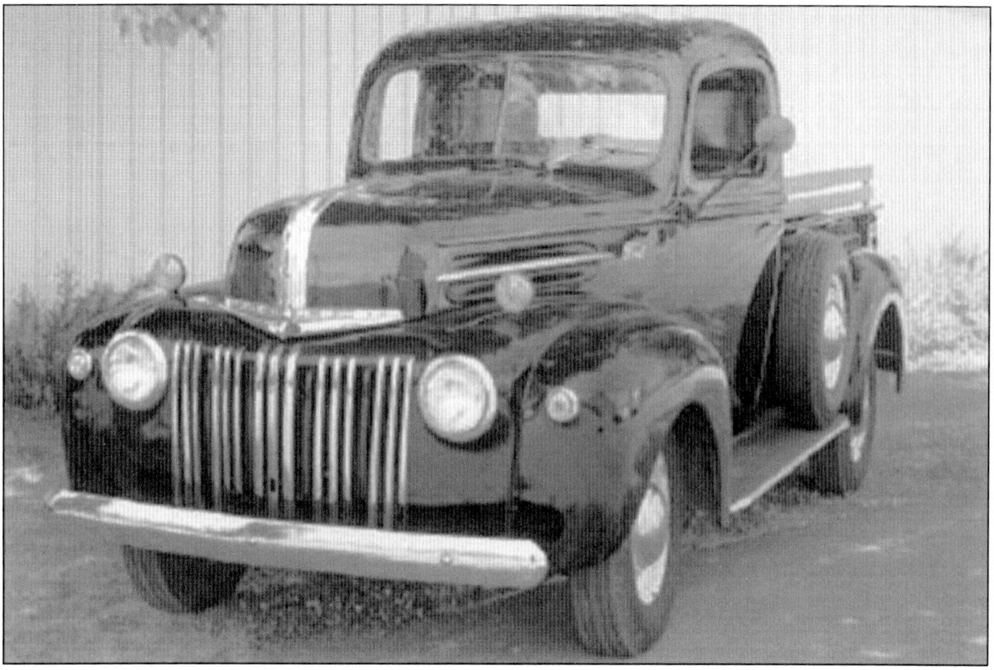

Truck farming became important in the early 1900s as an additional source of farm revenue. The problem of boll weevils in cotton farming was severe in 1903. With a reduction in cotton production, farmers sought cash crops to grow, including cantaloupes, cucumbers, tomatoes, onions, potatoes, corn, radishes, watermelons, and other garden products. The Bird Canning Company emerged in Eagle Lake in 1905. Fruits such as figs were marketed and sold. Truck farming and shipping produce by rail were common. Trains, trucks, and wagonloads of watermelons were shipped out of Eagle Lake.

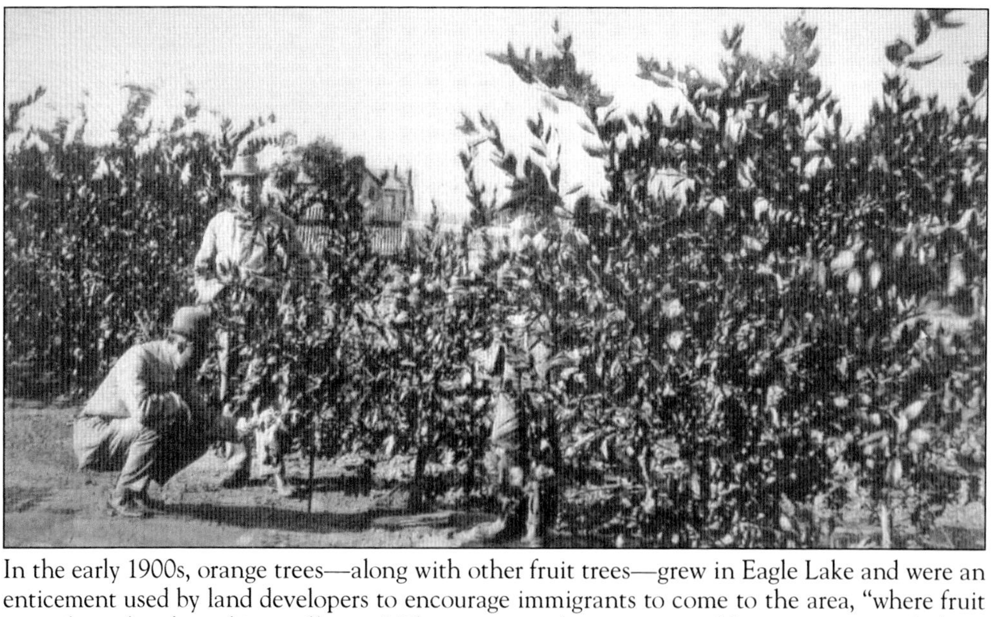

In the early 1900s, orange trees—along with other fruit trees—grew in Eagle Lake and were an enticement used by land developers to encourage immigrants to come to the area, "where fruit trees abound and anything will grow." These trees are being inspected by growers, one of whom may be Olaf Kolberg (standing).

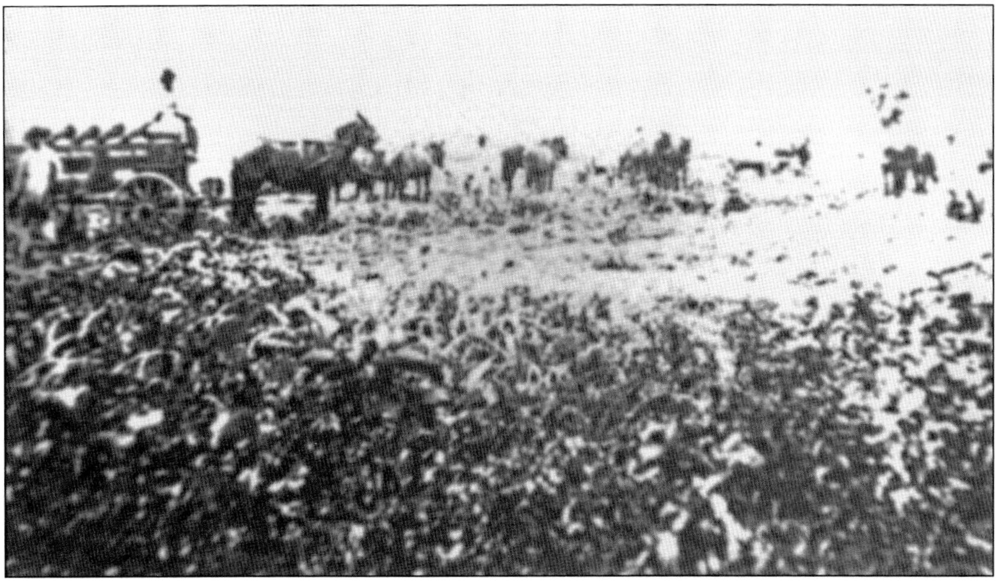

Local farmers had excellent potato crops in 1911. Potatoes were plentiful and were shipped in loaded railcars to markets in Kansas City and St. Louis. W.J. Wright and Chris Englehardt were pioneers in potato-growing in the county. Other notable potato farmers included J.W. Plunkett, Joe Helmer, Dr. Otto Rogers, Dr. P.T. Gordon, Ervin and Waldo Terrell, and the Evoritts. Calhoun, near Eagle Lake, was a major potato-farming area. Much of the bottomland around Calhoun was bought by potato farmers from Missouri and Nebraska, and the community's prosperity was based on potatoes, which were planted in February and harvested in May. Laborers from Mexico were brought in to assist with the farming. In a good year, as many as 1,000 loads of potatoes were shipped in cattle cars (for ventilation). The Englehardt brothers built a home in Calhoun; and as a farming community with a depot on the Atchison, Topeka & Santa Fe Railway, the town was active for 15 to 20 years. The weather, including floods and rain, of 1913 and 1914 heavily damaged the crops and destroyed the yield. Below, C.E. Evoritt stands with potato workers in the field.

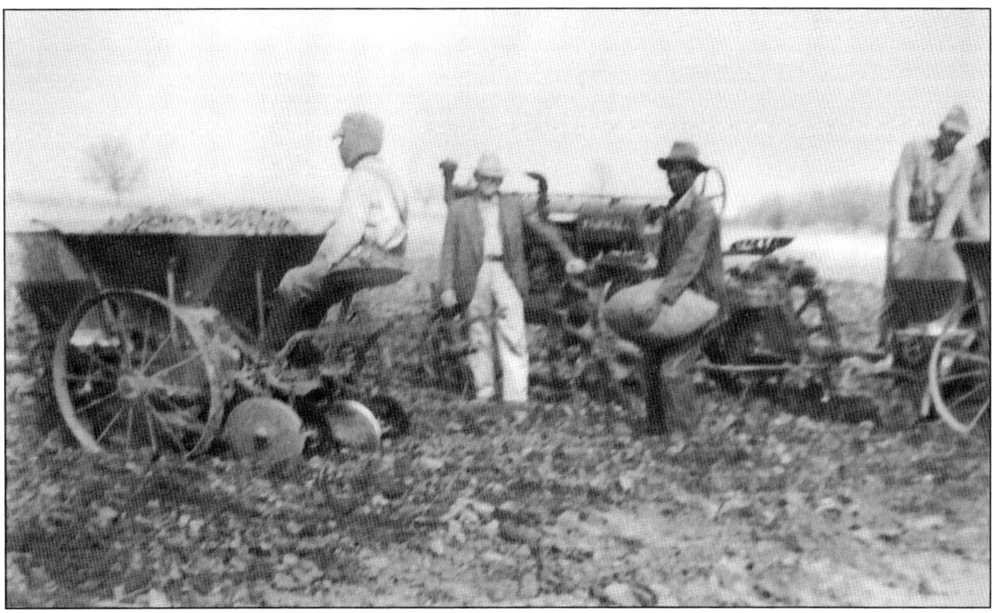

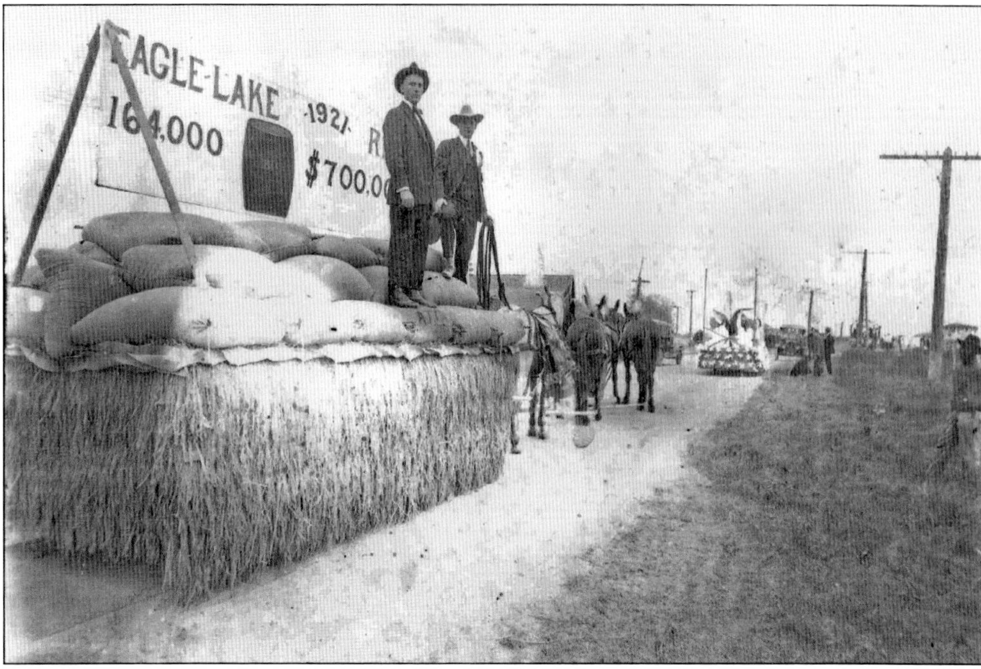

The Eagle Lake Rice Float highlights the industry at the Colorado County Fair in 1921. The county fair was a popular event that drew crowds from each community in the county to view farm products, livestock, canned goods, and displays of county agriculture. Charles Duddleston (left) and Lee Larson (mule driver) stand atop the parade float representing rice as Eagle Lake's most important crop.

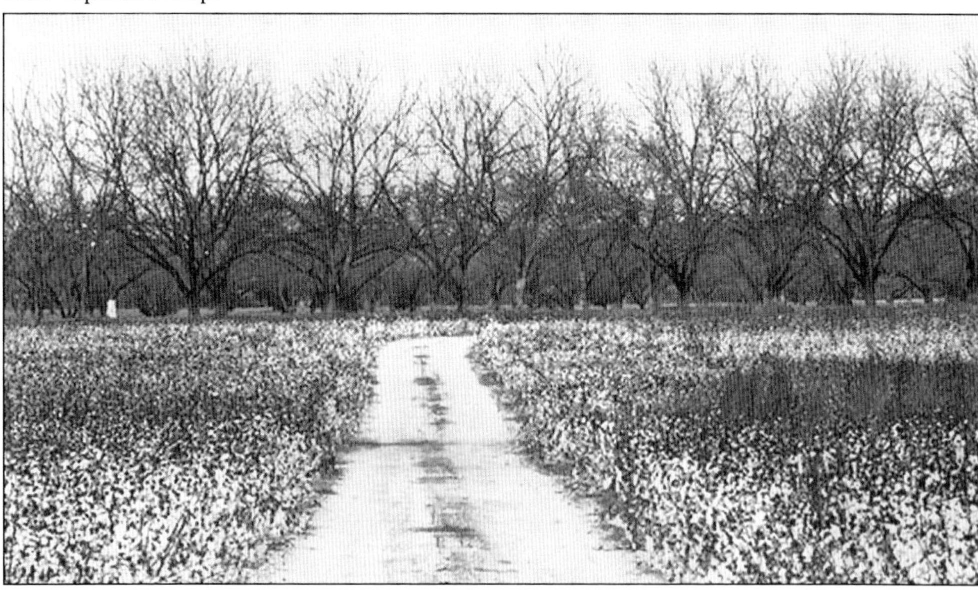

Early Eagle Lake agriculture included cotton, pecans, sugarcane, and grain for cattle. In 1896, the cotton crop was the best ever recorded in the area. By 1897, there were two cotton gins, cotton was the major crop, and a cotton farmer was the only type of farmer who could obtain credit. However, after the arrival of the boll weevil, by 1903, large cotton plantations were no longer financially successful, and cotton was replaced by sugarcane and rice.

Until the late 1800s, most of the prairie from Eagle Lake and beyond was open range. Drovers moved their cattle to market over the free rangeland. After fences were built, cattle were shipped to market by train—usually to Houston and Fort Worth, later to Kansas City and Chicago. Here, Ernest Seaholm tends his cattle near Eagle Lake.

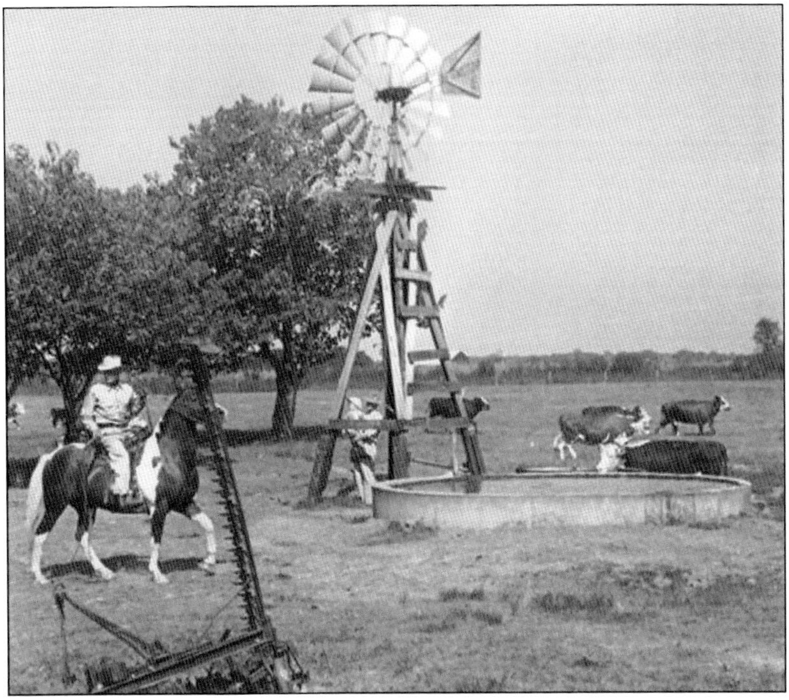

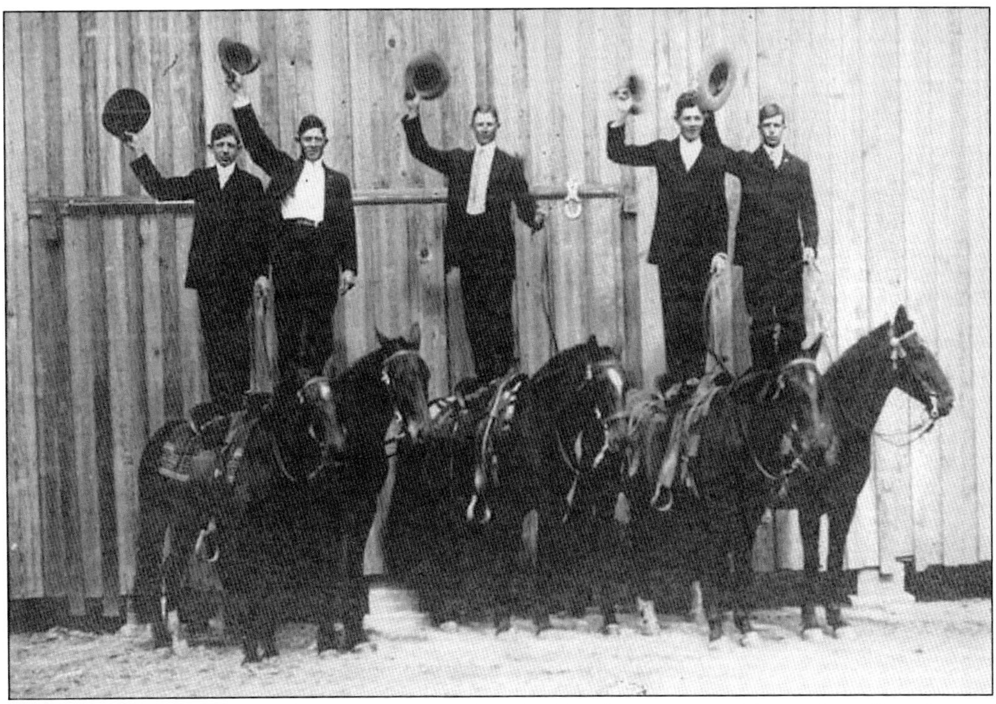

The Seaholm Boys (pictured from left to right)—Axel Seaholm's sons Helmer, Gus, Carl, Ernest, and their cousin Ed—were a popular group in the early 1900s. They excelled in music, playing in cornet bands, as well as farming and riding and were popular students. The Seaholm family emigrated from Sweden and had its own Seaholm School, No. 32, in the Chesterville area. Axel and his sons farmed rice and irrigated from some of the area's first wells.

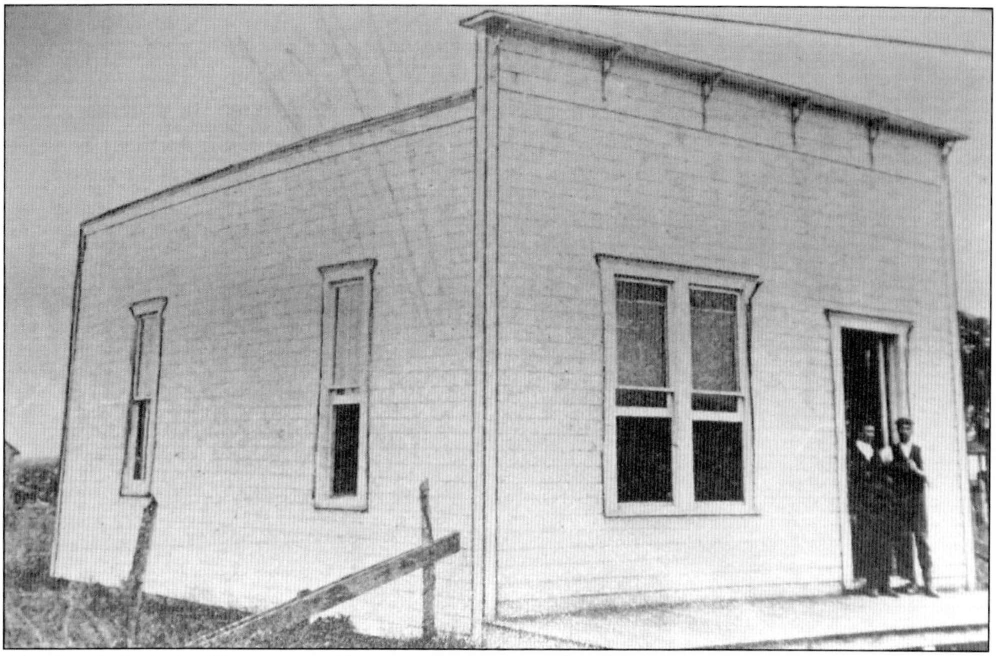

John Linderholm's office was in Chesterville. He was a land developer from Chicago who bought 60,000 acres near the Chesterville prairie and Eagle Lake to bring prospective buyers from the Midwest to the area. Partnering with a real estate/train company, Linderholm sent out four land opportunity circulars to help recruit settlers and their families.

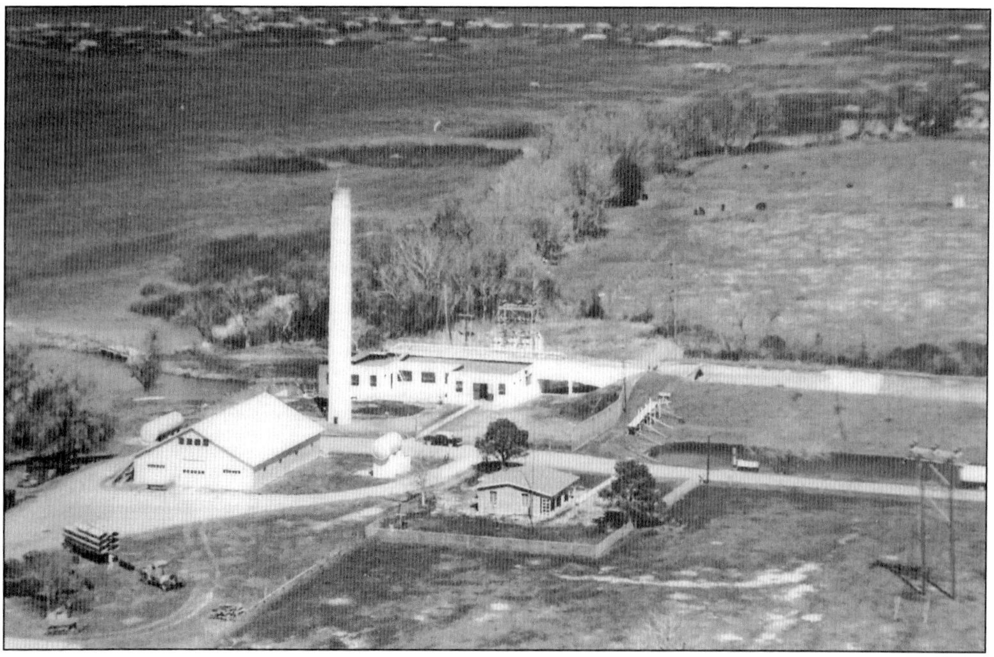

Lakeside Irrigation Company was incorporated in 1909 by Rudolph Wintermann, J.H. August Meyer, Don Raynor, and John Raezer. The Eagle Lake Rice Irrigation Company was formed in 1900, met financial difficulties, and was acquired by the Lakeside Irrigation Company. Both companies were set up to provide adequate water for farm irrigation.

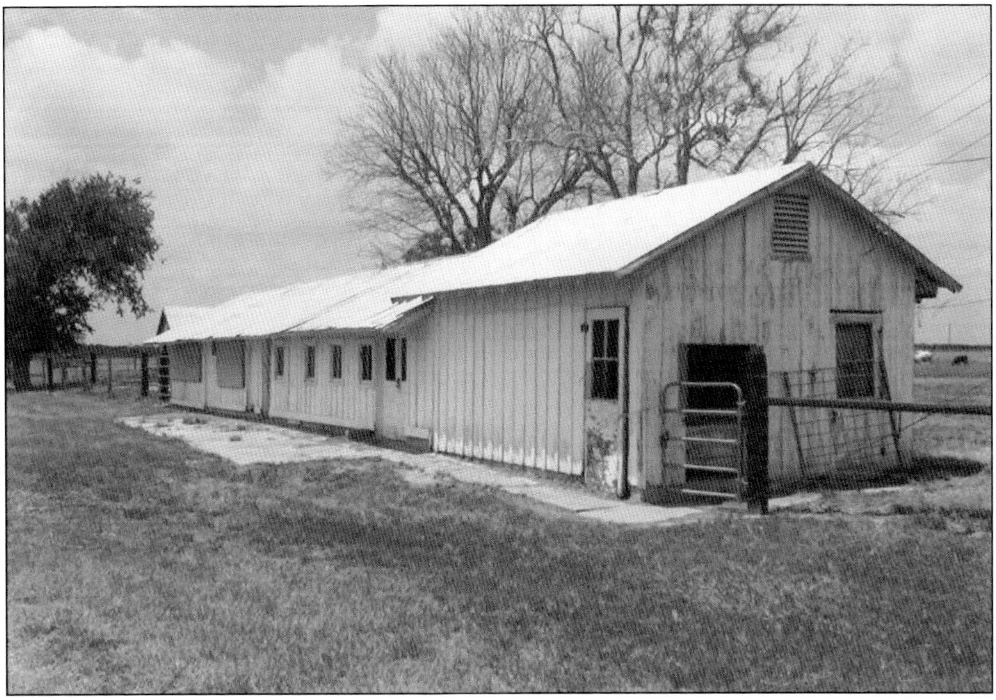

Located at the Mose Thomas Farm Camp on FM 102, the Thomas Riceland Dairy supplied milk to families and restaurants in town. "Bottle boys" were hired to carry the milk bottles door to door from the dairy truck, bring fresh milk to town daily. The white frame dairy barn with a cement floor was the mainstay of the Riceland Dairy and is still standing today.

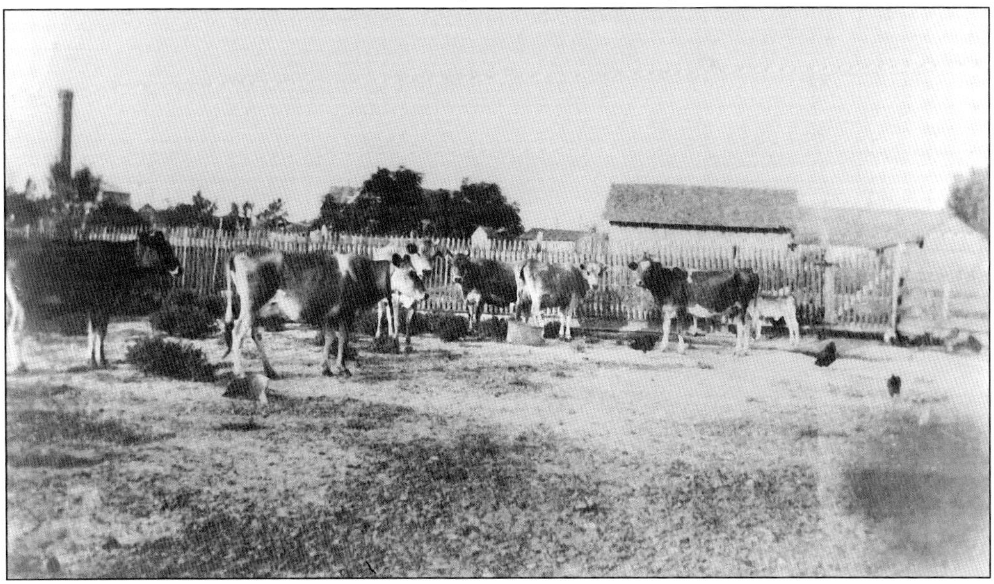

Before the 1900s, most families had their own cow or got milk from a neighbor. In the early 1900s, while many families still had their own cows, some larger operations became commercial dairies that supplied Eagle Lake residents with milk, cream, and butter. Brown's Dairy Garden (1922) sold and delivered milk from its 15 cows. Other dairies were owned by F.G. Smith, the Kolbergs, and L.J. Berger.

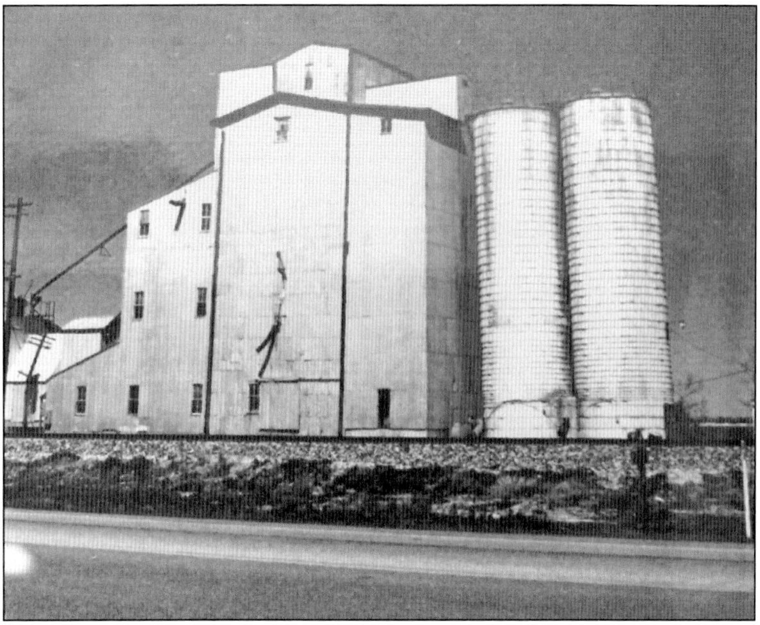

Rice elevators and dryers were essential to rice farming in the Eagle Lake area. The original elevator in this Lissie complex was built in 1908. It was converted to a dryer in the 1940s and had storage areas. It was especially accessible to the rice farms around Lissie and Chesterville. (Courtesy of Prairie Edge Museum.)

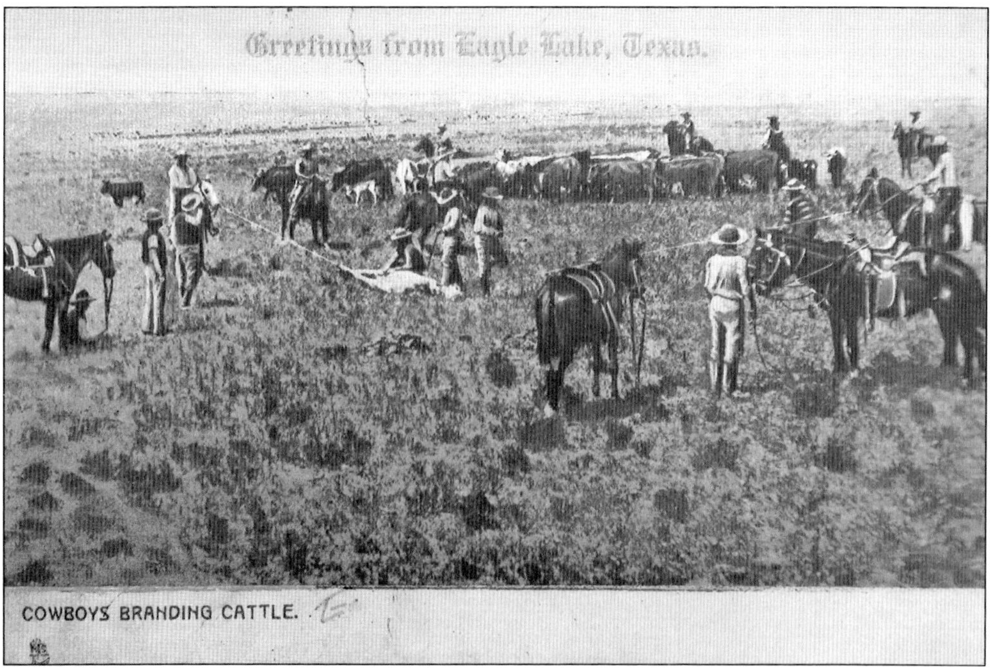

An early postcard depicts cowboys, cattle, and ranching around Eagle Lake. Cattle brands were registered in Colorado County as early as 1837. At the turn of the century, the prairie was open range until barbed wire was introduced to the area around 1912. Early cowboys used Mexican-style charro saddles and rawhide lassos while roping, tying, and branding their cattle on the open range. (Courtesy of Prairie Edge Museum.)

Oscar J. Wintermann, a native of St. Louis, arrived in Eagle Lake in 1912 to manage his family's interests in agricultural businesses. He helped salvage the bankrupt Eagle Lake Irrigation Company, renamed it the Lakeside Irrigation Company, and expanded the canal operation to approximately 200 miles of canals by 1942, servicing 20,000 acres of rice-farming land. Wintermann was a leader in the Eagle Lake American Rice Growers Association, as well as a philanthropist and a business, agriculture, and community leader. (Courtesy of Prairie Edge Museum.)

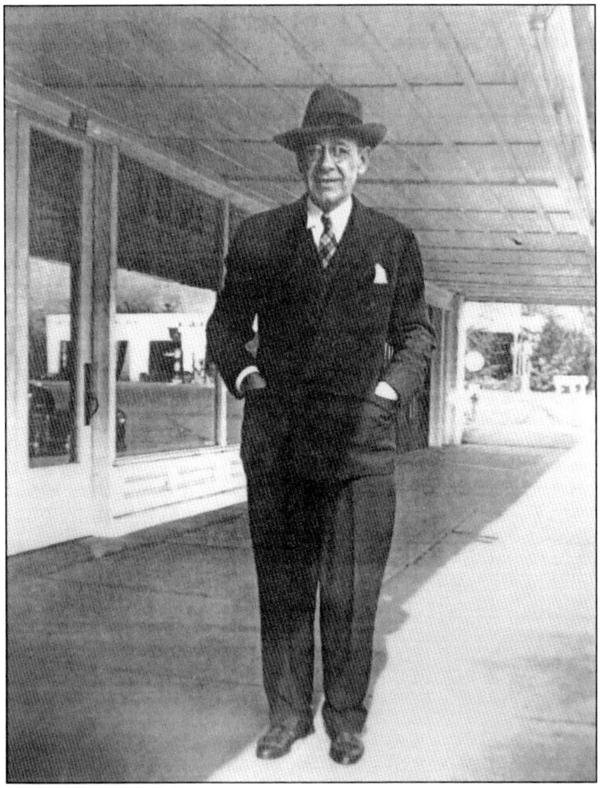

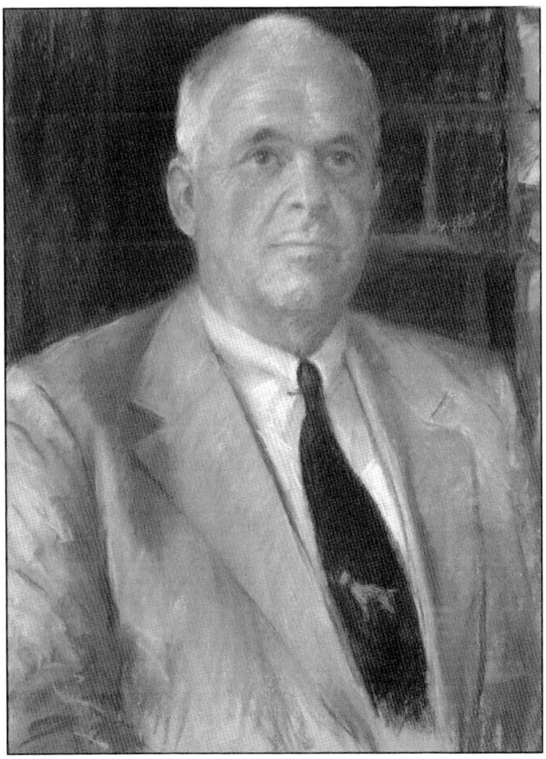

David R. Wintermann, son of Oscar J. Wintermann, was a sportsman and a member of the prestigious Eagle Lake Rod & Gun Club. He was a supporter of conservation practices and a leader in Ducks Unlimited, a wetlands and waterfowl conservation group. Wintermann successfully continued the family interests in agribusiness and irrigation from 1942, including the Lakeside Irrigation Company and thousands of acres of rice in Colorado and Wharton Counties. He was a leader in the Eagle Lake American Rice Growers Association and donated land and money toward the creation of the Attwater Prairie Chicken National Wildlife Refuge. He was a benefactor, businessman, and conservationist. He and his wife, Eula, both major philanthropists in the region, supported the library, scholarships, and many other community and state interests.

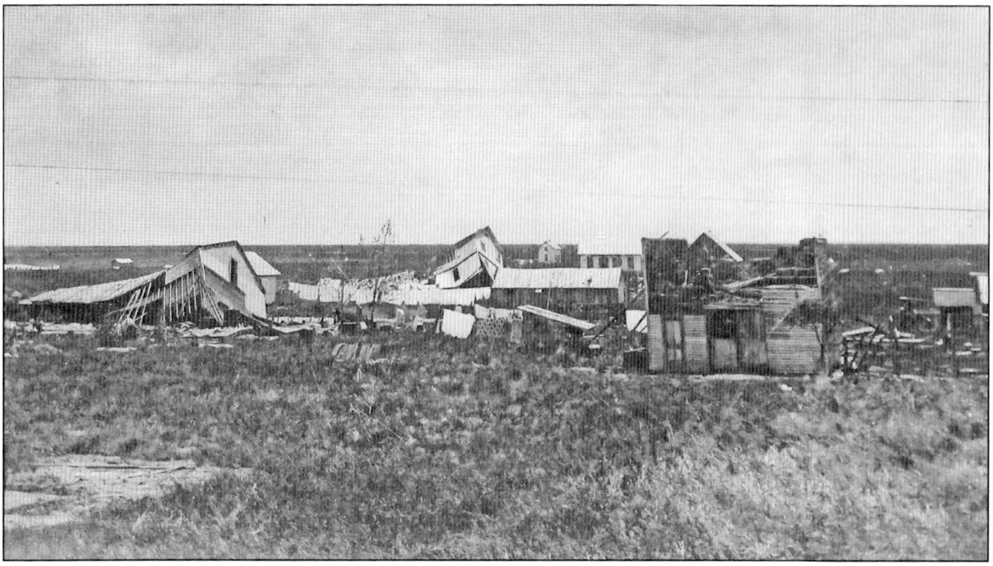

The Great Storm of 1900 left damages near Eagle Lake. In this image, Chesterville's buildings—including the first hotel, store, and post office facing Main Street; the Adams Livery Barn (to the left); and remnants of homes and barns— are strewn across the prairie. The hurricane was one of the largest natural disasters in the country and destroyed much of Galveston. (Courtesy of Prairie Edge Museum.)

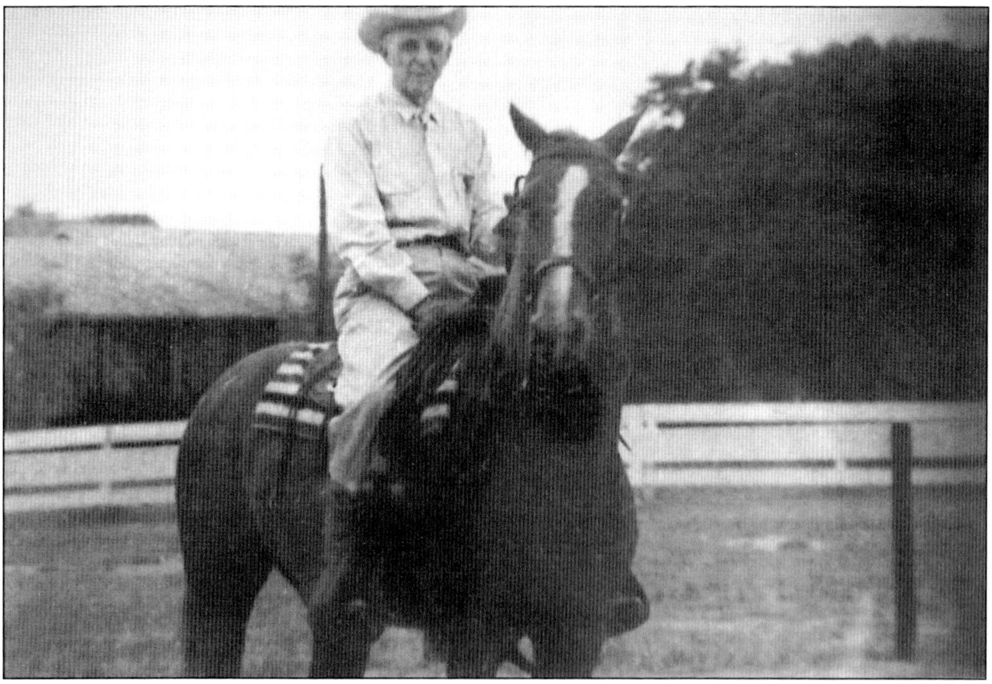

I.V. Duncan was among the area's most prominent ranchers and citizens. He had one of the largest cattle-raising operations in the area on his Retama Ranch just south of Eagle Lake. Duncan and his wife moved from Egypt, Texas, in 1910, where he had a successful ranching and farming operation. From his arrival until the middle of the 20th century, he delighted many with his ranch rodeos, where even the governor once came as a guest. (Courtesy of Diane Duncan Tucker.)

Five

The Town

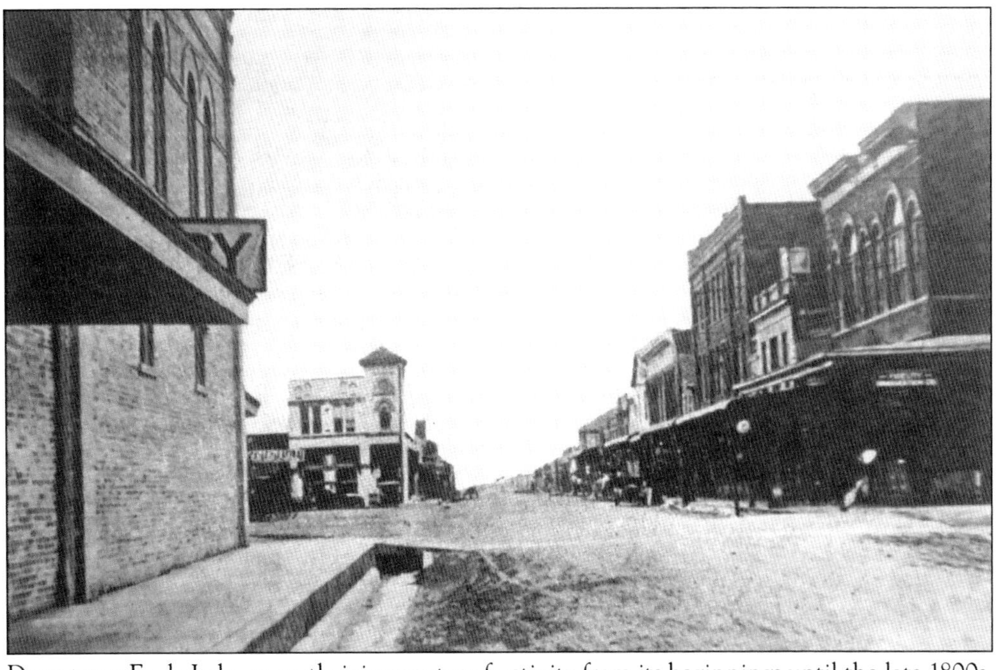

Downtown Eagle Lake was a thriving center of activity from its beginnings until the late 1800s. It had three banks, four substantial original brick buildings, an opera house, a city park, and bustling commerce. This photograph shows a view from East Main Street.

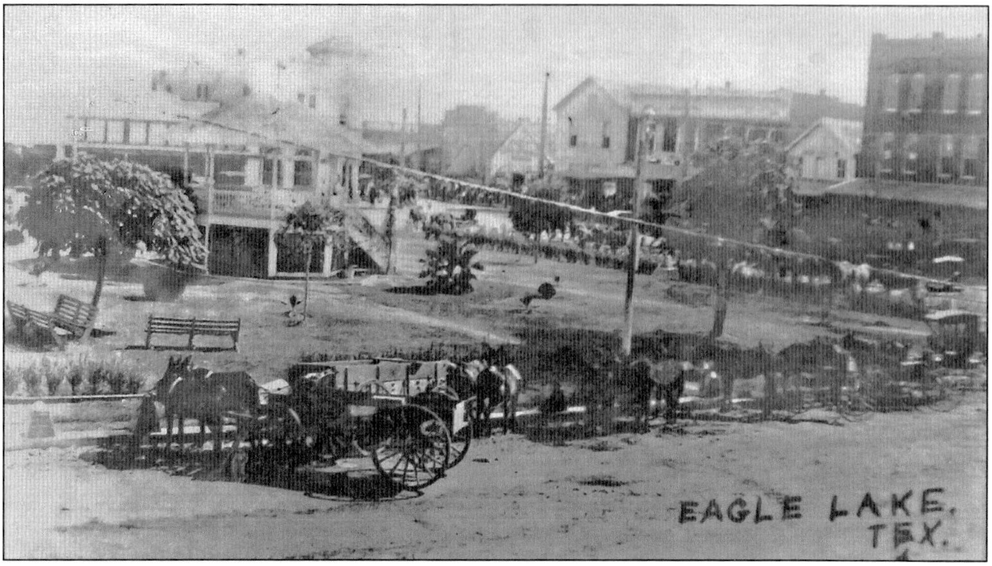

In 1897, the town square had a hitching rail and water troughs for horses, which made the square and the downtown area the center for commercial and social activity. The square, which was once a sand-covered area, housed the early Eagle Lake Water Works, which consisted of water troughs for livestock, two wells, and a windmill.

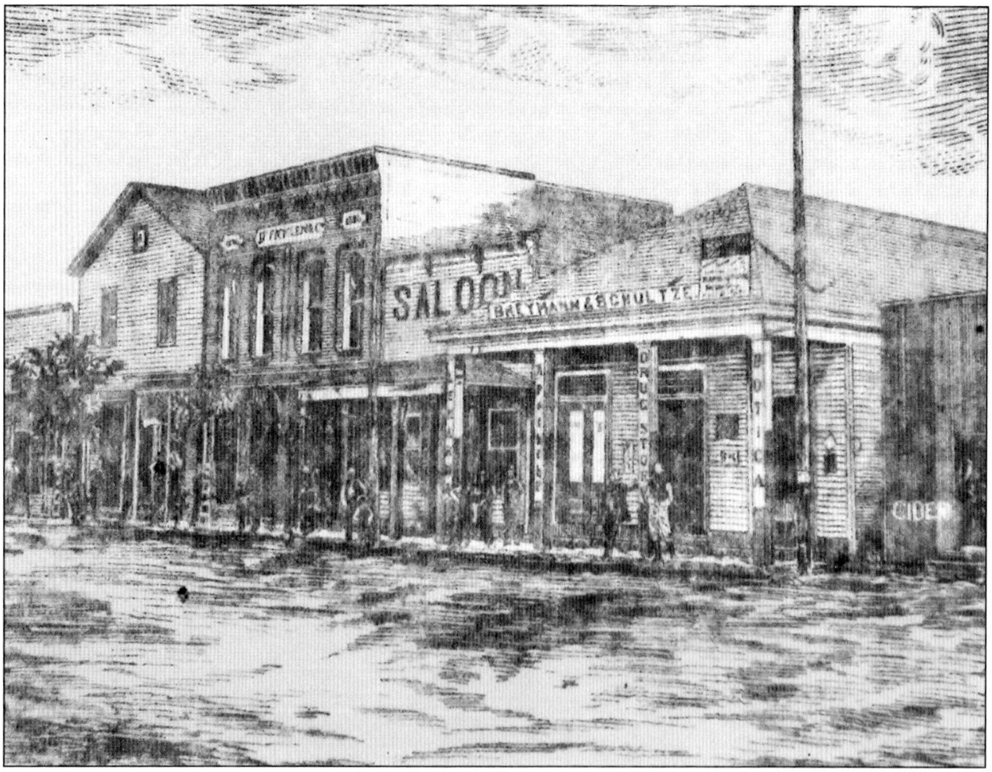

This 1887 drawing of the south side of the town square shows the wooden buildings, their galleries or porches, and one of several saloons. Later, after the arrival of Prohibition, authorities from Houston arrived to enforce gambling and alcohol laws and to help keep order in town.

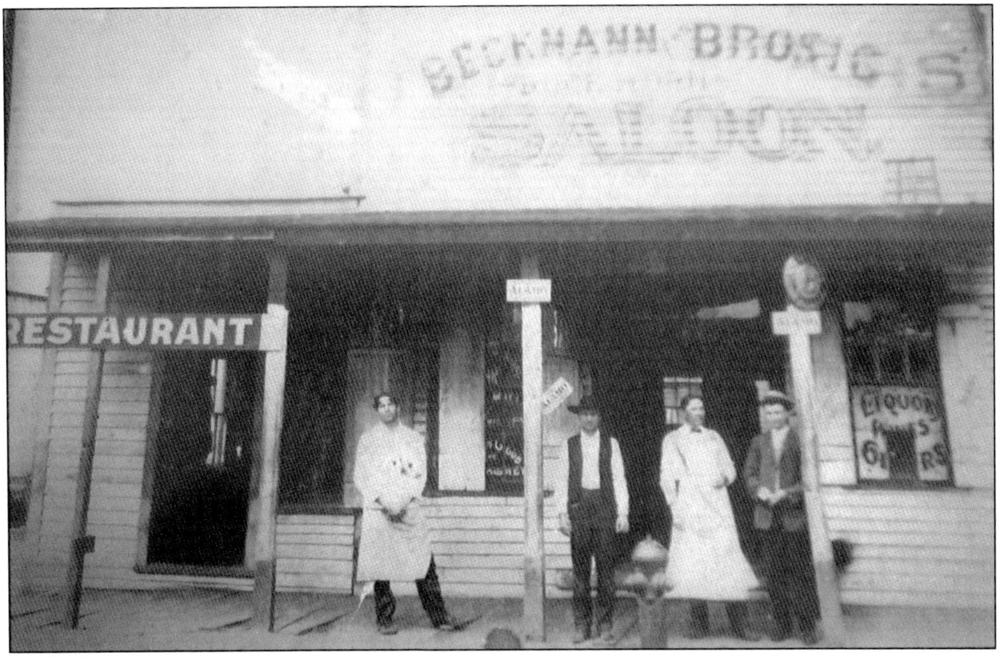

This saloon/restaurant owned by C.H. Brosig and Henry Beckmann in 1903—once called the Buckhorn Saloon—was across from the A.L. Baring Saddle Shop on what would later become the site of Miller's Store BBQ. In 1906, Brosig bought full interest in the Buckhorn.

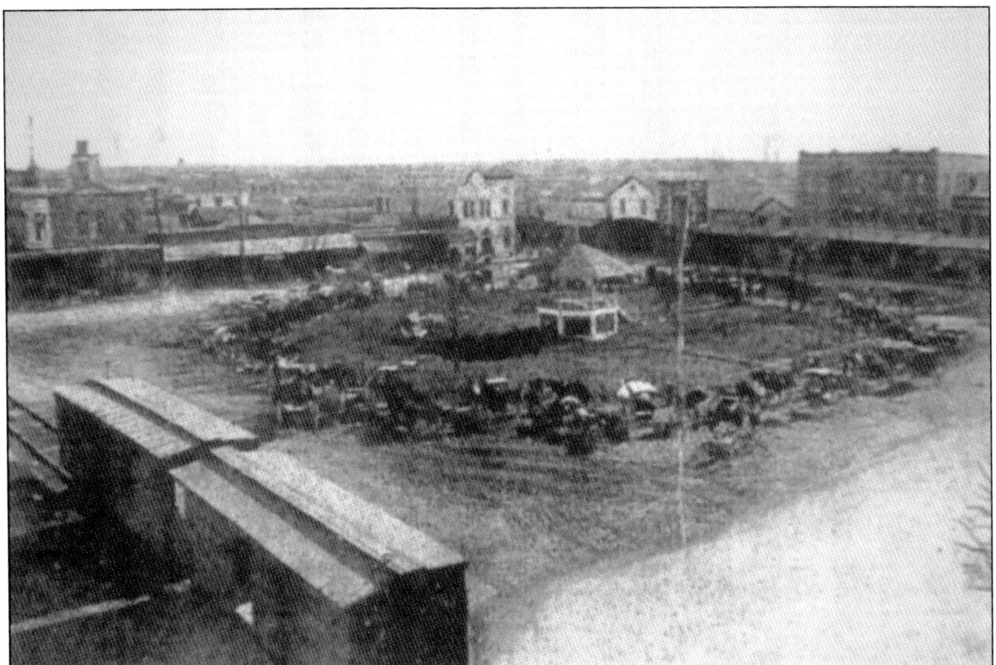

The city square, shown during a rare snowfall in 1906, was a center of commerce and railroad traffic. Boxcars are coated with snow. To the far left is the J.W. McCarty Building, with the First National Bank to the right. The public square offered hitching rails for horses and buggies, and the bandstand was located in the middle of the square.

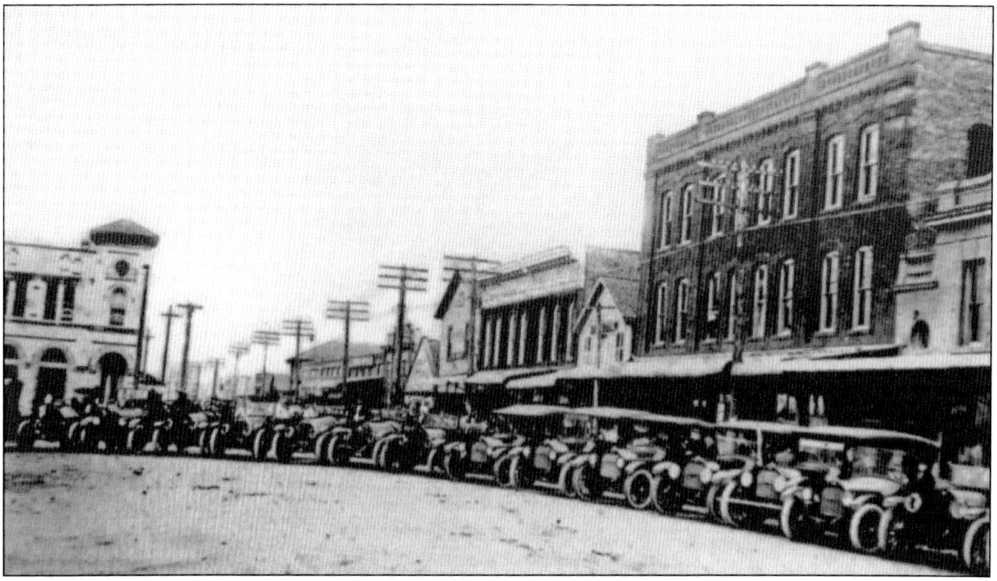

Early cars parked along East Main Street and the city square are on display in this 1912 image. The streets were unpaved at the time, but the tracks of horses and wagons indicate they were heavily used. Only a few people had automobiles. The First National Bank is at left, and the three-story Norris Building is at right.

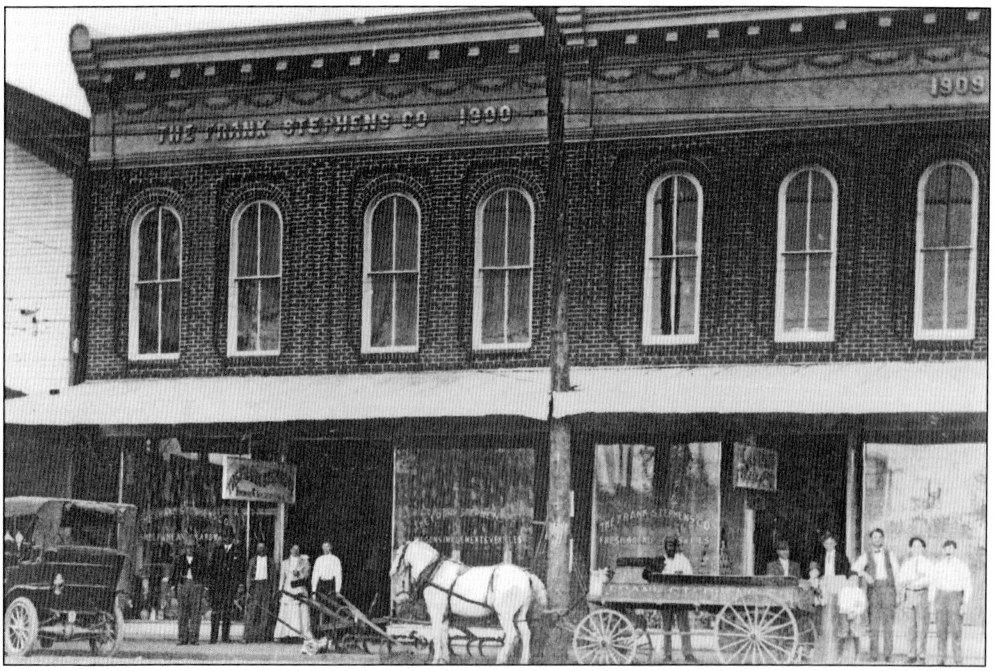

The Frank Stephens Company was a general store that sold groceries, dry goods, seed, hardware, farm equipment, and gasoline. The people pictured in front are preparing to load farm equipment from the store onto a freight wagon as onlookers watch. Stephens' trade tokens were issued as currency. In 1909, spaces were added to the rear of the building, which had a warehouse and a railroad siding. At one time, customers could trade eggs or chickens for supplies. In 1941, the Frank Stephens Company ended its downtown mercantile business; the building still stands.

On November 5, 1906, William Green opened the Eagle Lake State Bank on Main Street with a capitalization of $40,000. In 1912, it merged with the Farmers and Merchants State Bank of Eagle Lake, which was chartered in 1910. The combined assets of the two banks made the Eagle Lake State Bank the largest bank in the county and the 19th largest bank in the state. In 1932, the bank experienced financial difficulty and was liquidated. The bank directors were William Green, G. Duncan, J.R. Westmoreland, G. H. Northington, Haynie Matthews, John Matthews, A.C. McClanahan, W.E. Welford, and W.C. Strickland; M.E. Guynn was cashier.

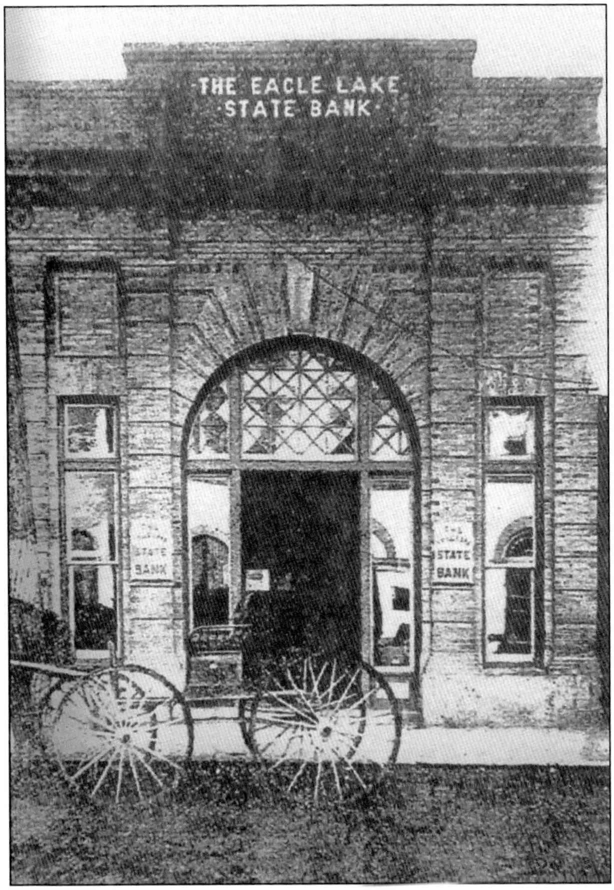

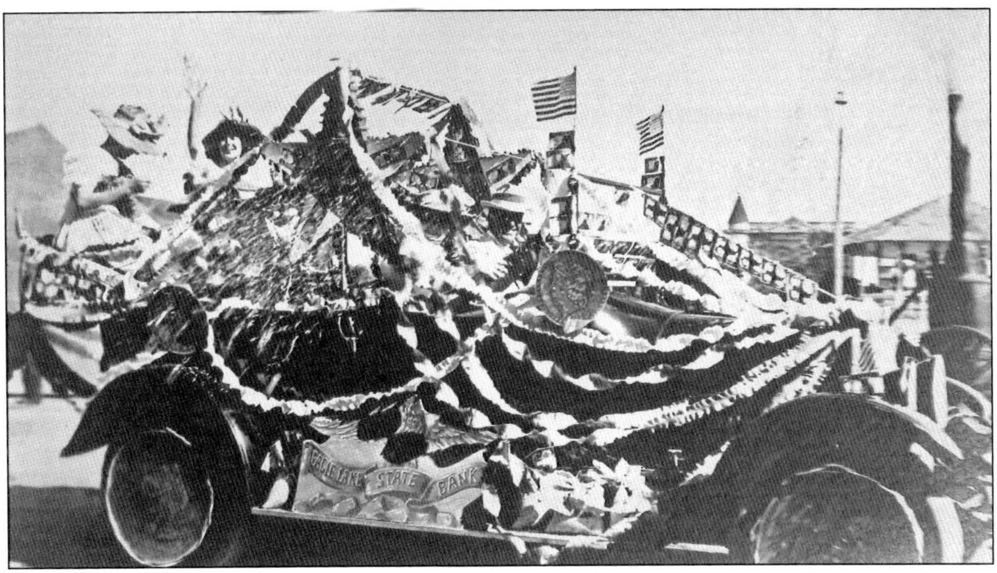

The Eagle Lake State Bank parade float is decorated for the 1916 Independence Day Celebration along Main Street. Agnes Chew is on the left, and Beth Fitzgerald is on the right; Milby Guynn is the driver.

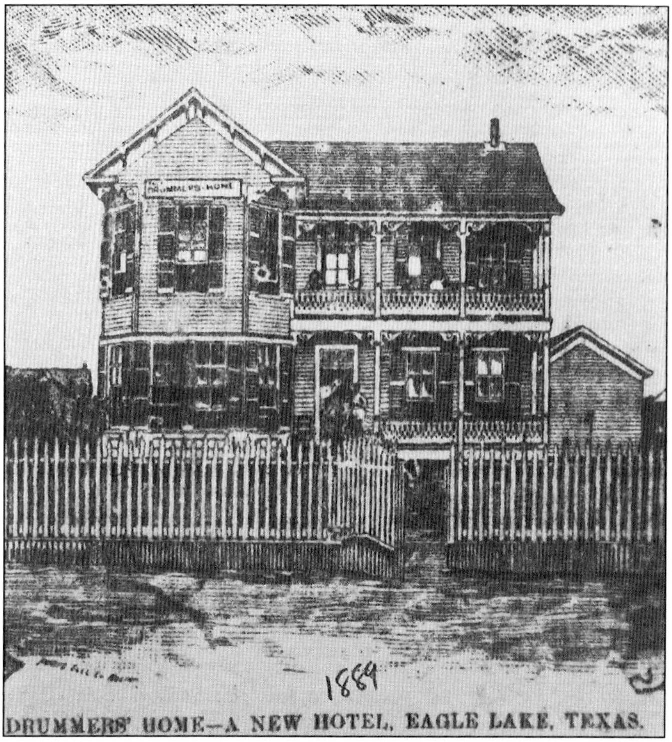

In 1889, the original Drummers' Home hotel was built as an inn to primarily accommodate traveling salesmen, also known as drummers. Many traveled by train. Located across from the train depot on the east side of the current fire station, the hotel also offered lodging for short-term visitors and tourists. According to some sources, it was the most popular hotel between Houston and San Antonio. After the second Drummers' Home was built, the original became the Annex and continued to operate.

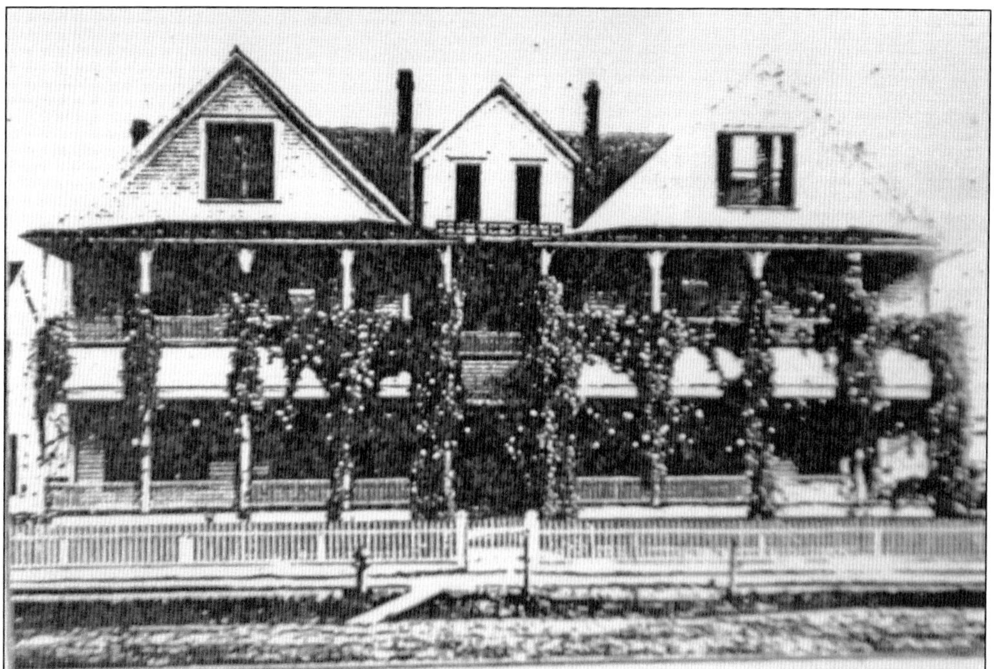

Eventually, a second Drummers' Home was built—a large two-and-a-half-story frame structure with balconies and 25 rooms. Known for its pleasant accommodations and excellent food, it was a popular destination and important to local commerce. The hotel was famous for its fragrant morning glories and moon vines along the front porches.

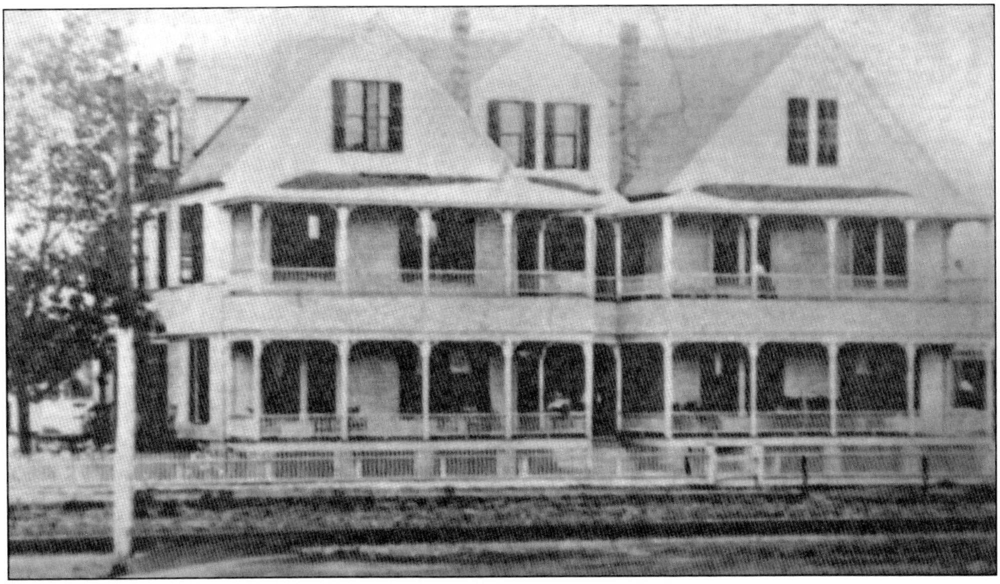

In 1902, a new Drummers' Home was built by W.T. Eldridge, and the old hotel, which still offered accommodations, was then renamed the Annex. When Eldridge retired and a Mrs. W. Watson, who was related to Eldridge, ran the Drummers' Home, the delicious meals earned a reputation far and wide. Drummers and others came, especially on Sundays, to dine at and enjoy the hotel. In 1925, Lena Schattenberg arrived to manage the inn. She married a drummer named P.P. Ramsey, and they bought the Drummers' Home from Eldridge. The Ramseys later purchased the Hotel Dallas and renamed it Hotel Ramsey. Classes were held at the Drummers' Home when the new school was being constructed on Prairie Avenue. Due to a storm in the early 1930s, the hotel was damaged beyond repair and was demolished; the Ramseys then constructed a two-story redbrick apartment building on the site. The home pictured below was the residence of W.T Eldridge; it was located to the right of the second Drummers' Home (which has been replaced by another building) on Post Office Street.

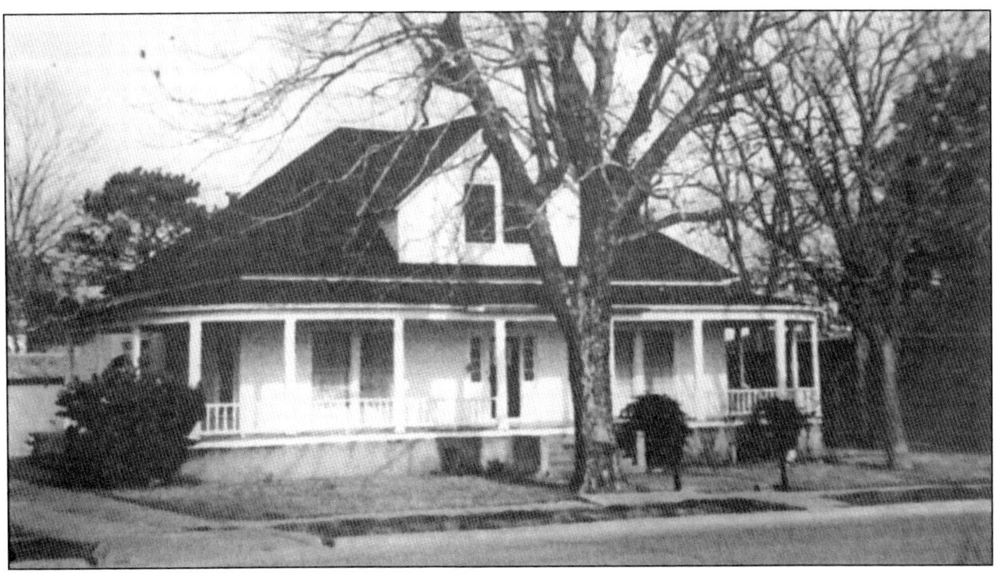

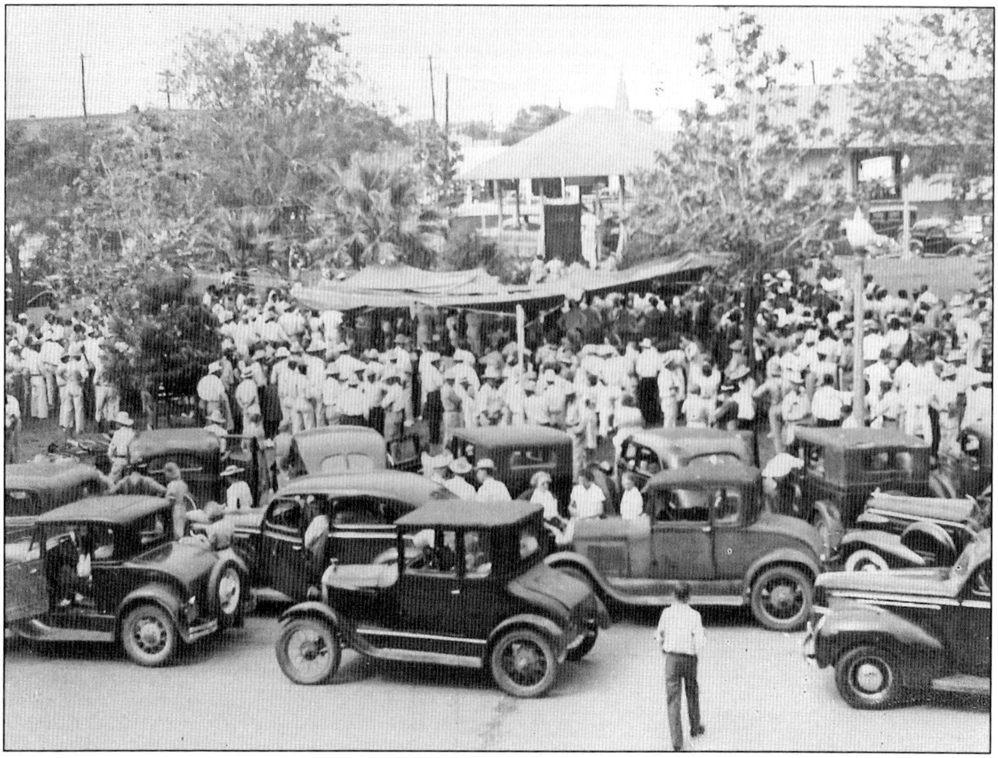

In the early 1900s, Eagle Lake Trade Days and community activities were held in City Park and along Main Street, where people gathered for social and business reasons. The downtown area was bustling with commerce and vehicles. Trade days brought farmers to town to sell livestock and products. These events often had traveling carnivals and tents, Ferris wheels, and activities for children and families. Entertainment programs were often held in the bandstand.

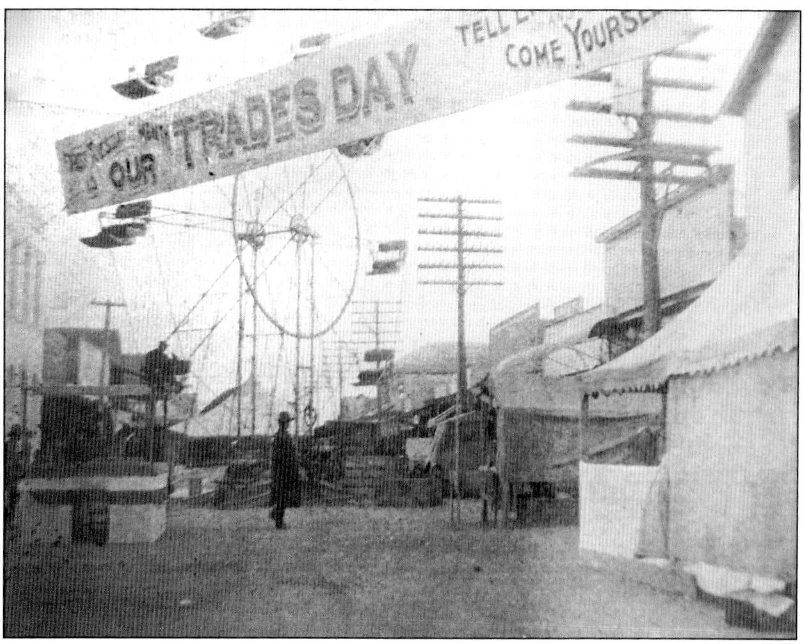

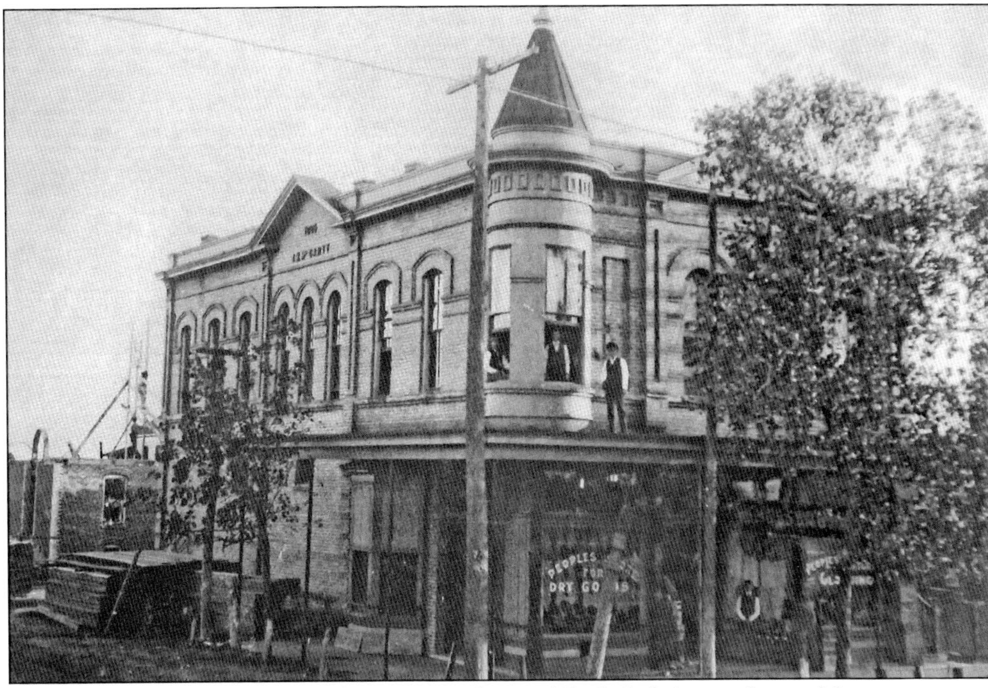

The J.W. McCarty Building, built in 1895 and one of Eagle Lake's most beautiful structures, was one of the first four brick buildings in the city. Offices for the Cane Belt Railway and Dr. Jaquelin Bruce were located here, as well as the first office of the *Eagle Lake Headlight*. There was once a small movie theater on the east side of the building. The building was owned by Capt. James William McCarty (1835–1903), Eagle Lake's first mayor. It was demolished in 1949.

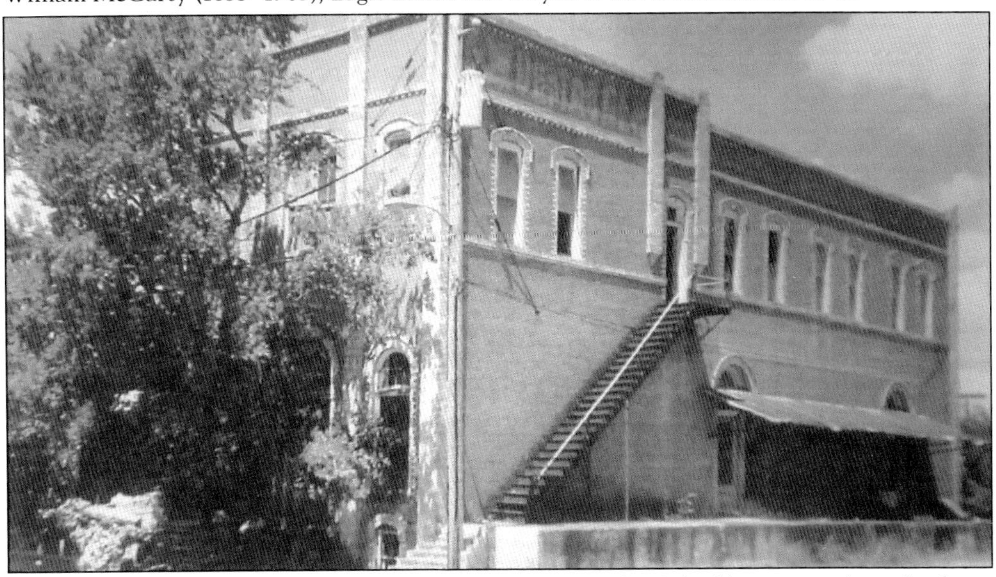

Built in 1903 by G.W. Deaton and Company, the two-story brick building across from the depot and the railroad tracks was home to the Schumacher Wholesale Grocery Company. It had loading docks on the front and sides. The structure was used as a dance hall, church, and warehouse. The building provided three schoolrooms between 1922 and 1925, while the new school was built. (Courtesy William H. Harrison.)

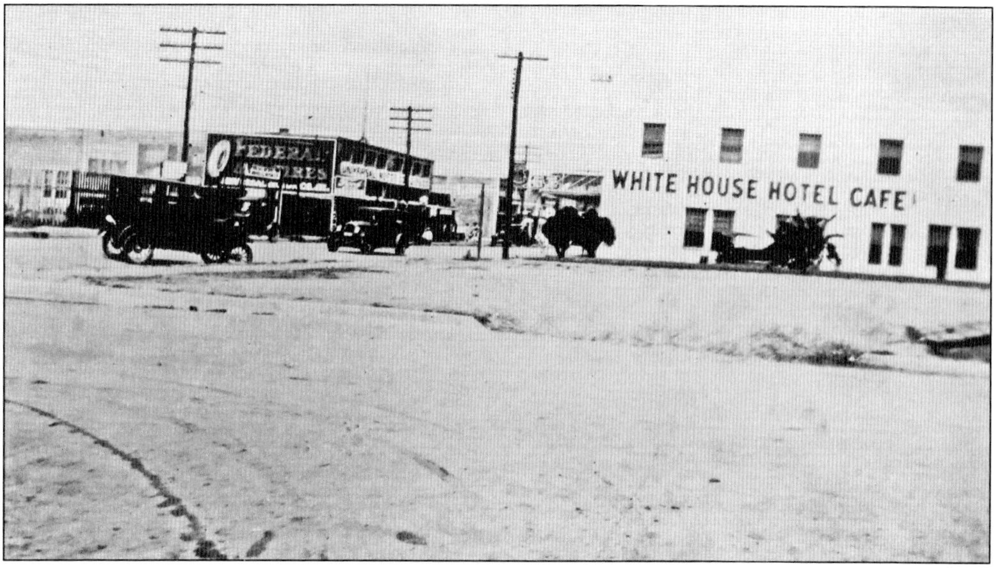

The White House Hotel and Café, seen in the snow, was built in 1927 by R.M. Eggers, contractor for A.C. McClanahan of the McClanahan Lumber Company. The structure housed a 16-room hotel on the second floor, with a restaurant on the first floor. Located on East Main Street near the depot, it served as a Western Union telegraph office and an active Greyhound bus depot. The hotel and café served as a popular meeting place for diners and travelers until it closed in 1970. (Courtesy William H. Harrison.)

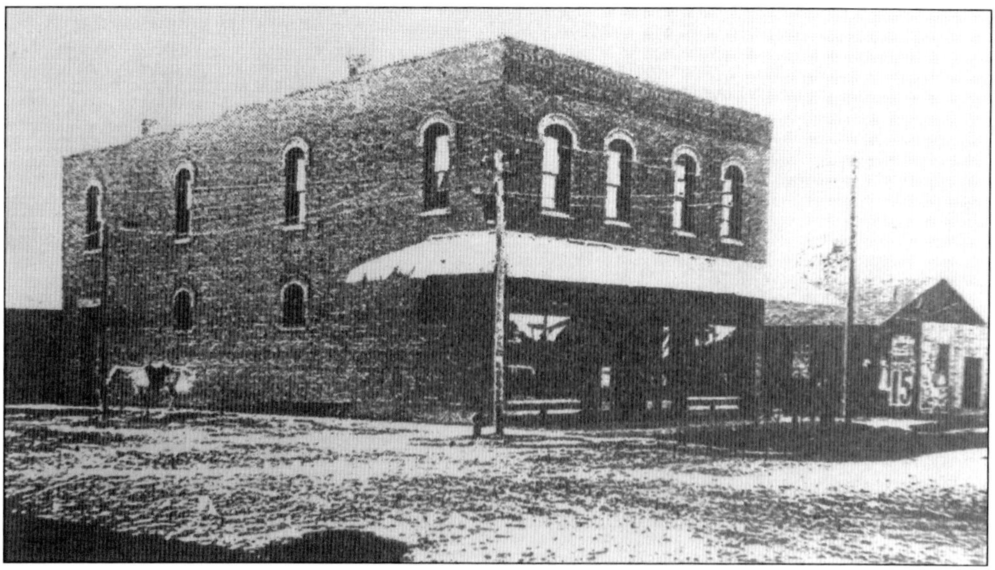

In 1907, the two-story Gottlieb Herman Building on the corner of Main and McCarty Streets opened as Gottlieb Furniture and Undertaking Company, a furniture store and funeral parlor. Herman sold the business to A.H. McCreary in 1919. The McCreary funeral parlor was upstairs and the furniture store was downstairs. The funeral parlor was eventually moved to the building next door. In 1921, McCreary died and left the business to his son, J.H. McCreary.

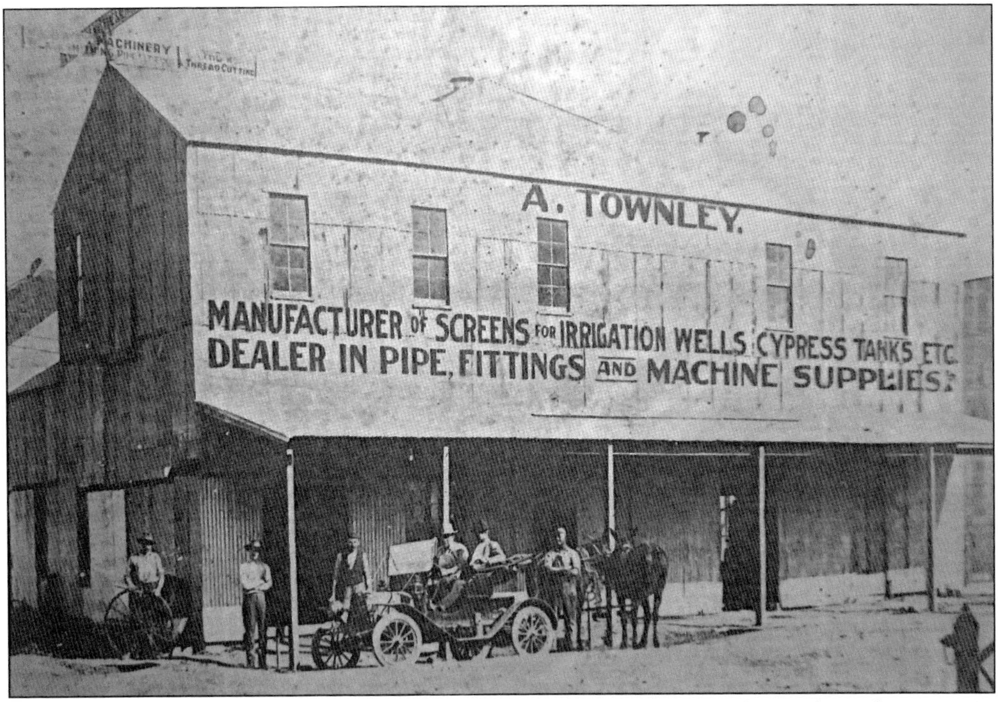

In 1902, Arthur Townley arrived in Eagle Lake from Illinois. He opened a machine shop in 1904 near the depot in a building formerly owned by Capt. William Dunovant. Townley's work was very important to farming and business enterprises: he provided irrigation well fittings and mechanical supplies. Townley's business was sold in 1946 and became Eagle Lake Iron Works.

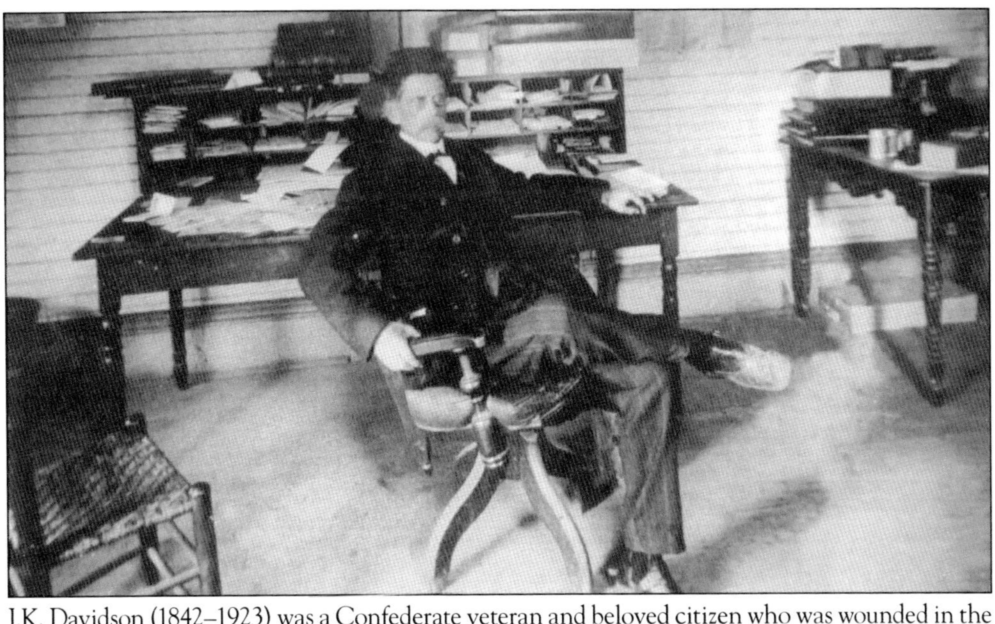

J.K. Davidson (1842–1923) was a Confederate veteran and beloved citizen who was wounded in the war. Born in Alabama, he went to medical college there. In Eagle Lake, he served as a physician, four consecutive terms as mayor, and as justice of the peace from 1890 until his death. This photograph shows Davidson at work in his office on the second floor of the Norris Building.

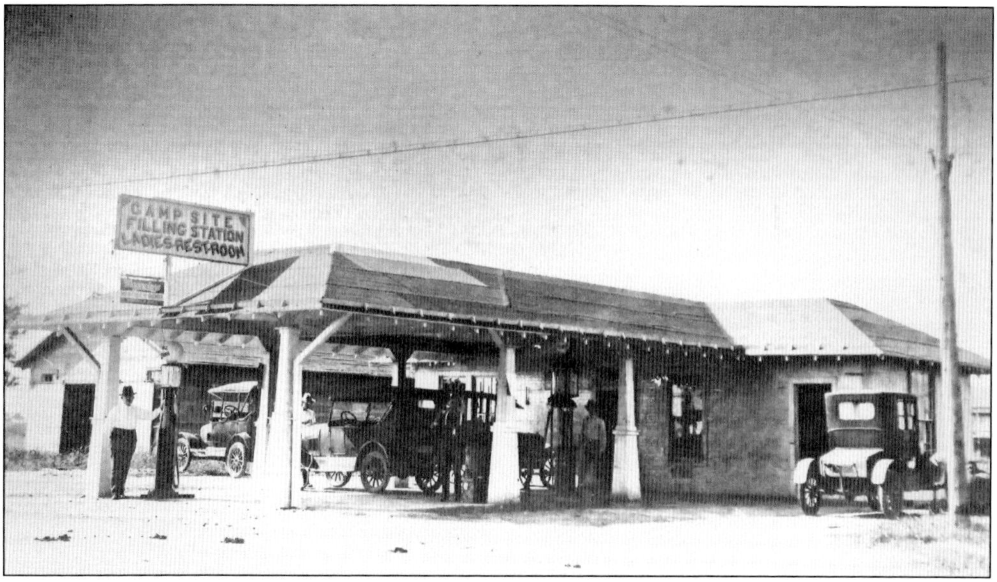

In the early 1920s, the Hanly Campsite Filling Station served farmers, travelers, and locals by supplying gasoline, oil, air, and minor automobile supplies. It was an important stop for residents from nearby farms, who came to town on Saturdays for supplies and socializing.

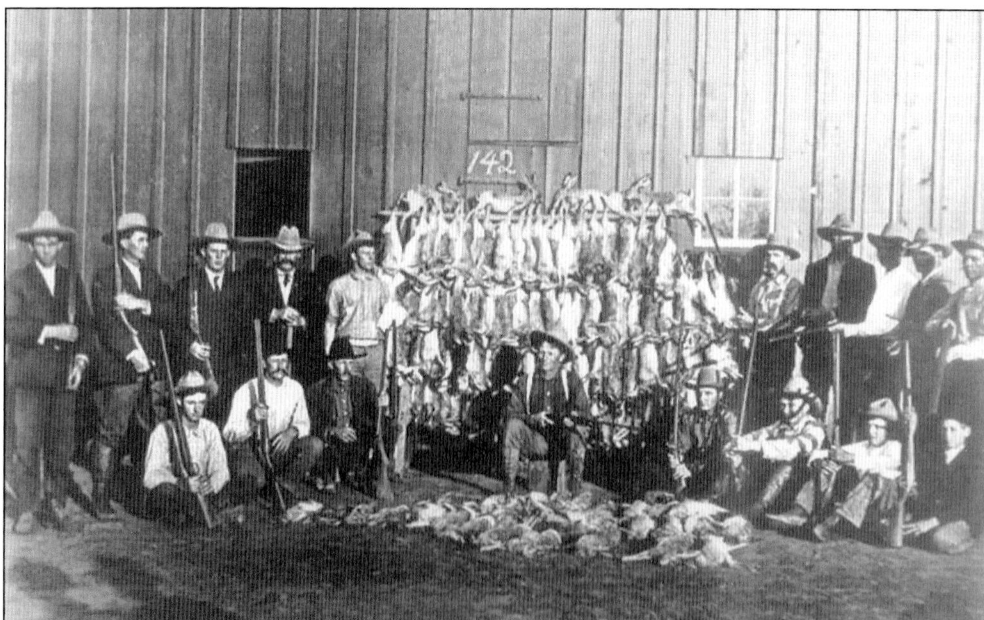

These jackrabbit hunters assembled at the old John Carlson place, located about six miles from Eagle Lake, on a Sunday in the early 1900s. The hunt covered a strip of prairie about three miles wide. There was a reward for killing jackrabbits, as they had become so plentiful that they were a nuisance to farmers. In two Sundays, the men killed 201 rabbits.

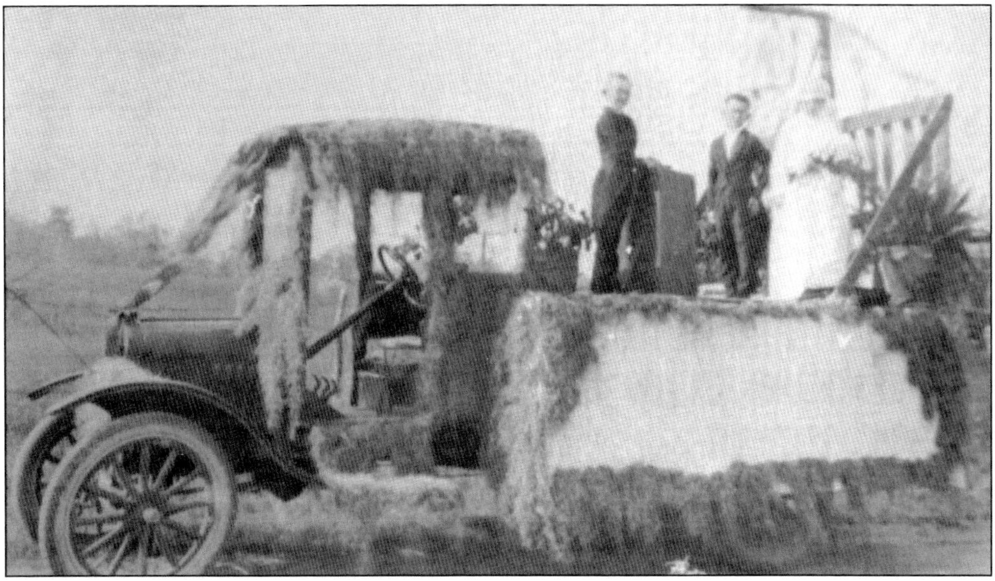

In the early 1920s, this Eagle Lake Furniture Company parade float—covered in moss and displaying the slogan "You Furnish the Girl, We'll Furnish the Home"—was a popular entry. Pictured here are Caroline Smothers (bride), Harry Reading Jr. (groom, center), and Newton Fox (preacher). The furniture company, owned by the McCrearys, was located at Main and McCarty Streets.

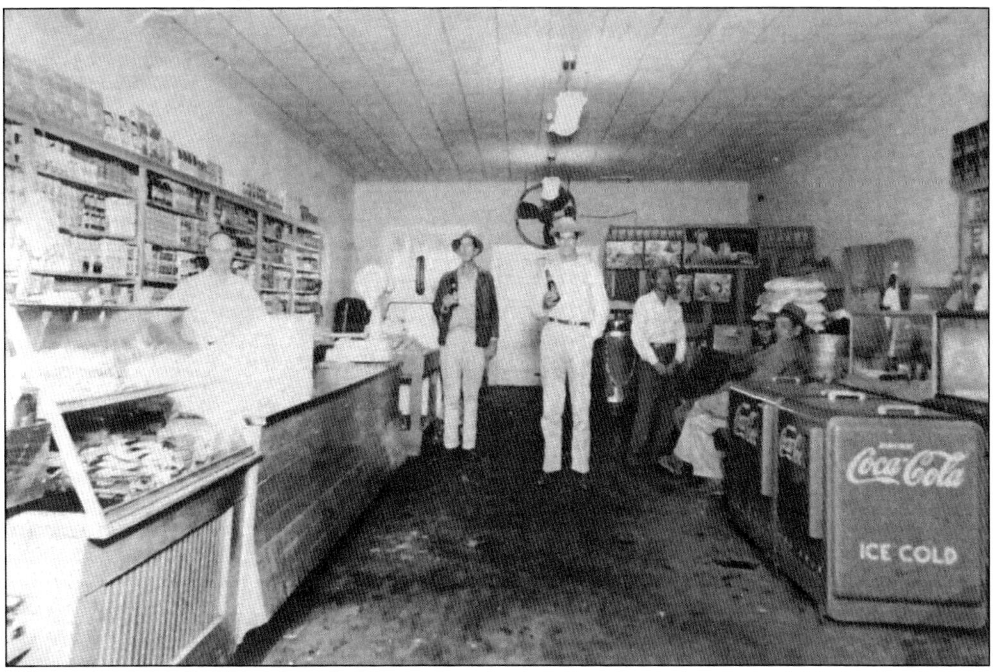

The Austin Grocery began at 505 East Main Street when Sam Austin and J.B. Barker bought the property and store from E.W. Smith on November 9, 1922. It was a popular destination for all members of the community. In 1928, the Austins built a popular 100-by-48-foot roller-skating rink with a maple floor. Dances were held there often. In 1951, the rink was taken down. The Austin family—descendants of Stephen F. Austin—lived in a home next to the store until 1952. Carl Austin bought the store and property from his father in 1957.

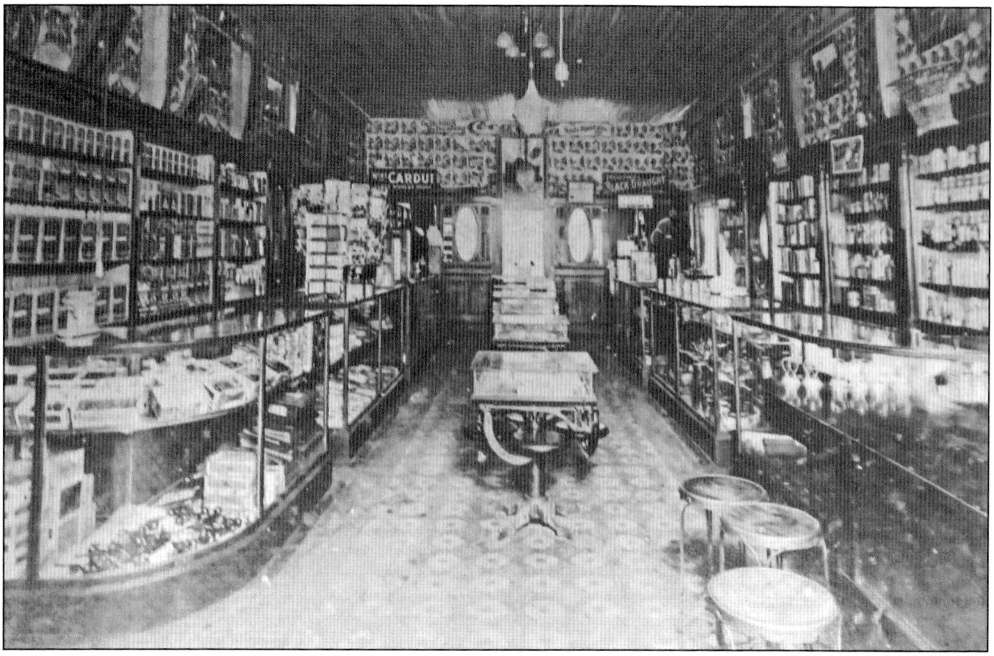

Well-known citizen Mont G. Calvert entered the drug business in 1900 with Dr. Howard H. Fitzgerald. In 1906, the enterprise was called Calvert's Drug Store. The drugstore also sold pianos, organs, and other musical instruments, and in 1916, Calvert provided the first piano tuner in town. The first local lending library started at the Calvert Drug Store in 1930. Membership was $1, and book rentals were 5¢ per day. The library later moved to the city hall above the fire station. In 1919, Calvert bought the Eagle Lake Drug Company.

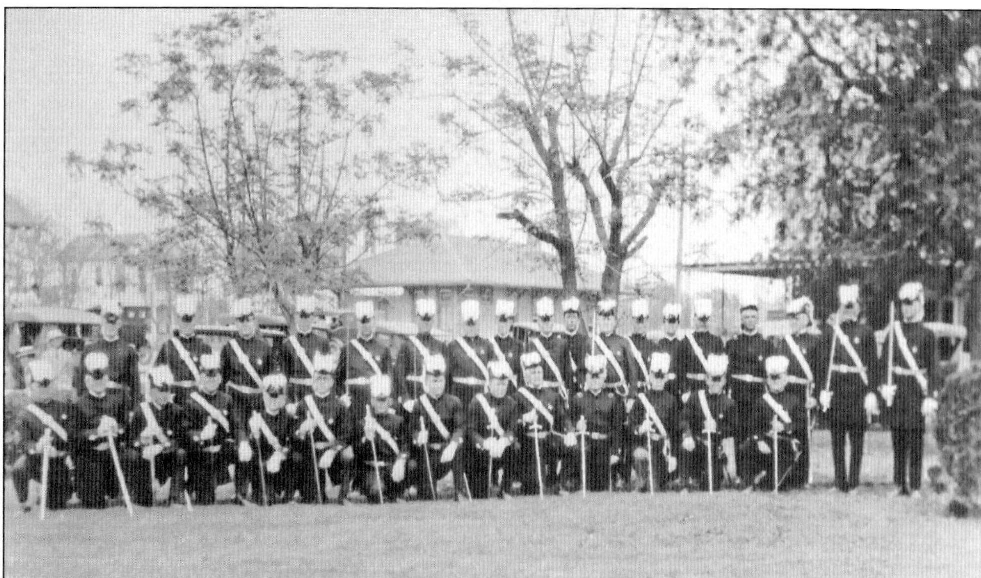

The Knights Templar Order, part of the Ancient Free and Accepted Masons organization, is pictured on the town square next to the McCarty Building and the train station. In 1873, a group of local Masons organized the first Eagle Lake Masonic lodge just 16 years after the townsite was designated. The lodge has played an active role in Eagle Lake's history.

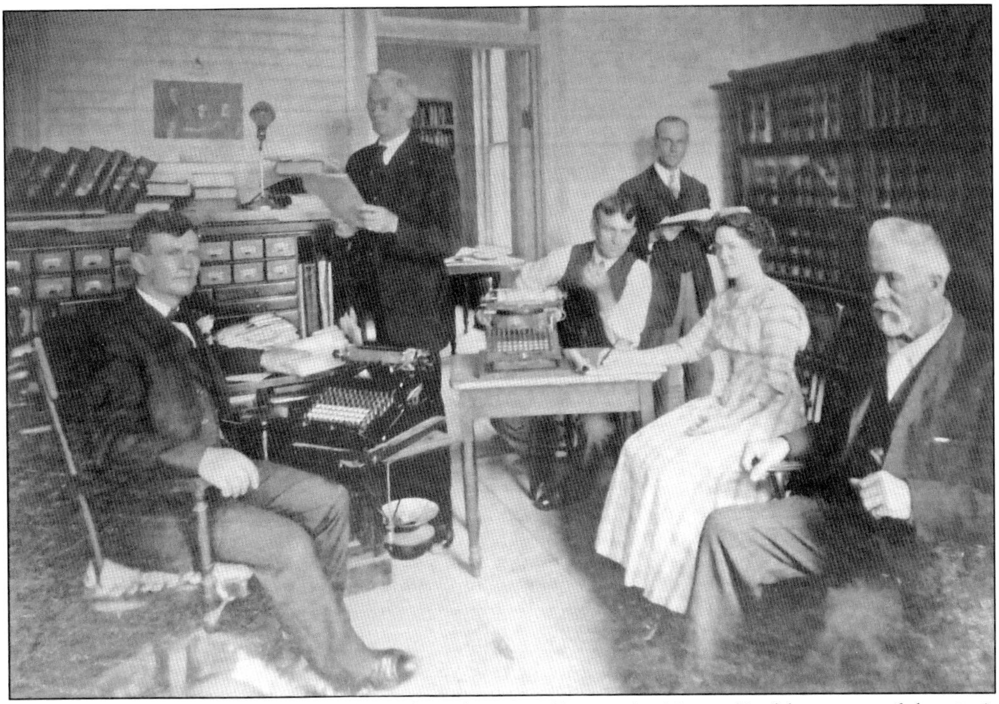

A group of Eagle Lake professionals gathered in an office in the Norris Building, one of the city's original buildings. They are, from left to right, Walter Strickland, Dr. F.O. Norris (standing), Dr. P.T. Gordon, Emanuel Roos (standing), stenographer Mary Thomas, and Tom Roberts. (Courtesy of Prairie Edge Museum.)

The Hotel Brown, built in 1890 and remodeled in 1908, was the first cement block structure in Eagle Lake. It was constructed with three floors, 30 guest rooms, and a large dining room. In 1915, it became the Heiney Hotel and was later named the Eagle Hotel. The building, near the train station and behind city hall, was demolished in 1974 to make way for a parking lot.

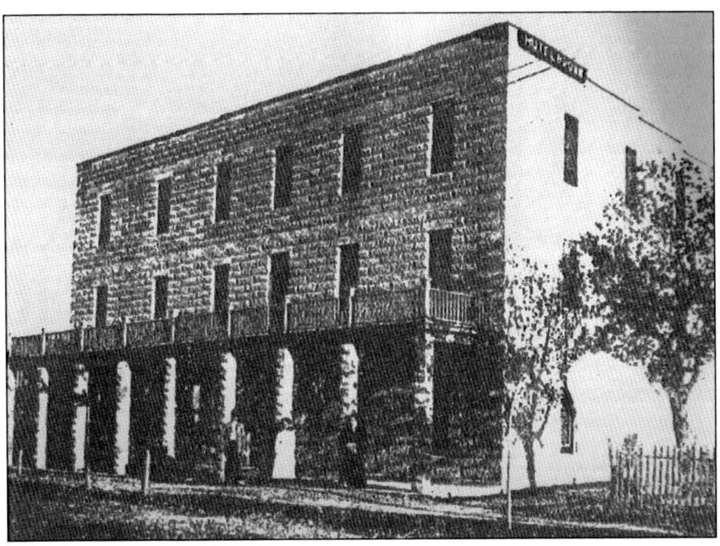

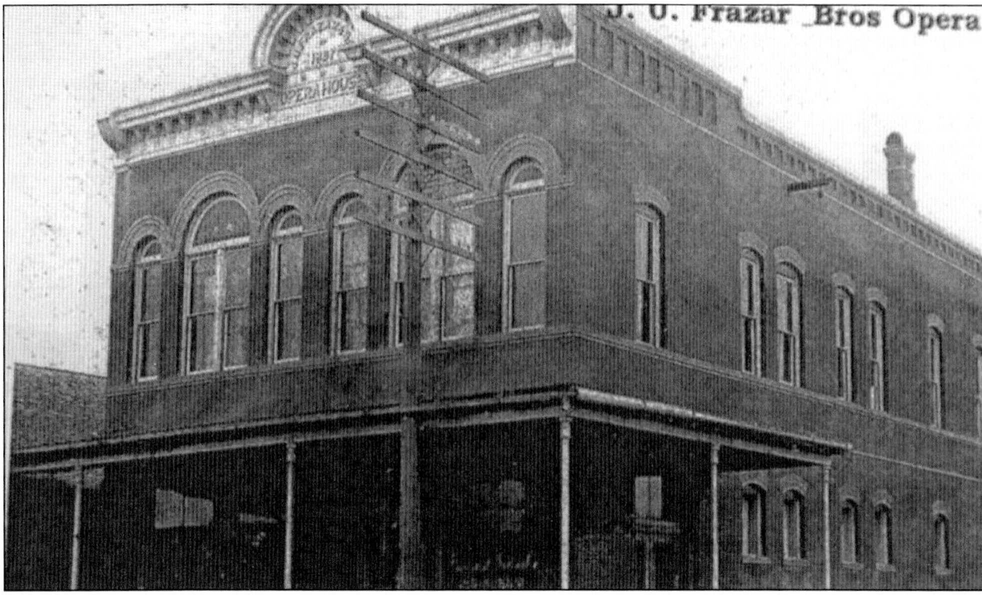

The Frazar Opera House was built in 1886 as a two-story, all-brick structure with the opera stage and auditorium on the 40-by-110-foot second floor. The downstairs of the building was divided into two stores, each about 20 feet wide. The corner store housed the Vineyard and Walker Bank, and the business on the left side was a saloon and domino parlor called the Welford and Beckman Saloon. (Courtesy of Prairie Edge Museum.)

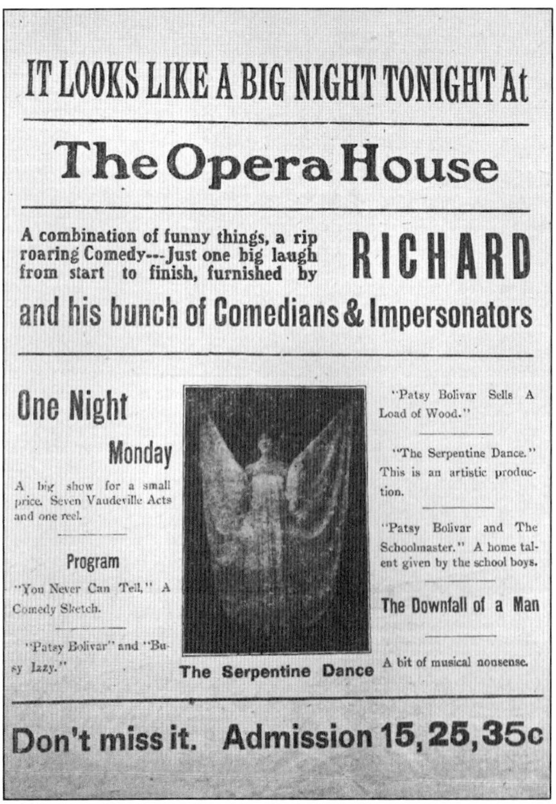

The opera house auditorium was used for musicals, plays, visiting road show entertainment, dances, and sporting events such as wrestling and boxing. In 1921, there was a 10-round boxing match at the opera house. After a dance in 1925, the building was destroyed by an accidental fire but rebuilt in 1926 as a one-story building measuring 40 by 90 feet. The original bricks were made in a brick oven situated along the Colorado River. The new building was constructed from the old bricks, which were cleaned by high school boys for 1¢ per brick. The Sugar Boys' Ball, sponsored by employees of the Lakeside Sugar Refinery, was a popular event at the opera house. Other events included the Children's Masked Ball and concerts by the Cornet Band. The opera house was a popular cultural and entertainment center in Eagle Lake.

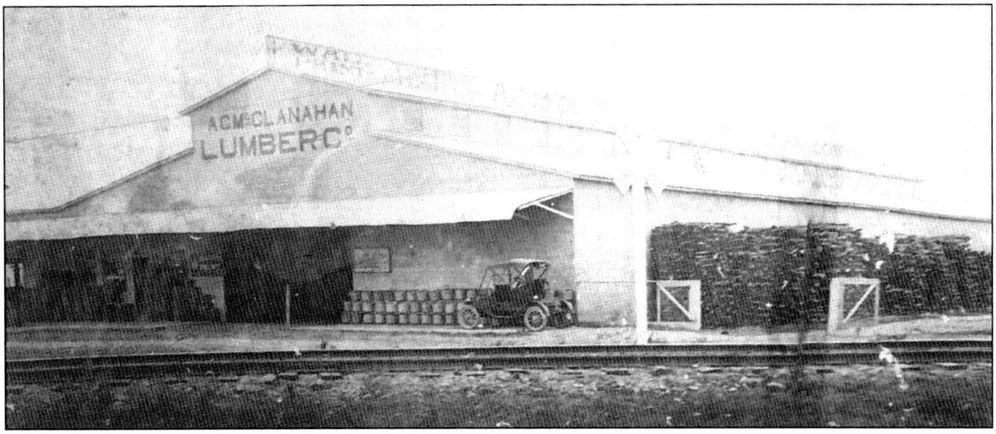

One of the oldest local lumberyards was started in 1901 by George W. Keith; the A.C. McClanahan lumberyard (pictured above) began in 1903. The Conner brothers also owned a small lumber company, which they later sold to McClanahan in 1903. The McClanahan company did a thriving business and was conveniently located near the freight tracks.

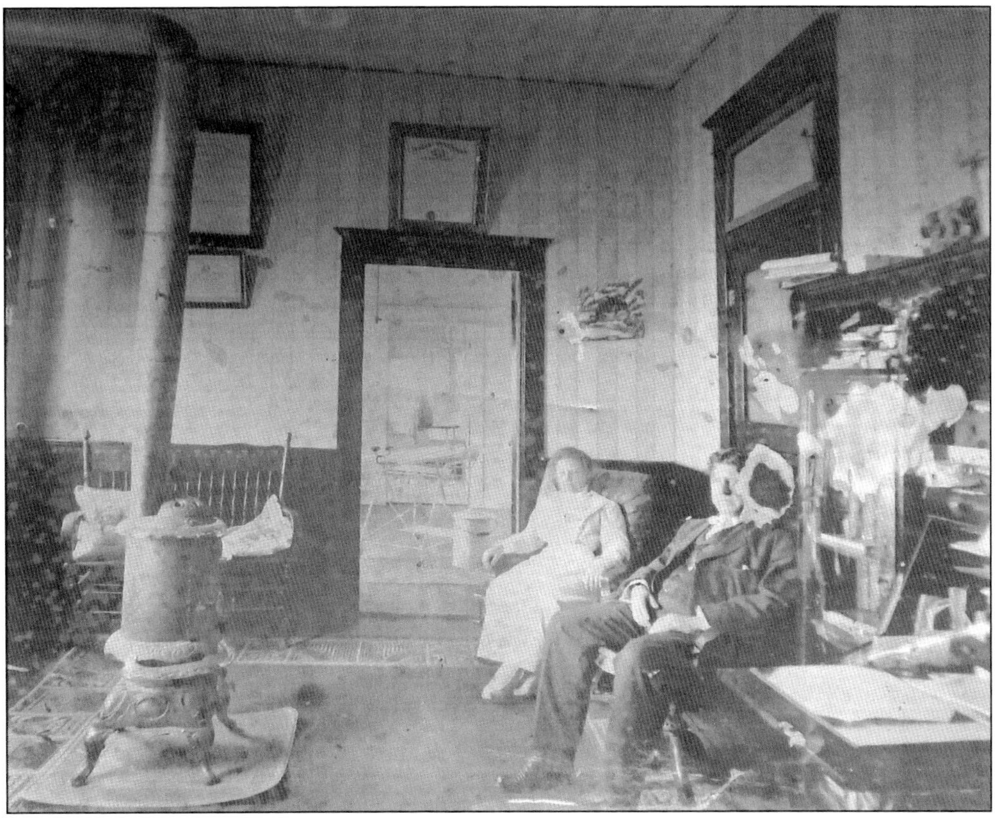

The two-story Fitzgerald Building on McCarty Street was constructed in 1912 by T.J. Roberts. Dr. Harold Fitzgerald, physician and surgeon, occupied offices on the upper floor from 1912 to 1918. This c. 1915 photograph shows Fitzgerald and his unidentified nurse in his office, with the examining room through the door and a bench, which served as the patients' waiting area, near the woodstove. (Courtesy of Prairie Edge Museum.)

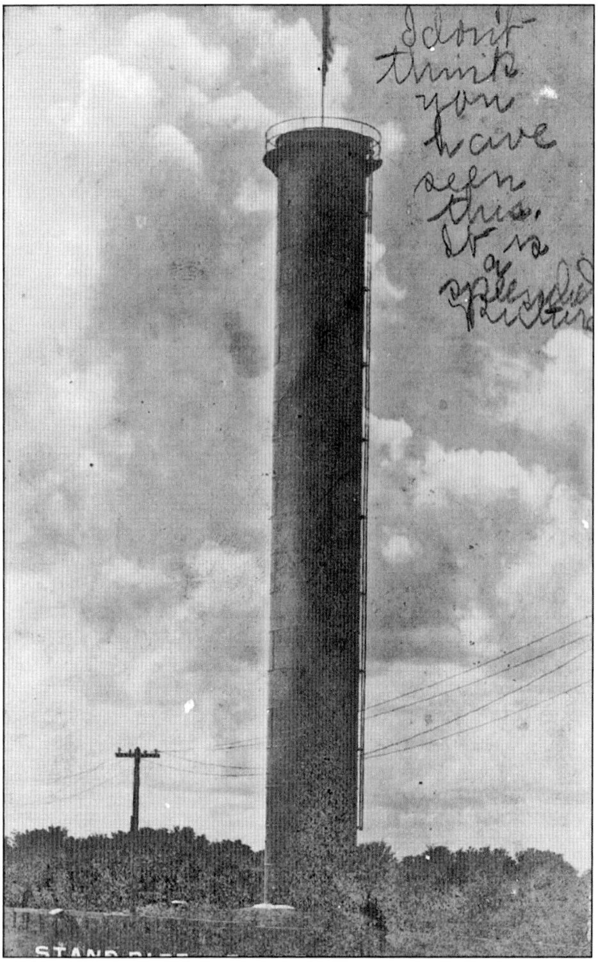

The standpipe of the Eagle Lake Water, Light, and Gin Company was 105 feet high and 12 feet in diameter, and there was a flagpole on top from which the American flag flew. The standpipe was a symbol of progress indicating the abundant water furnished to the town. As the tallest structure in the area, it could be seen from a distance and became a symbol of town progress. It was light-colored, with a ladder extending from near the bottom to the top.

A tractor parade heads down Main Street, with Hayes Stephens (at right) looking on. The parade showed the newest models of tractors on its way through the downtown area. The Frank Stephens Company sold farm machinery and equipment; Hayes and Frank were brothers.

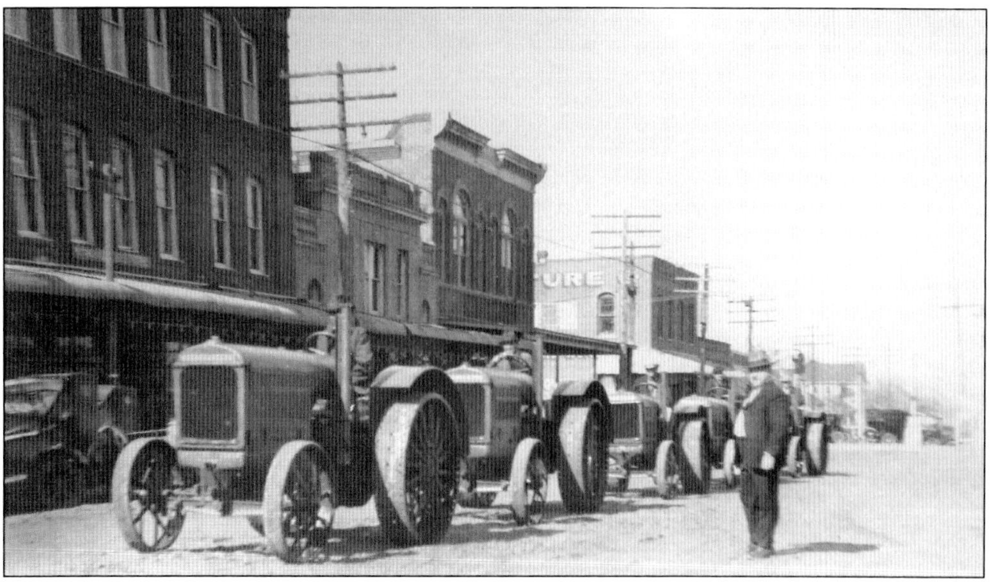

The First National Bank float is shown in an Independence Day parade, possibly around 1916. The bank, covered in white tile, was one of the town's most beautiful buildings. On the parade float are, from left to right, Agnes Chew, Mrs. W.E. Lenhart, Archie Douglass, Fox Stephens, and W.E. Lenhart.

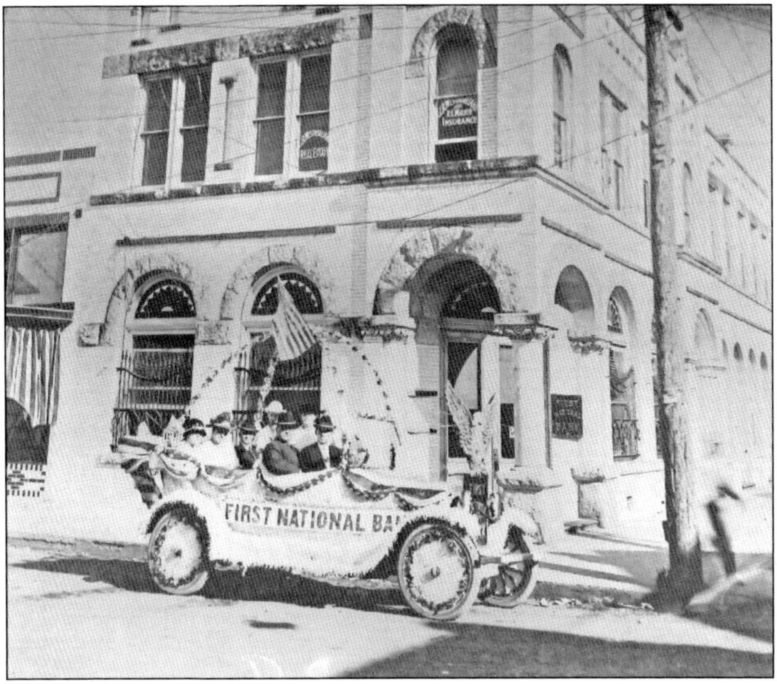

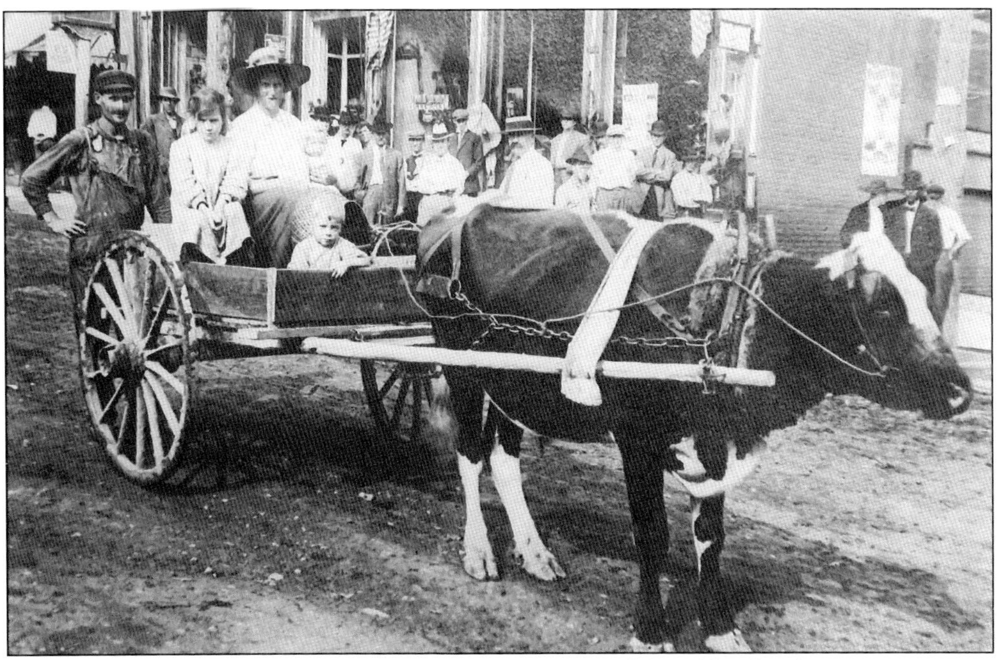

Dressed in their finery. Harvey Cutshawl (far left, in overalls) and his family came to town in their oxcart on Saturdays. Weekend shopping and socializing were important activities. When dry, the unpaved streets made it easy to maneuver carts to the hitching rail.

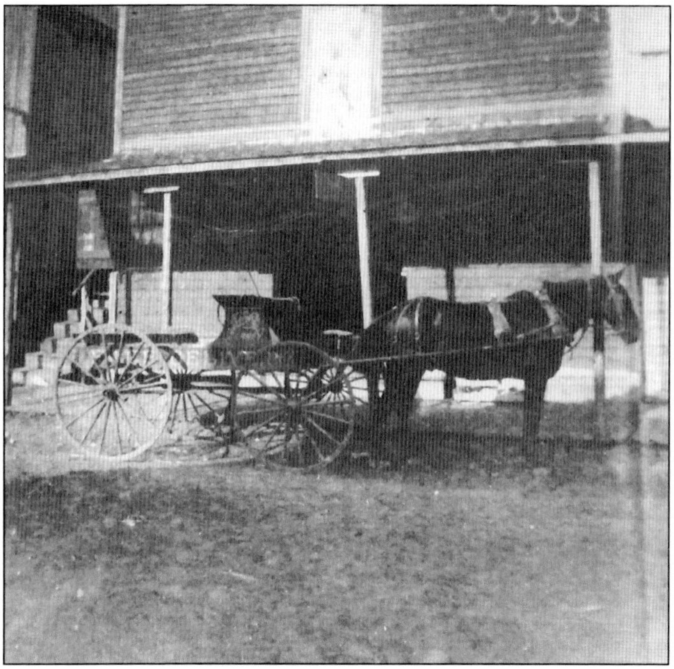

Toliver and Carney Horse and Delivery Cart, which offered free delivery, sits in front of a wooden building owned by James W. McCarty and located on Main Street at the present-day site of the Norris Building. Toliver and Carney had an early grocery store in 1906. Many stores in the early 1900s were built of unpainted wood with front galleries and side stairways to the second floor.

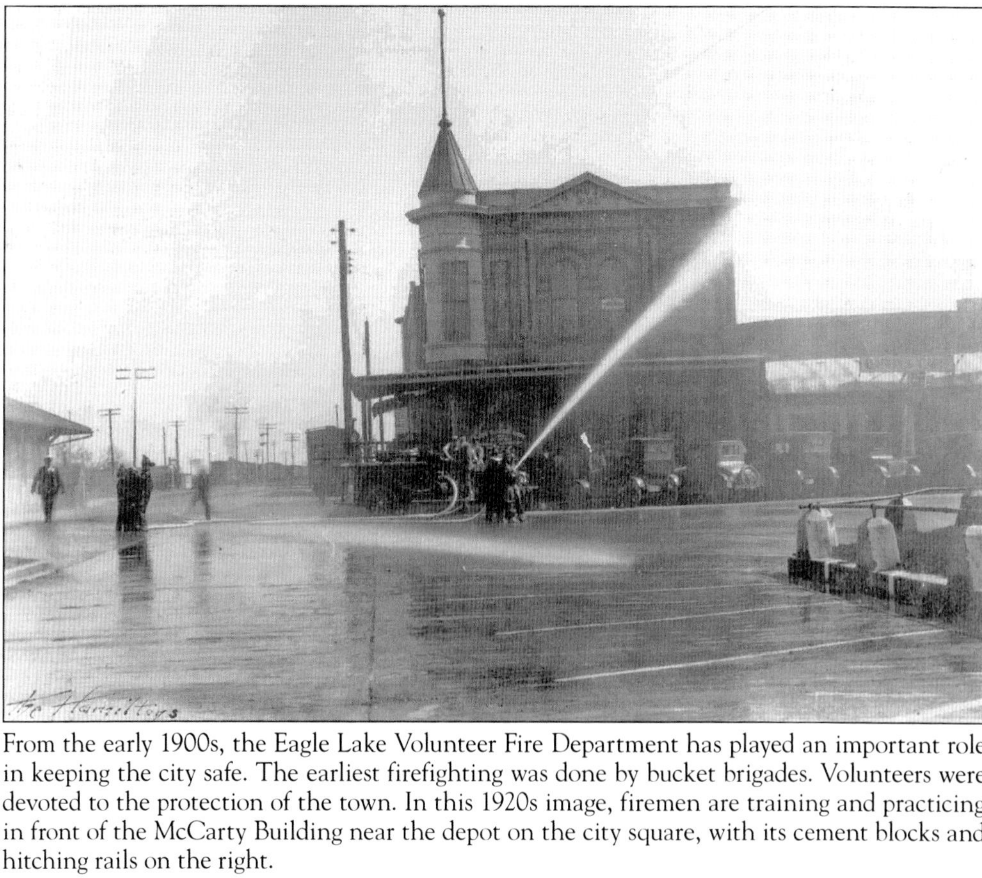

From the early 1900s, the Eagle Lake Volunteer Fire Department has played an important role in keeping the city safe. The earliest firefighting was done by bucket brigades. Volunteers were devoted to the protection of the town. In this 1920s image, firemen are training and practicing in front of the McCarty Building near the depot on the city square, with its cement blocks and hitching rails on the right.

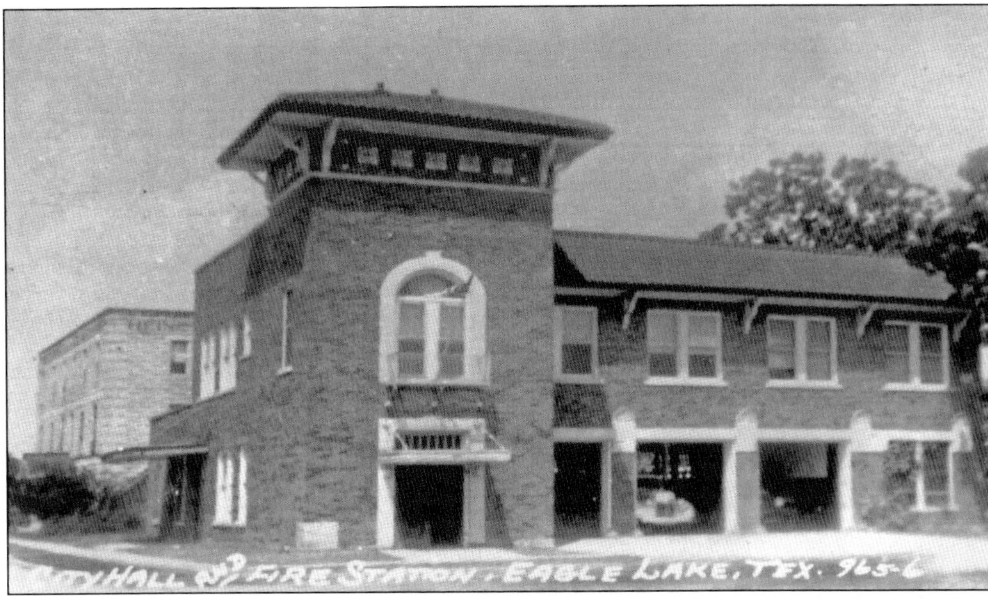

The Eagle Lake City Hall and Fire Station buildings were erected of brick with tile roofing at a cost of $20,000. They were built between the Southern Pacific passenger station and the Heiney Hotel. The lower floor had space for a courtroom and a room for public gatherings; three center bays to accommodate fire trucks; and rooms on the back, plus a toilet and shower for firemen. The second-floor tower section held the mayor's office. There were separate rooms for the tax collector, city records, and a city council chamber. There was also a 40-by-28-foot room used as an assembly hall and for public gatherings. Mayor R.T. Westmoreland began moving equipment and city records to the building in 1926. Later, a city jail and police station were added on the Heiney Hotel side. The upstairs also served as the town library for many years. In 1888, George W. Keith lost his house to fire and resolved to help start a fire department. (Both courtesy of William H. Harrison.)

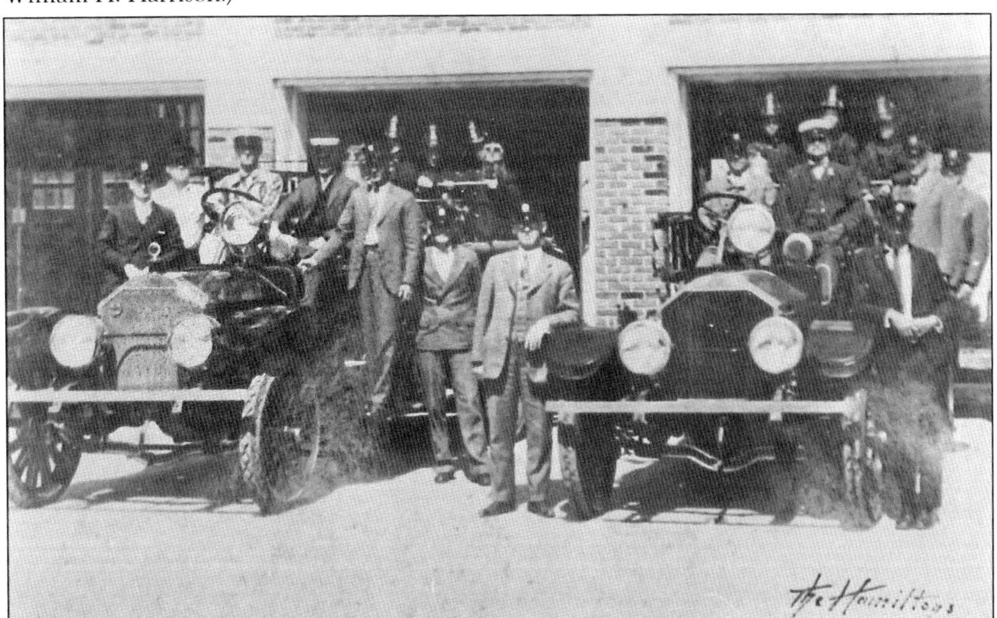

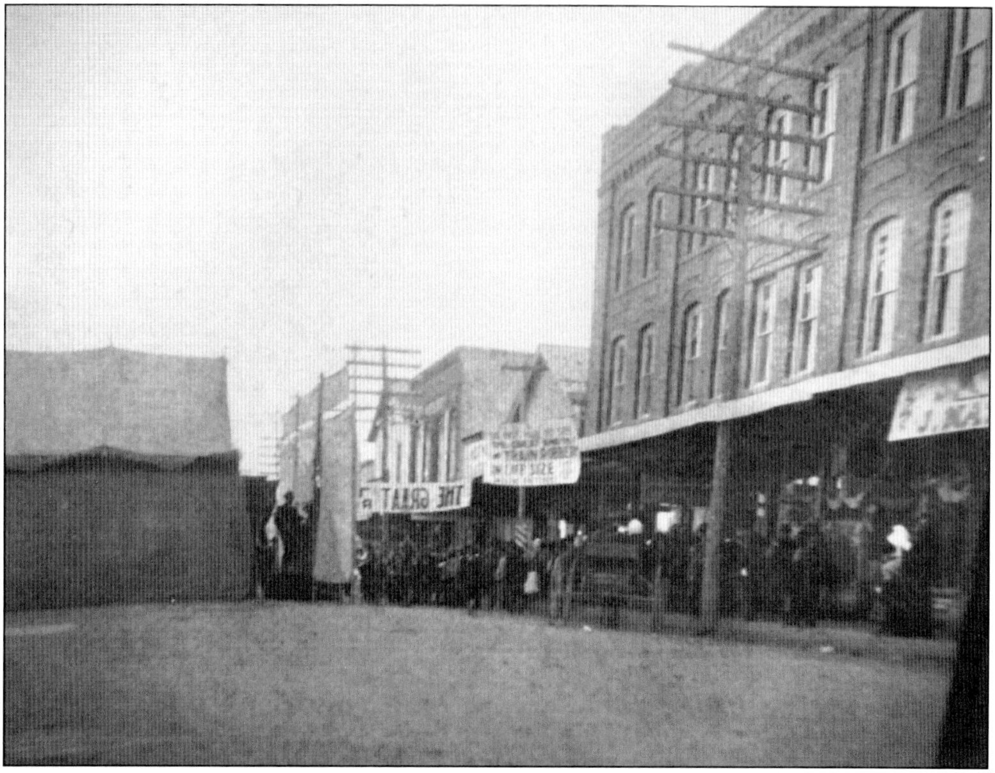

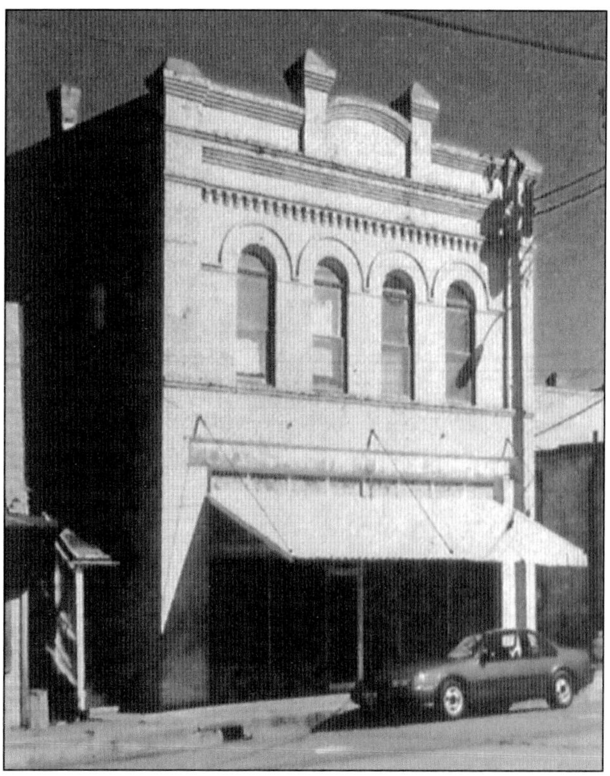

The first movie to play in Eagle Lake, *The Great Train Robbery*—a 12-minute Western made in 1903—was shown in a tent on Main Street as a part of a 1904 carnival. The event made local history and laid the groundwork for later movie houses.

Lee Hughes built the two-story brick building that housed the first stand-alone theater in the area. It opened in January 1913 and later that same year merged with the Dixie Theater and took its name. In 1919, it was renamed the Queen Theater and then the Rex Theater, which continued operating until the mid-1920s, when the establishment closed. The last owners were Carl Milentz and Mark Cole, who moved their business to the Avalon Theater in 1929. The 1913 building still stands on West Main Street.

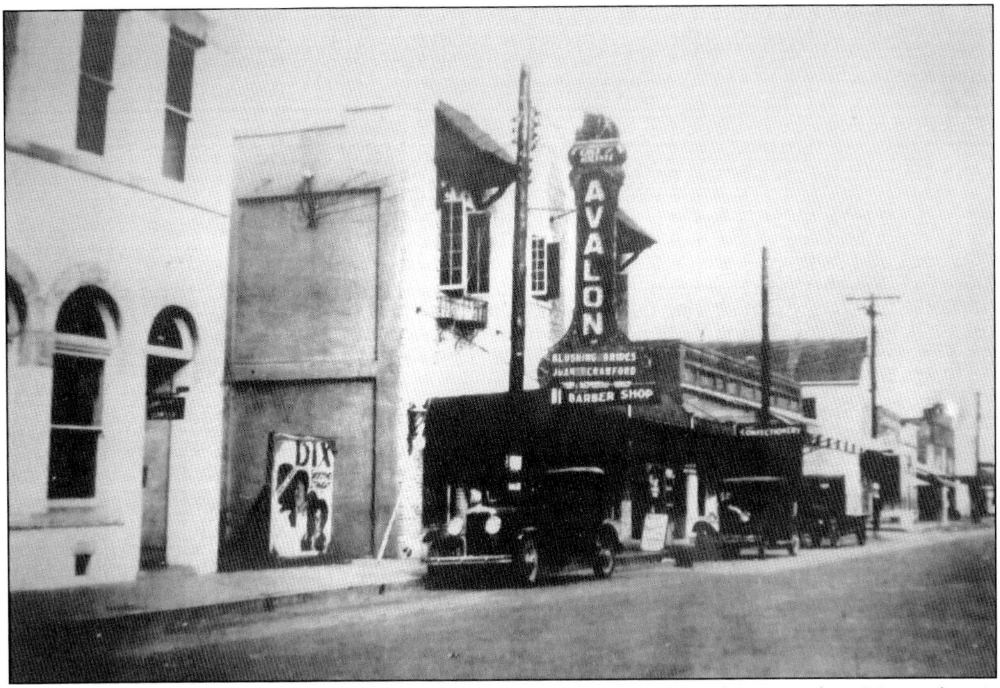

The Avalon, on Main Street next to the original First National Bank, opened on November 4, 1929, with a talking picture, *Young Nowheres*. Built for $20,000, the theater seated 520 on the first floor and 120 in the balcony and showed both silent and talking films. It was later renamed the Cole Theater and, in 1951, the Rice Theatre, the last movie house, which closed in 1968.

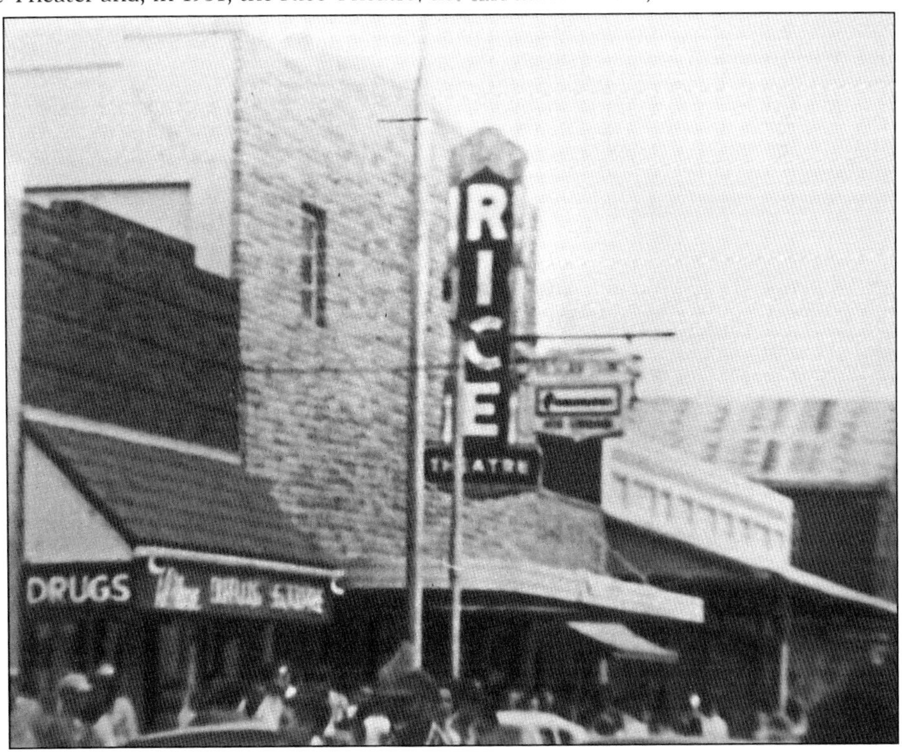

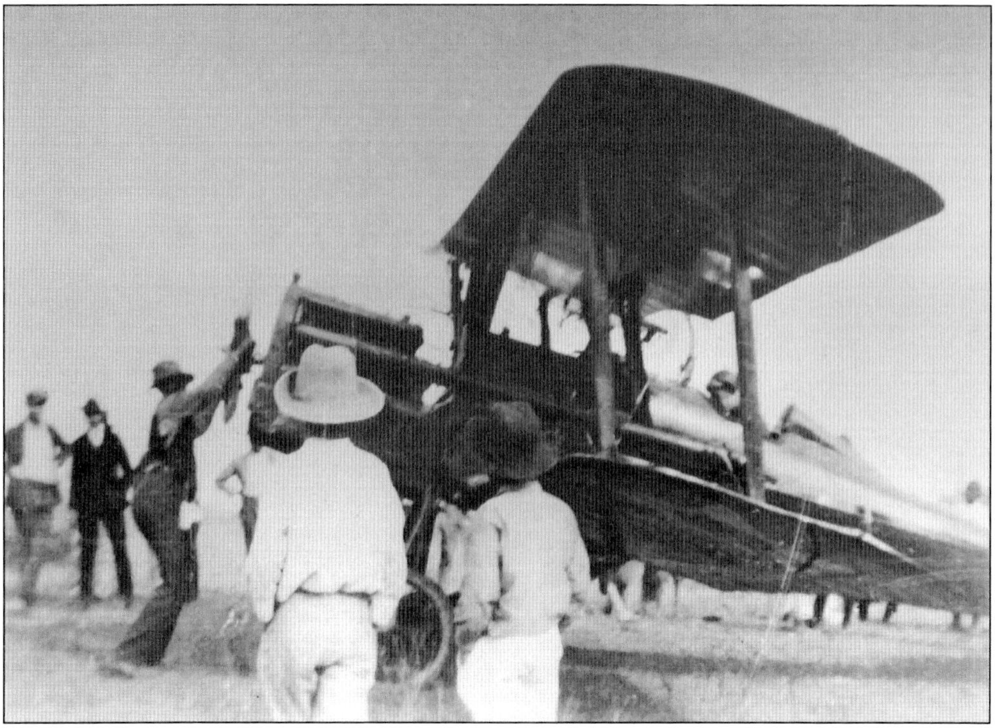

During World War I, between 1917 and 1918, Eagle Lake became the site of an aviation school and landing field for US Army Air Service planes from Ellington Field in Houston. The local airfield, called Griffin Aviation Field, became a training area for pilots. Ellington Field was built in 1917 to train pilots for combat in World War I. To meet the demand for pilots, there were numerous smaller pilot bases. Most planes were Curtiss JN-4s ("Jennys"). The Army plane was the first ever seen in Eagle Lake, and around 100 people came out to watch it land at Griffin Aviation Field.

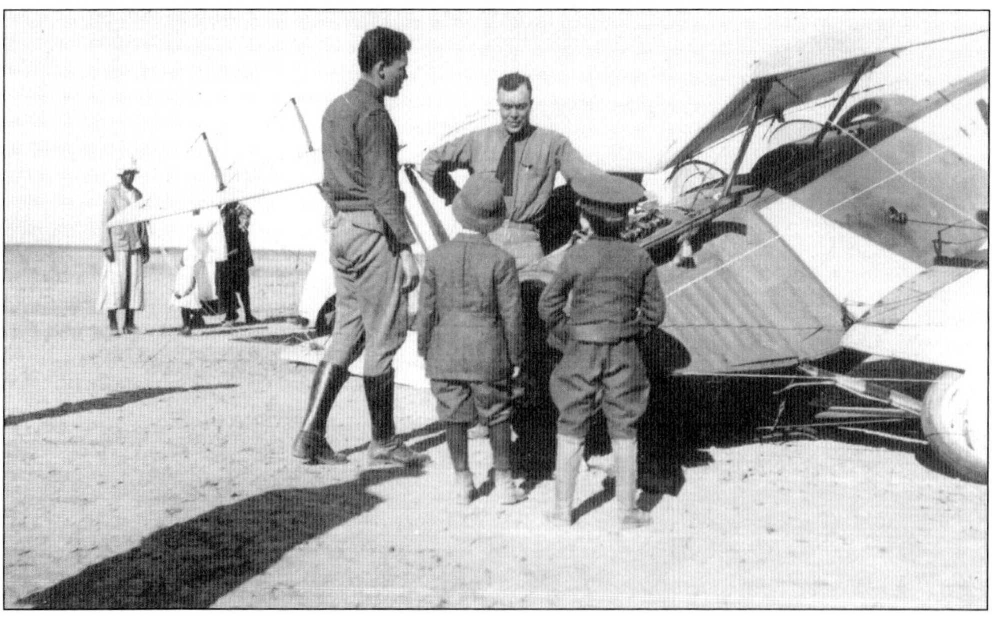

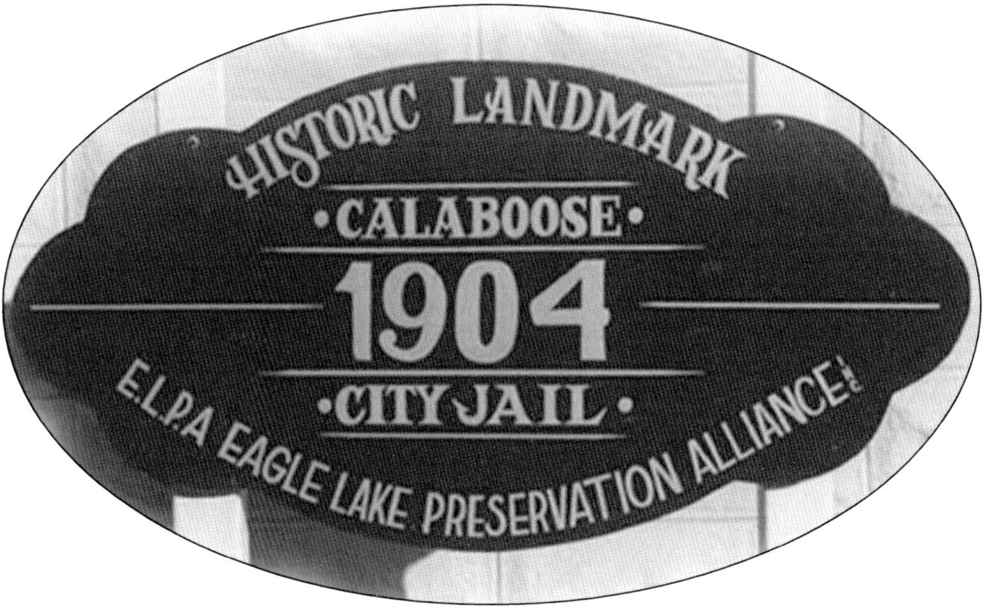

The first jail in Eagle Lake was located on South McCarty Street. It was built in 1904 by G.W. Keith as a one-room cement building, which cost $250. With saloons and gambling halls—as well as men frequently carrying guns—in the area, law enforcement was important. Later, during the Prohibition and speakeasy era, a new jail was built in October 1929 behind city hall. It was known to be "a modern jail with perfect sanitation and all of the latest jail improvements." The site of the first jail bears a historic marker. The building was rebuilt and dedicated as a Girl Scouts' hut.

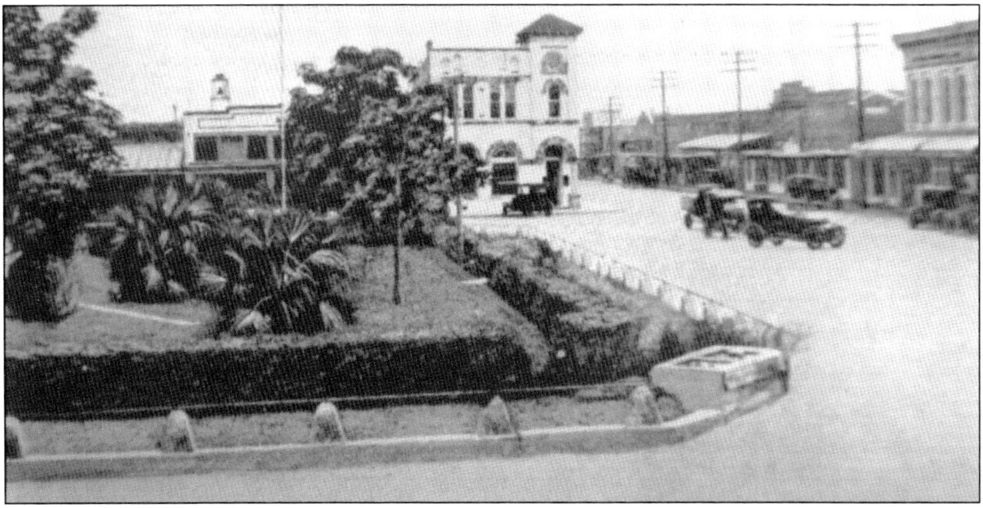

City Park, pictured here around 1926, was a place of beauty in the center of town. One could see palmetto trees and abundant vegetation, including a hedge surrounding the park. The iron hitching rail, supported by cement blocks, was surrounded by horses and buggies until they were displaced by the automobile. A double cement water trough stands at the corner, and the popular bandstand is in the center of the park. The First National Bank is in the background. The foliage and bandstand were gone by the 1950s, and City Park was renamed "The Square," or city square.

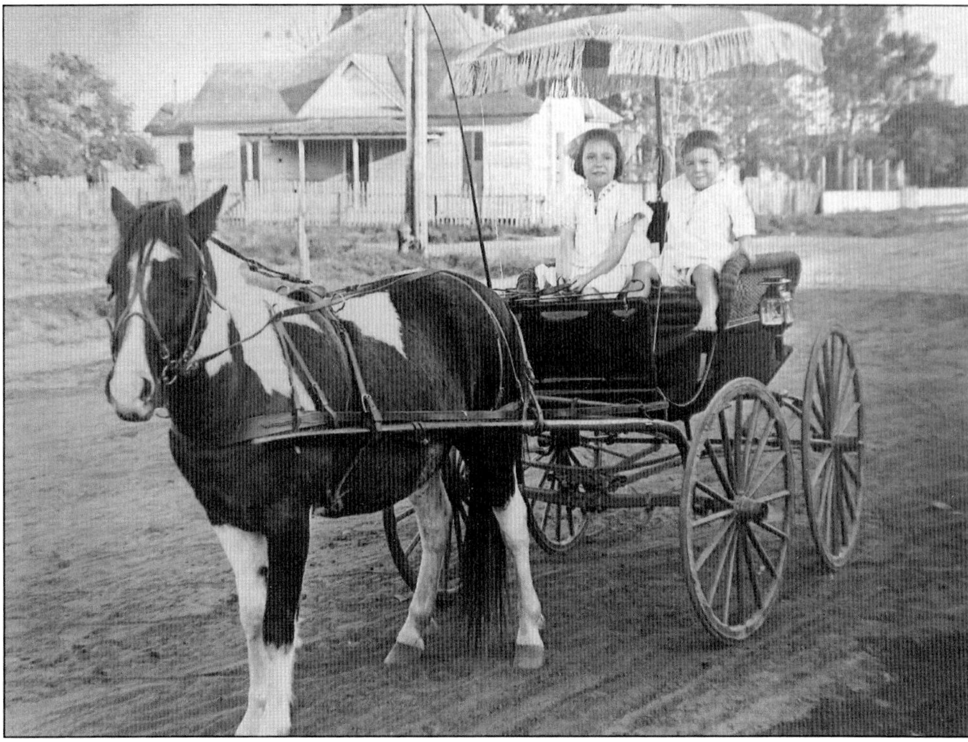

Virginia Guynn and her cousin, Bruce Oliphant, are out for an afternoon buggy ride. Virginia's father, M.E. Guynn, was a cashier at the Eagle Lake State Bank. In the early 1900s, streets in Eagle Lake were unpaved, making it difficult to travel after it rained. Sometimes, rice straw would be put in the mud to help prevent travelers from getting stuck.

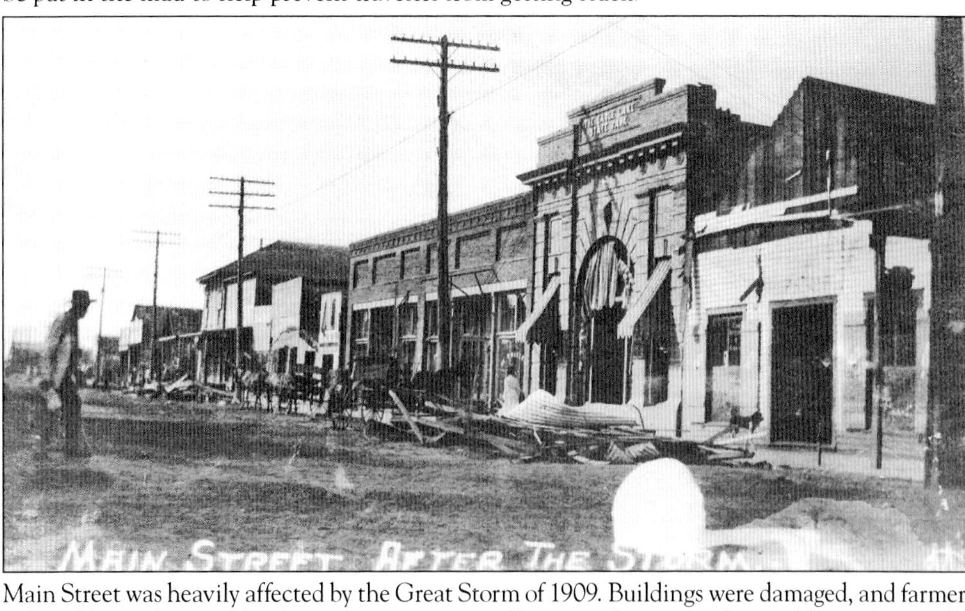

Main Street was heavily affected by the Great Storm of 1909. Buildings were damaged, and farmers suffered heavy losses. The downtown awnings, galleries, and some roofs were blown down. The frame building next to the State Bank was badly damaged. Cleanup was a slow process, with the work mostly done by men and wagons.

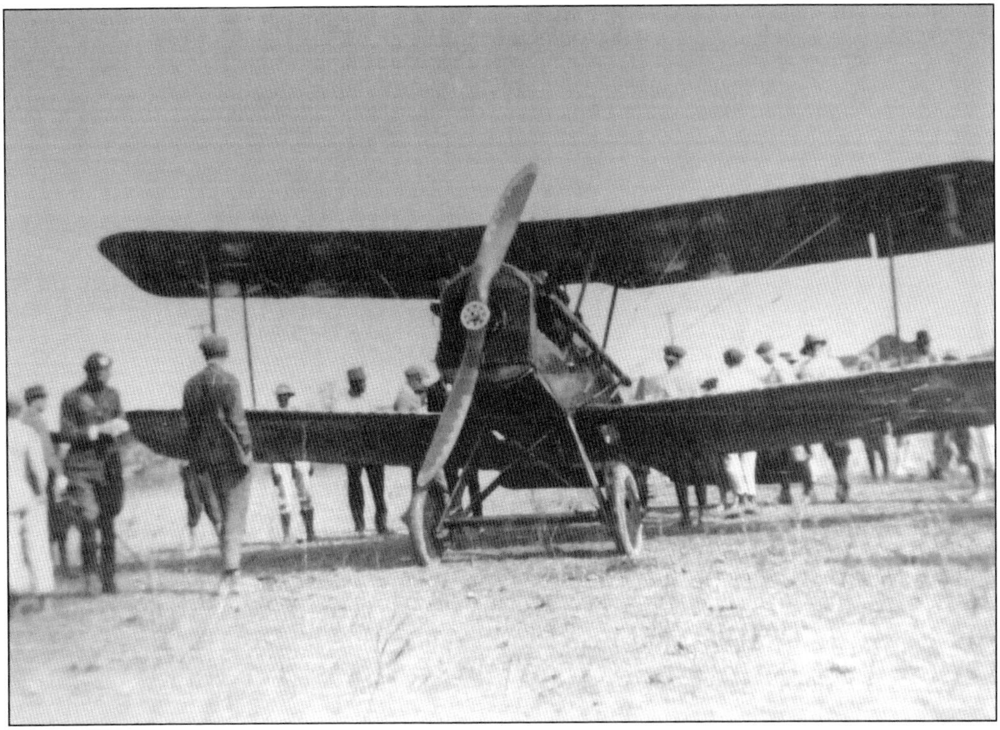

The first airplane to offer rides to passengers landed in Eagle Lake in 1930. The occasion drew a large and excited crowd, with the mayor acknowledging the momentous event. For $1 each, passengers were taken up one at a time to fly over the lake and the town. The popular planes were Curtiss JN-4s ("Jennys") purchased after World War I.

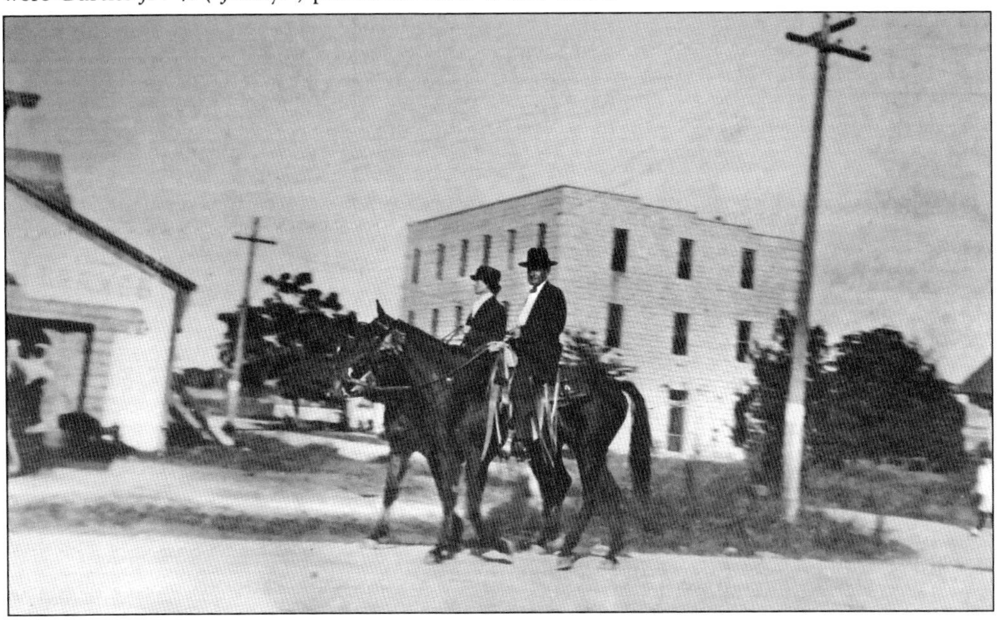

Business leader Hayes Stephens and his wife, Lillie, take a horseback ride through town, with the Heiney Hotel in the background, across from the train depot. The Stephens were involved in successful banking, agribusiness, and mercantile and farm equipment establishments.

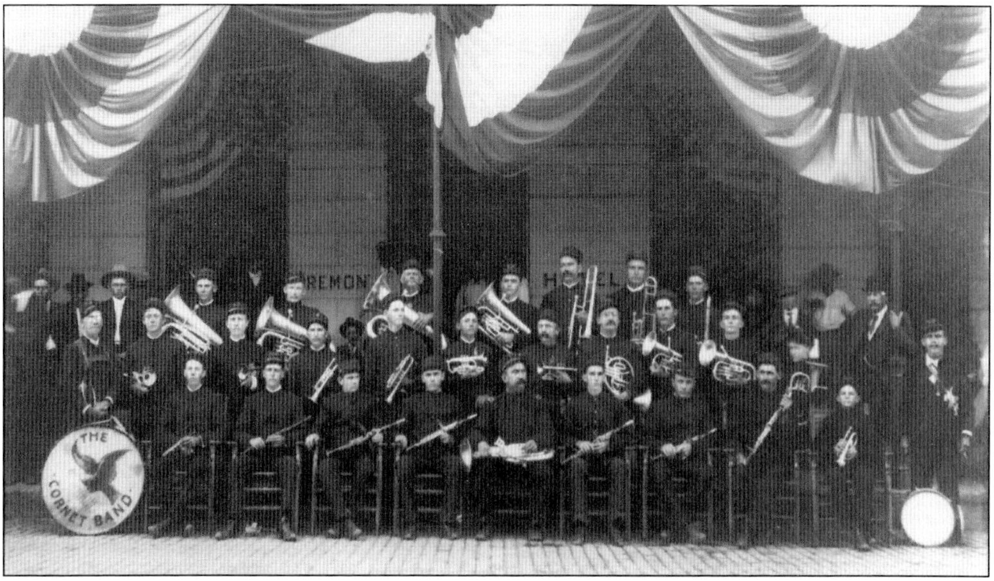

The Eagle Lake Cornet Band, established in 1905, was outstanding and won second place in an international competition in San Antonio in October 1905—the National Band of Mexico took first. The band made trips to Houston, San Antonio, and other areas in the state to compete in musical contests and to represent and advertise the town. This photograph was taken in front of the Tremont Hotel in Houston.

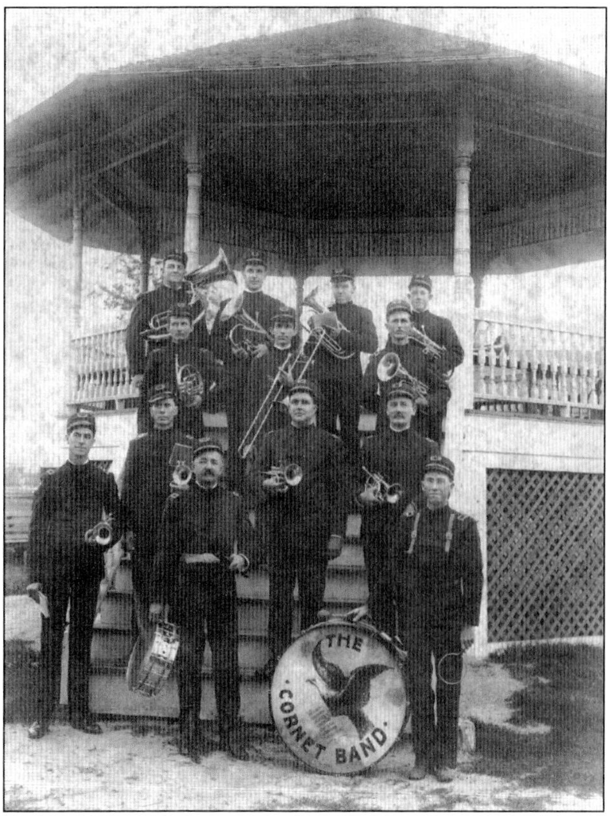

The cornet band, pictured at the town bandstand, sports new uniforms of dark green, black, and gold. The band began as the Eagle Lake Brass Band, organized in October 1904 and first called the Seaholm Band. It was made up of a small group of men from Eagle Lake and Chesterville. In 1905, the band became the Eagle Lake Cornet Band. Its symbol was an eagle painted on the bass drum. The Eagle Lake Cornet Band was active for almost 20 years.

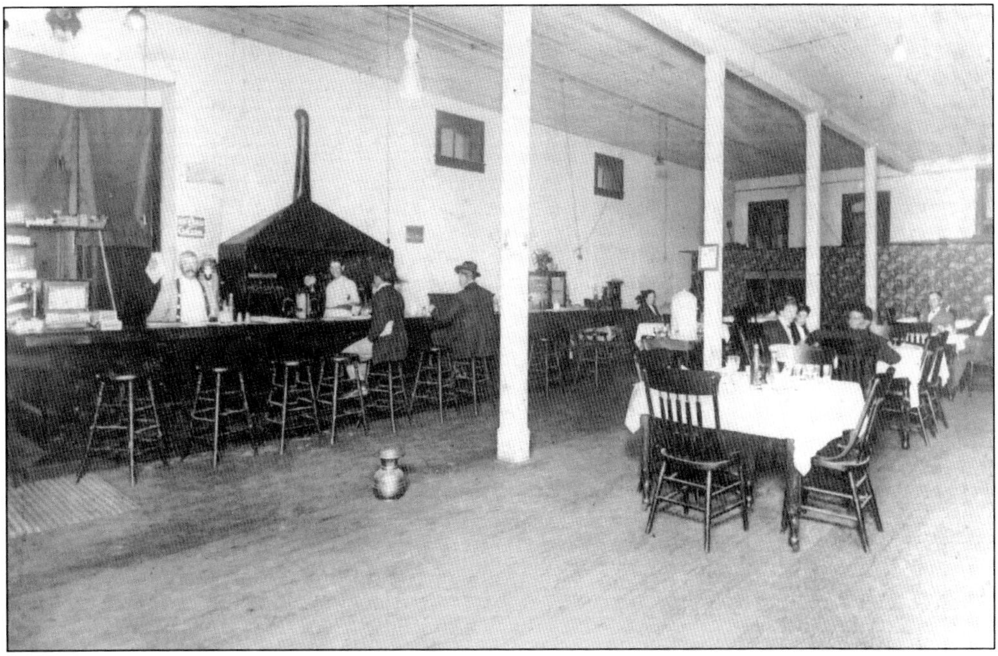

The Hanly Café, which specialized in fish and oysters, was a popular downtown café frequented by merchants, farmers, and ranchers. Located opposite the city square, near the depot, it was a gathering place for people to discuss news, weather, and crop and cattle prices. In 1912, at the café, a pearl was found in an oyster by A.T. Helmer, who sold it for $500.

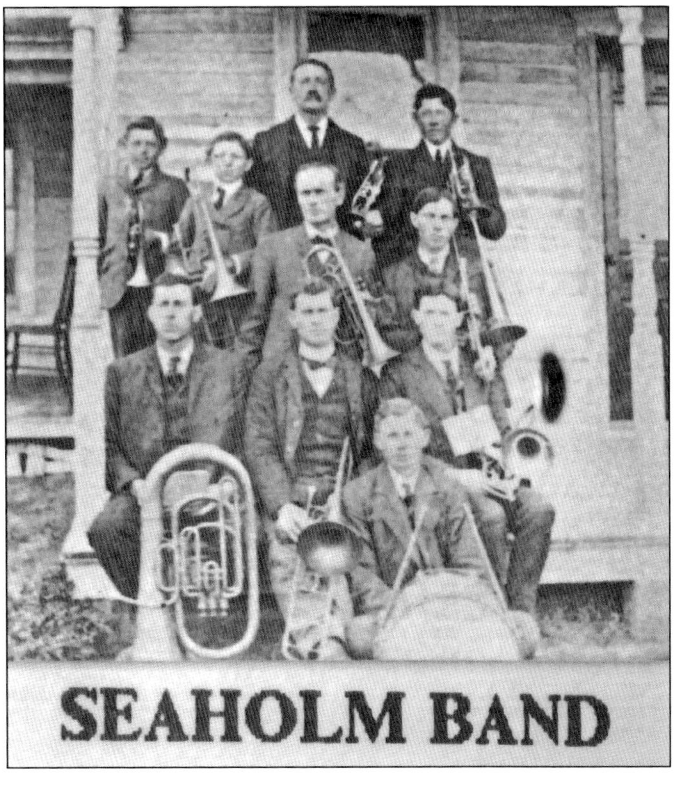

The Seaholm Band was organized around 1900 by Axel Seaholm, who had served as a musician in the Swedish army and played several instruments. He started a cornet band for his sons and other young men in Chesterville, which continued in Eagle Lake. Identified in this photograph are (first row) Carl Seaholm (with drum); and, from left to right, (fourth row) Ernest, Helmer, Axel, and Gus Seaholm.

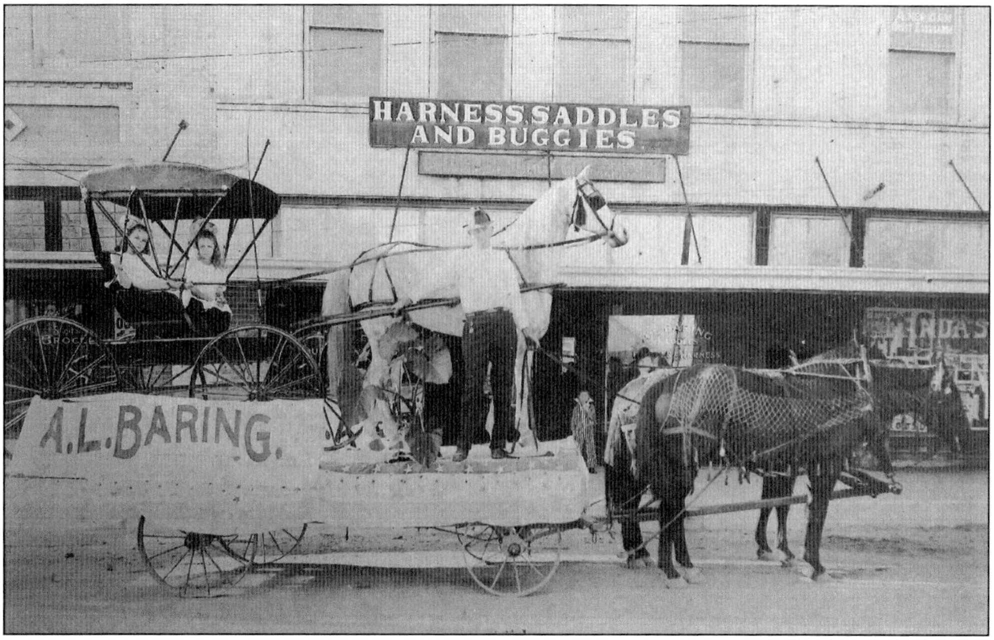

The A.L. Baring parade float in the Women's Community Fair of 1915 is in front of Baring's saddle and harness business on Main Street, which he began in October 1890, later adding buggies and surreys to his services offered. In 1929, he began selling Chevrolet automobiles. Baring died in 1936 and was succeeded in his enterprise by his son, Edgar, who was also a successful businessman.

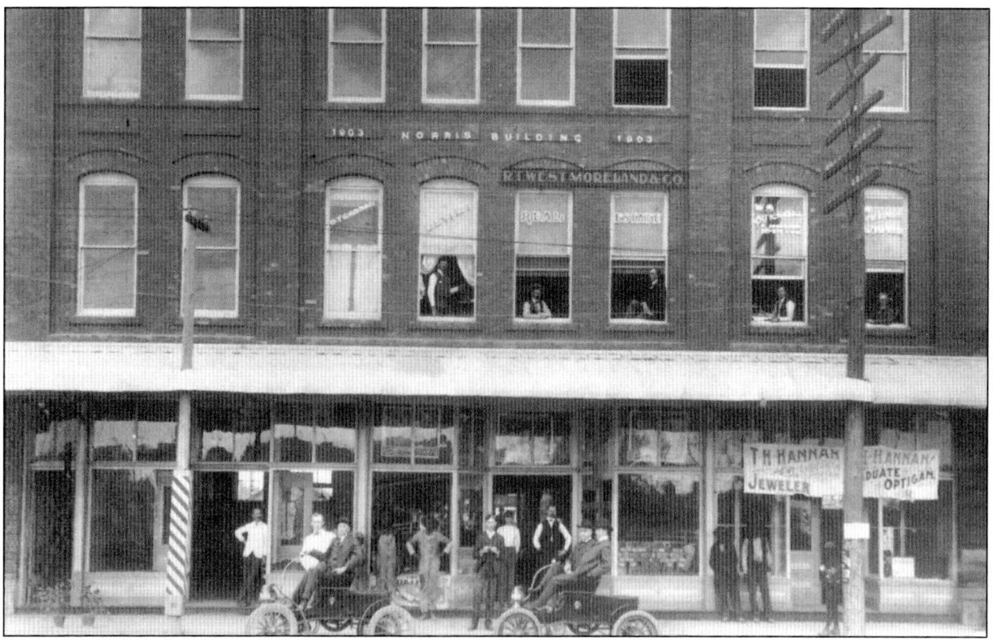

The first cars in Eagle Lake are pictured in front of the three-story Norris Building, built for Dr. F.O. Norris in 1903 for $12,500. Norris is in the first car, with John Matthews and George Vick in the second. The structure was described as the finest office building between Houston and San Antonio. The Norris Building's first floor was used for retail, the second for offices, and the third as a hall for meetings, socials, and programs.

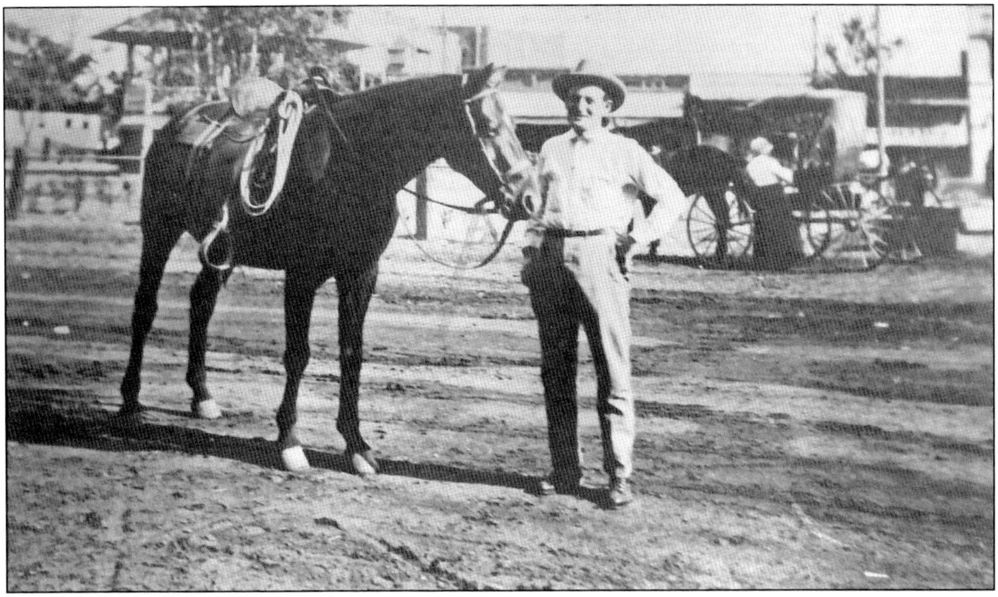

Born in Eagle Lake, "Mr. Max" Conner (1877–1960) was a well-known figure. He was in the lumberyard business from 1903 until the closing of the Eagle Lake Lumber Yard, located near the former Wilcox-Minimax grocery store. Conner was often seen visiting along the city square and served as justice of the peace for many years until he retired in September 1958. His father, Henry Conner, came to Eagle Lake in the late 1800s.

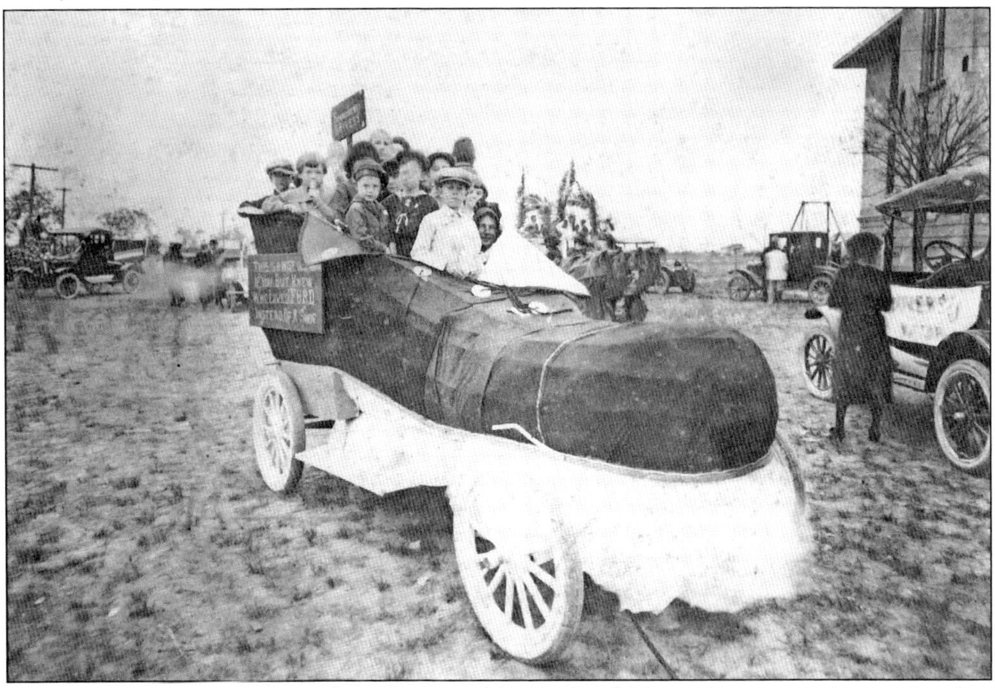

"The Old Woman in a Shoe" float, sponsored by the Ford Motor Company, advertised with a sign that reads, "This is a wise old woman, if you but knew, that lives in a Ford instead of a shoe." Meriwether L Anderson is the wise old woman, and her "children" included Louis Nathan, Mary Jacquelyn Oliphant, Joe Newton Frazar, and Ada Thomas.

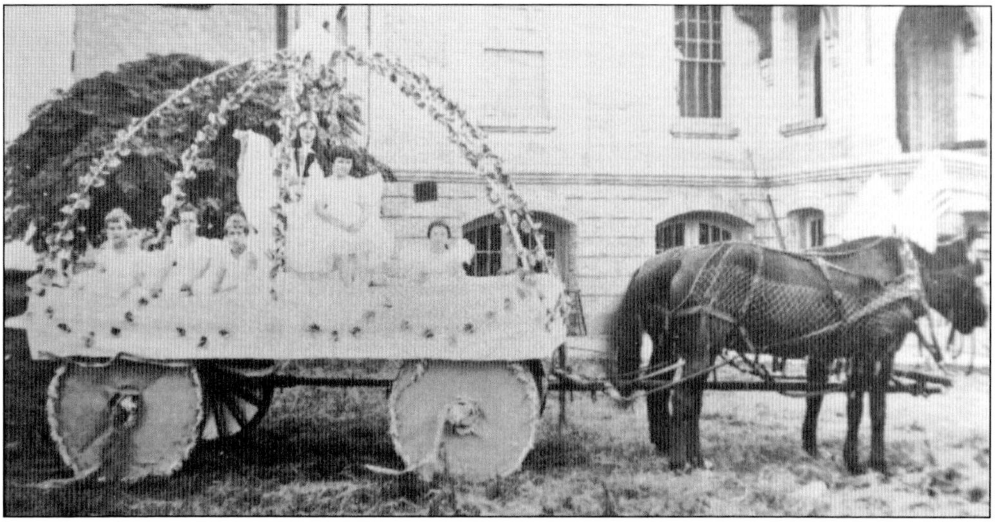

Horses sporting American flags and horsefly mesh and pulling a well-decorated float prepare to leave from the Eagle Lake Public School in 1916. Riding on the float are, from left to right, Corinne Bentley, Irene Davidson, Genevieve Calvert, Sophia Daily, Earlene Wicker, and Florence Evelyn Waddell.

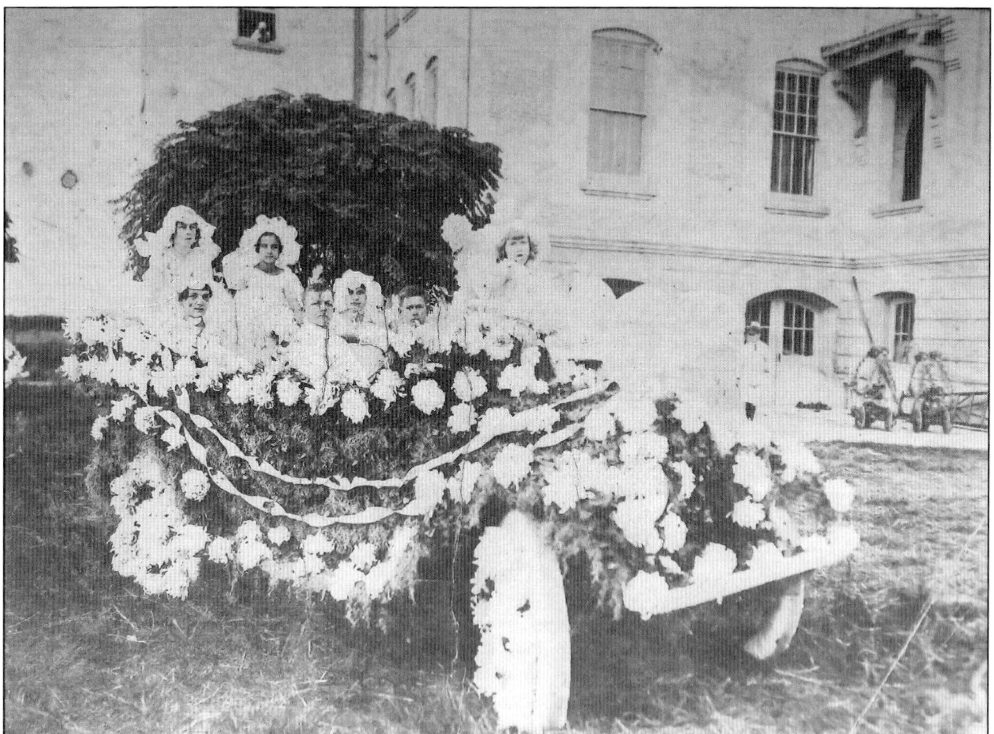

Riding in this elaborately decorated automobile for a 1916 Eagle Lake parade are, from left to right, (front seat) Brian S. Westmoreland, Reid Westmoreland, and Elizabeth Westmoreland; (backseat) Francis McClanahan, Josie Westmoreland, Janie Westmoreland (later Mrs. Joe Luna), and Jessie Vineyard. The building in the background is the first all-brick Eagle Lake Public School.

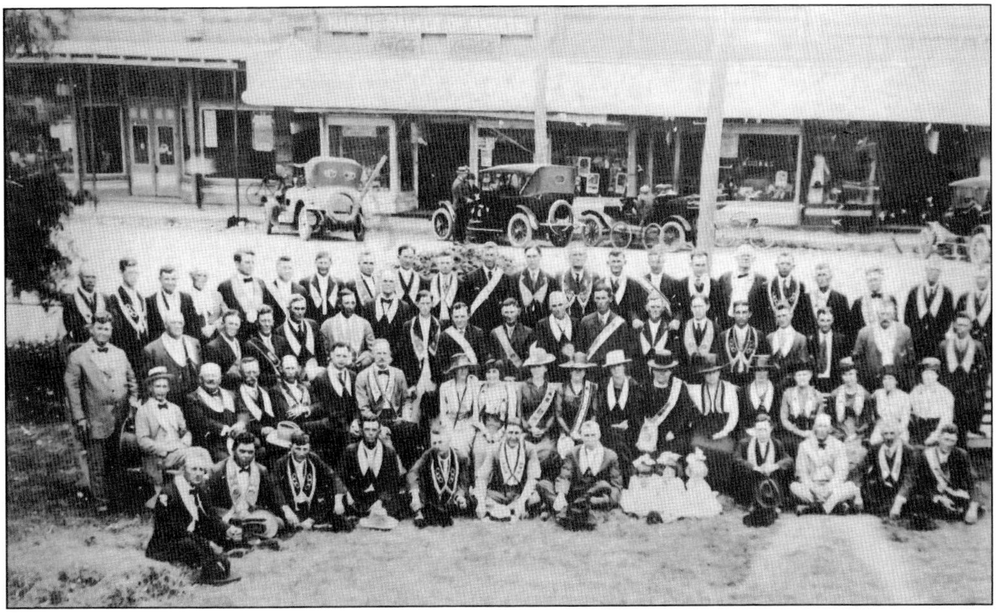

This photograph shows an Odd Fellows meeting at the city square in 1918. The fraternal Independent Order of Odd Fellows (IOOF) was dedicated to improving character through friendship and example, offering community support, aid to the less fortunate, and a helping hand to travelers and youth. The Eagle Lake IOOF lodge was established in 1907.

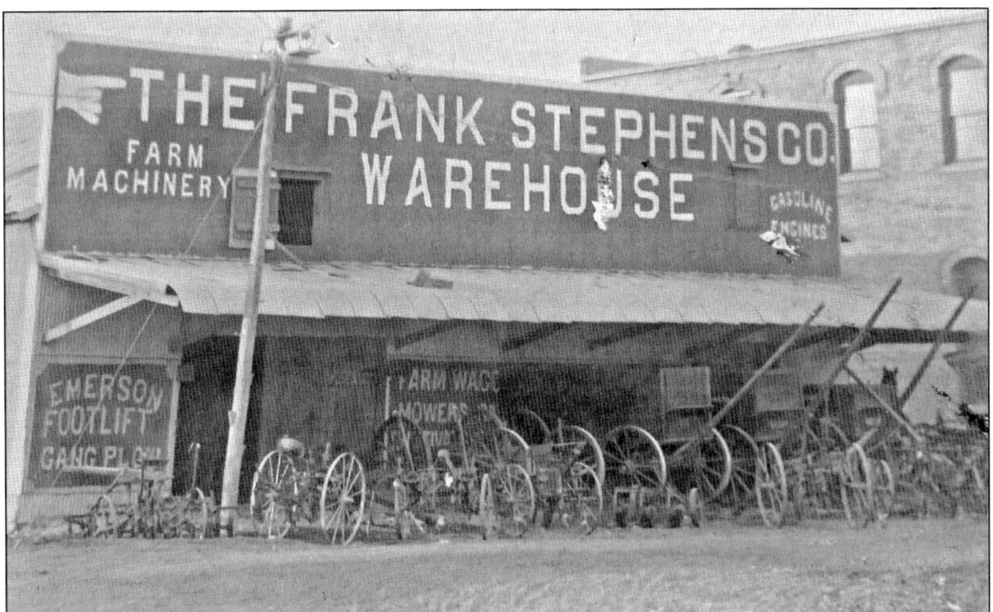

The Frank Stephens Co. warehouse, located on South McCarty Street behind the furniture store, was an important business for farmers. There, they could purchase farm machinery, plows, gasoline engines, wagons, mowers, discs, and other farm implements.

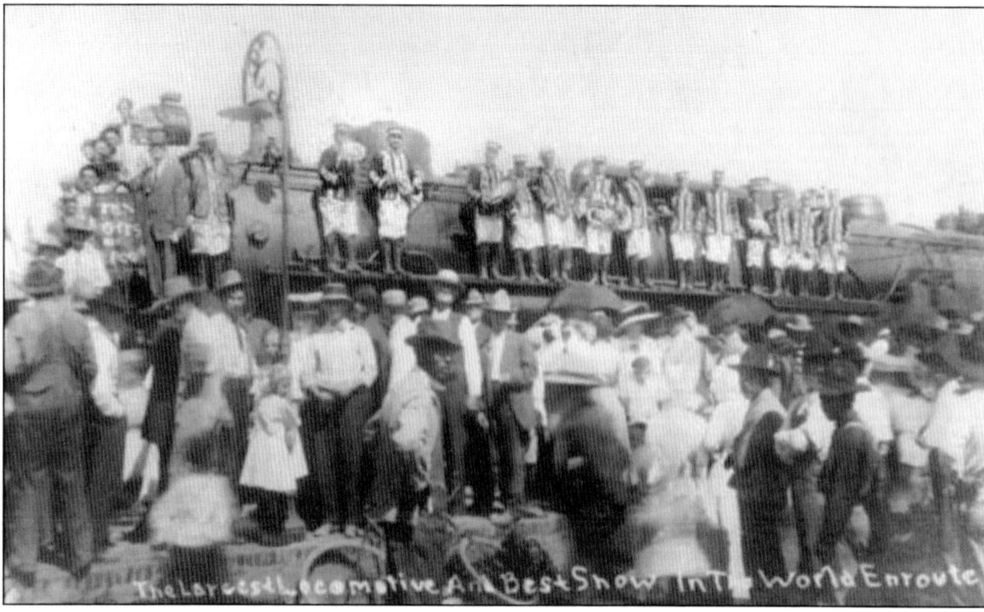

The "best show in the world" came to Eagle Lake in the early 1900s. People in small towns like Eagle Lake were delighted to see traveling shows, which often performed in the opera house or at the city square. The Eiler's "Ten Nights in a Barroom" show arrived by special train in a flurry of excitement, thrilling onlookers with its previews of the show. Cast members in colorful costumes presented previews aboard the locomotive to create interest and sell tickets.

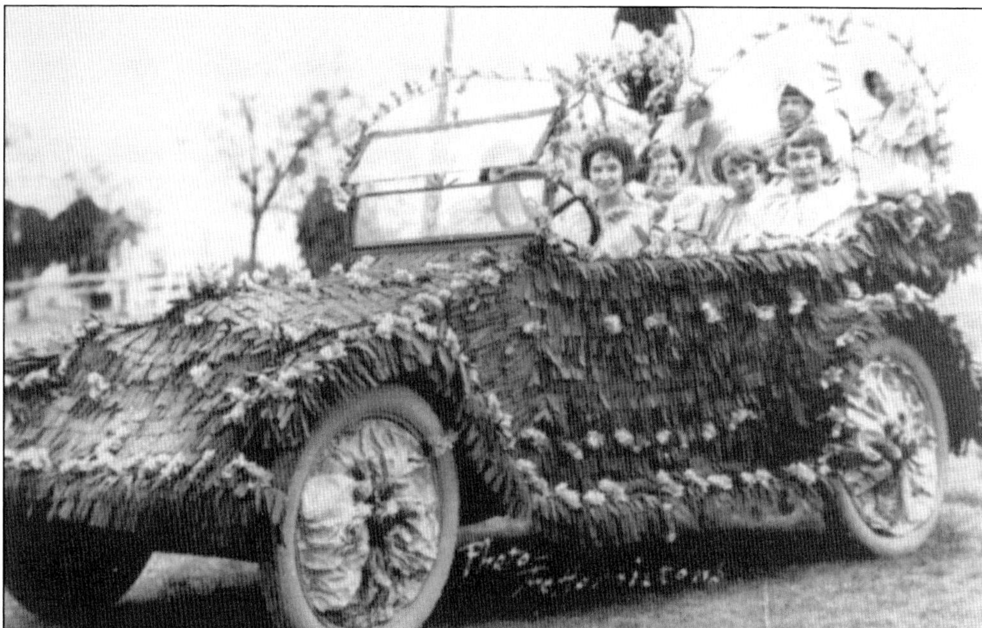

A 1923 automobile, decorated for the fair, graces the parade with popular local ladies. They are, from left to right, (front seat) Loueva Bunge, Louise (Mrs. Herbert) Matthews, Hetty Carey, Mrs. Ray Munn Fitzgerald, and Mrs. John Matthews; (back) Mary Waddell, Lorease Carey, and Ruth Waddell.

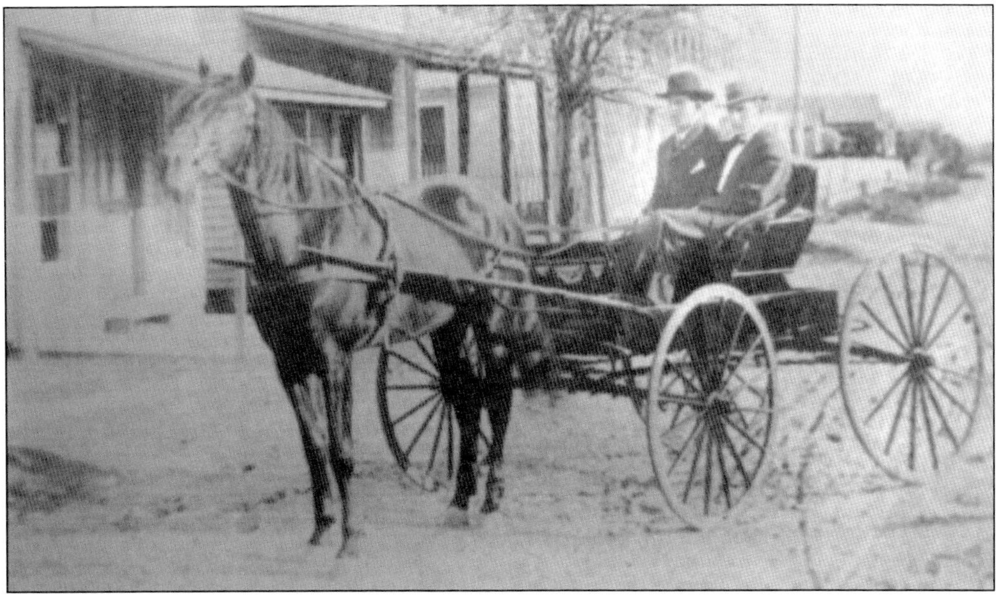

Howard Shortt (left) and an unidentified friend are parked in front of the old post office building on Post Office Street. In 1882, the post office was moved here from the present-day Prairie Edge Museum area on Main Street, which was then the Samuel Norris store. The post office remained in this location—between the present-day fire station and the former Meitzen's Service Station—from 1882 until 1902. The Drummers' Home hotel is visible in the background. The first Eagle Lake post office was established on June 19, 1849, with George W. Thatcher as postmaster.

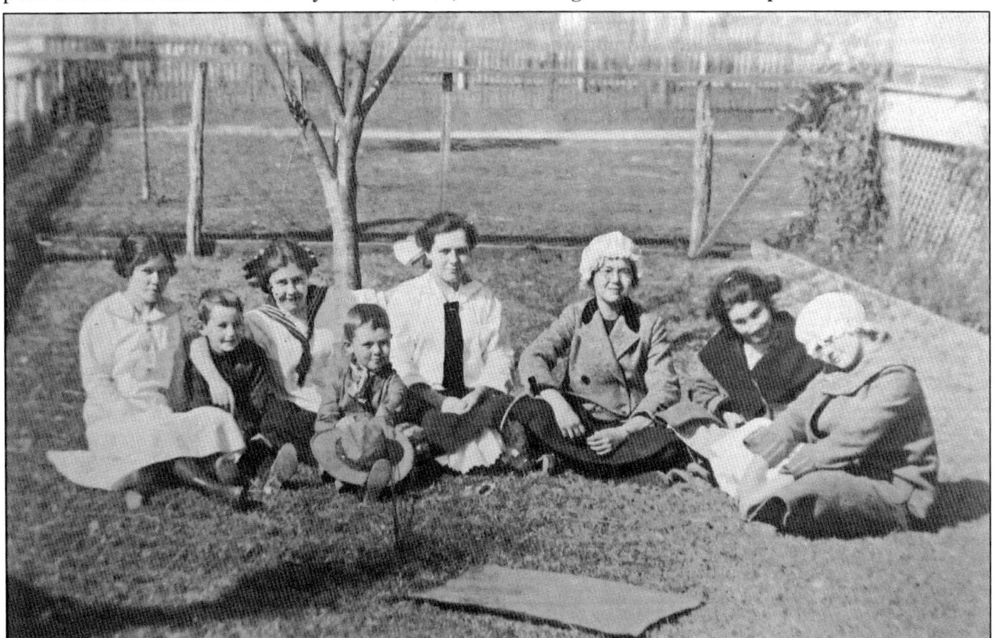

On New Year's Day 1913, youngsters gather for a celebration at the Drummers' Home hotel, located across from the train station. Pictured here are, from left to right, Agnes Chew, Gene Welford, Eloise Frazar, Max Conner, Annie Margaret Thatcher, Rowena Walker, Bunny Frick, and an unidentified friend.

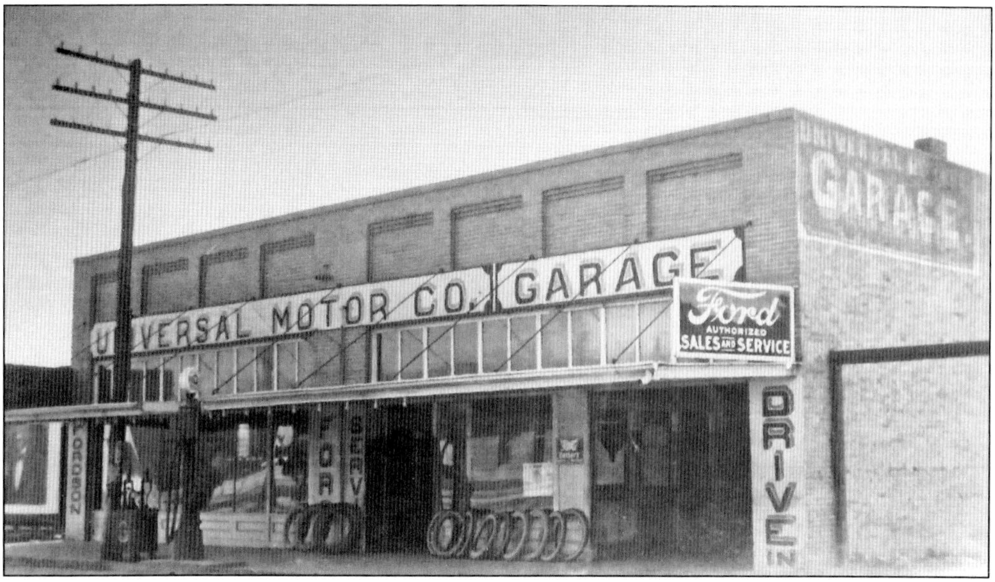

In 1917, the impressive new Ford service station, established by Hayes Stephens and B.S. Field, was known as Universal Motor Company Garage. In 1921, O.E. Sinclair purchased a one-fourth interest from Field, with Stephens owning the other three quarters. The building was later the John Deere Tractor Company, and was owned by Eagle Lake Implement Company in 1978.

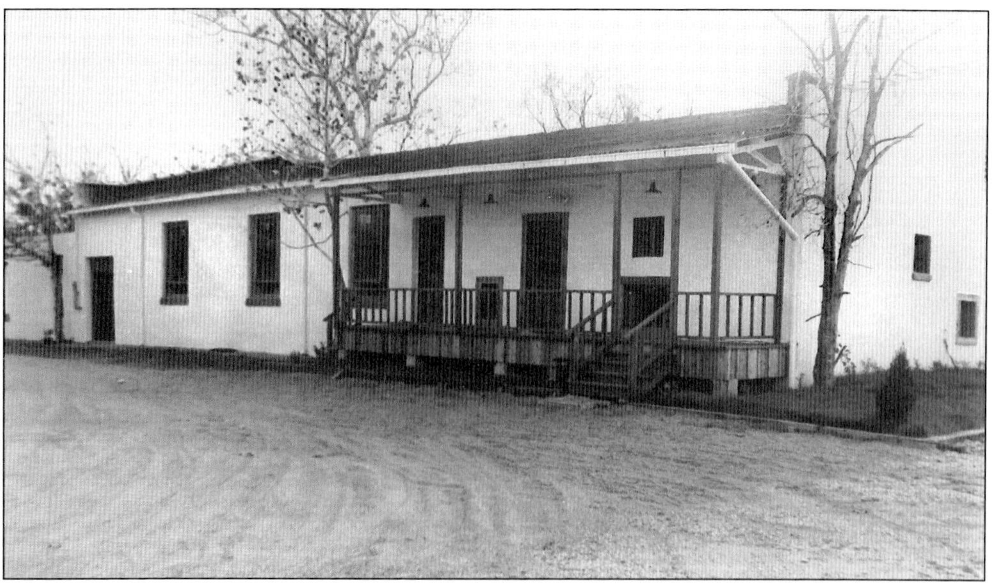

The new icehouse was completed in 1924 at a cost of about $3,300. When iceboxes become widespread, block ice was available at the refrigerated icehouse. Ice was first available for use in restaurants and saloons and was later delivered to neighborhoods by wagon. In the summer, children would jump onto the back of the ice wagon to fetch a piece of broken ice.

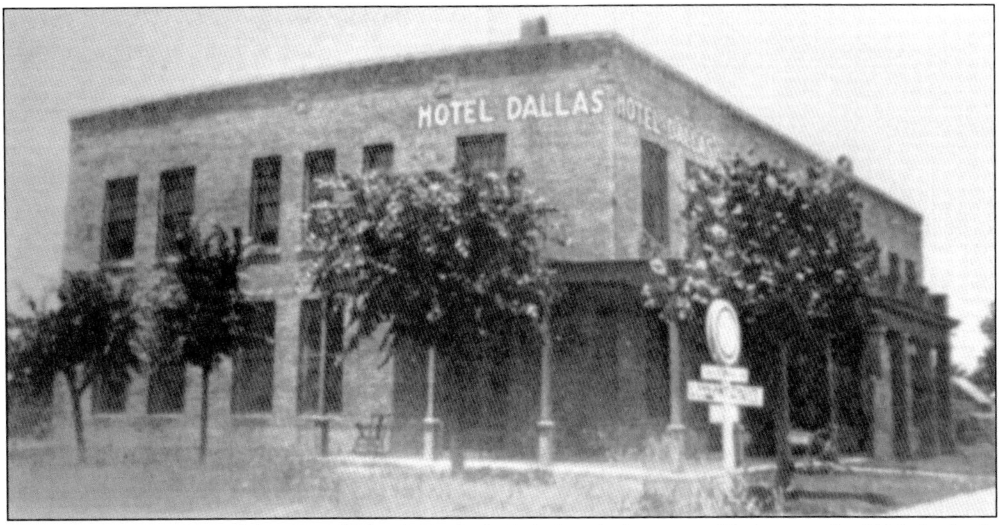

W.A. Dallas purchased the Good Hotel, Eagle Lake's first lodging establishment. In 1912, he built the Hotel Dallas—a $12,000 modern, brick hotel—on the site, with 20 bedrooms, public rooms, and large columns supporting a second-floor balcony. It had a central solarium and a large staircase and was an elegant hotel and meeting place. Its long gallery was a gathering spot for drummers after dinner, and it also had a drummers' room where salesmen could display their samples. The Hotel Dallas was sold in 1926 and renamed the Ramsey Hotel. After it was purchased by William and Helyn Farris, who restored the hotel to its former beauty in the mid-1970s, it became the Farris 1912 Hotel.

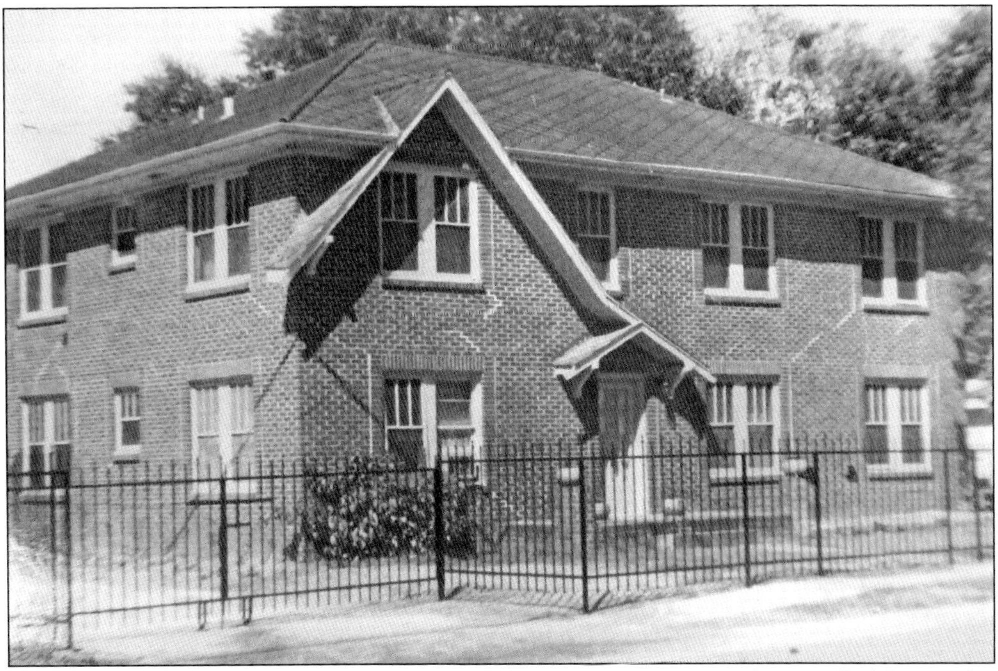

In 1931, the Charles W. Bentley family built a modern, two-story, 12-room house called the Bentley House to provide room and board for teachers, retired residents, and visitors. The dining room served three meals a day and was frequented by businessmen and other guests. Boardinghouses were an important part of Eagle Lake's history.

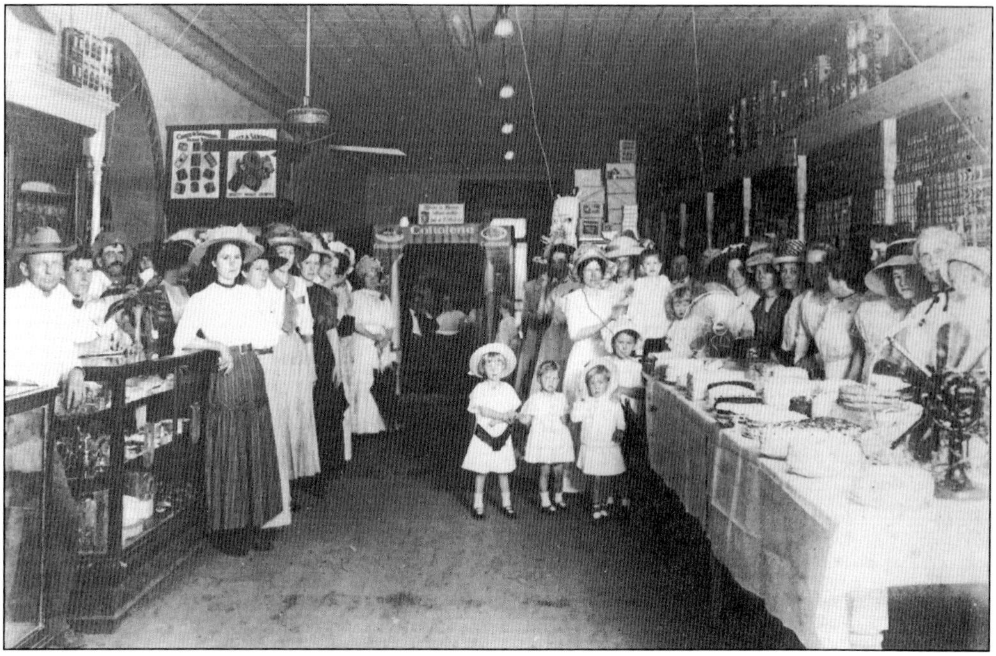

As seen in this c. 1924 image, the town turned out when the ladies of the local churches held a bake sale to raise money. With cakes, cookies, baked goods, and sweets of all kinds, these sales, often held along Main Street, were popular occasions, bringing in both merchants and shoppers who wanted to taste the homemade delights.

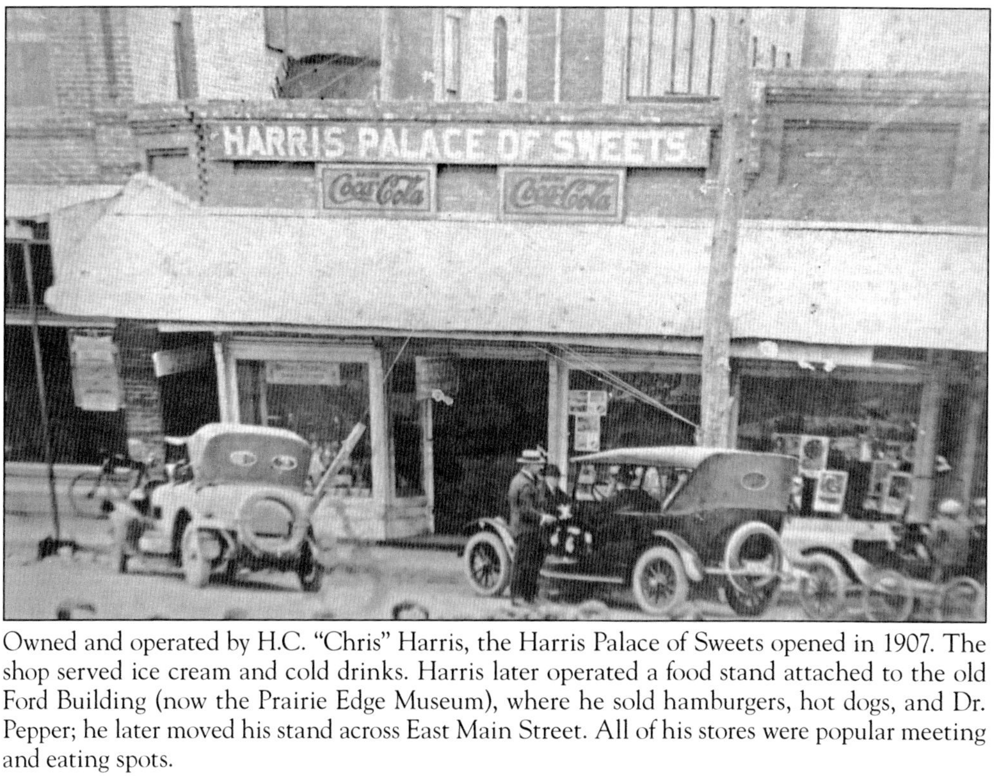

Owned and operated by H.C. "Chris" Harris, the Harris Palace of Sweets opened in 1907. The shop served ice cream and cold drinks. Harris later operated a food stand attached to the old Ford Building (now the Prairie Edge Museum), where he sold hamburgers, hot dogs, and Dr. Pepper; he later moved his stand across East Main Street. All of his stores were popular meeting and eating spots.

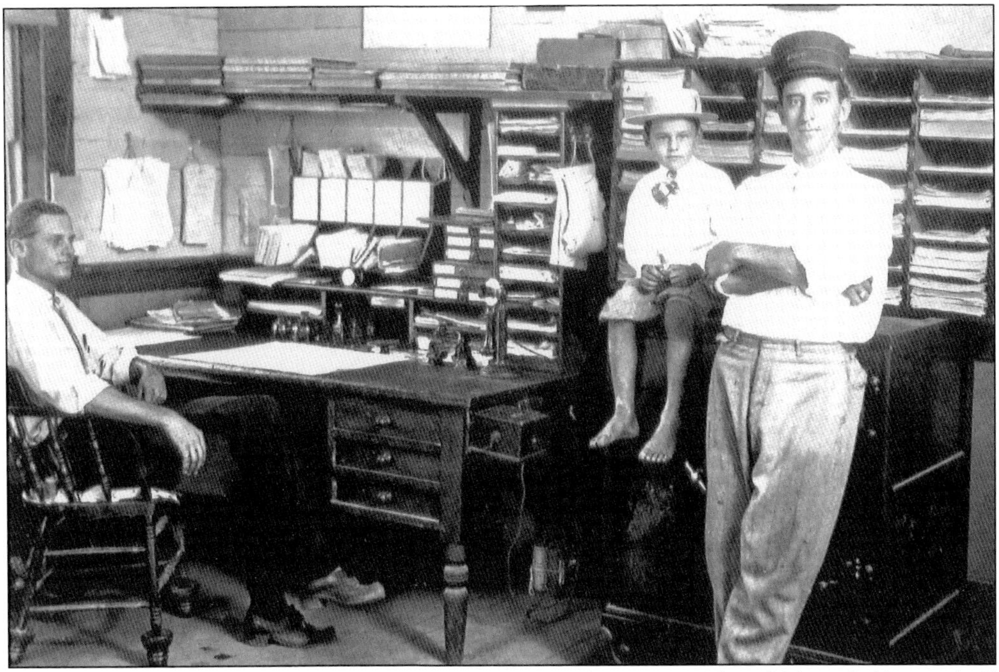

Awaiting the next train in the Eagle Lake depot around 1915 are Edward Blum (left), Marshall Nye (center), and Nicholas Charles Nye, who was the station agent in Eagle Lake for 35 years. With three railroads, Eagle Lake became a busy rail center. Cattle pens (for loading) and a water tower once stood along the tracks.

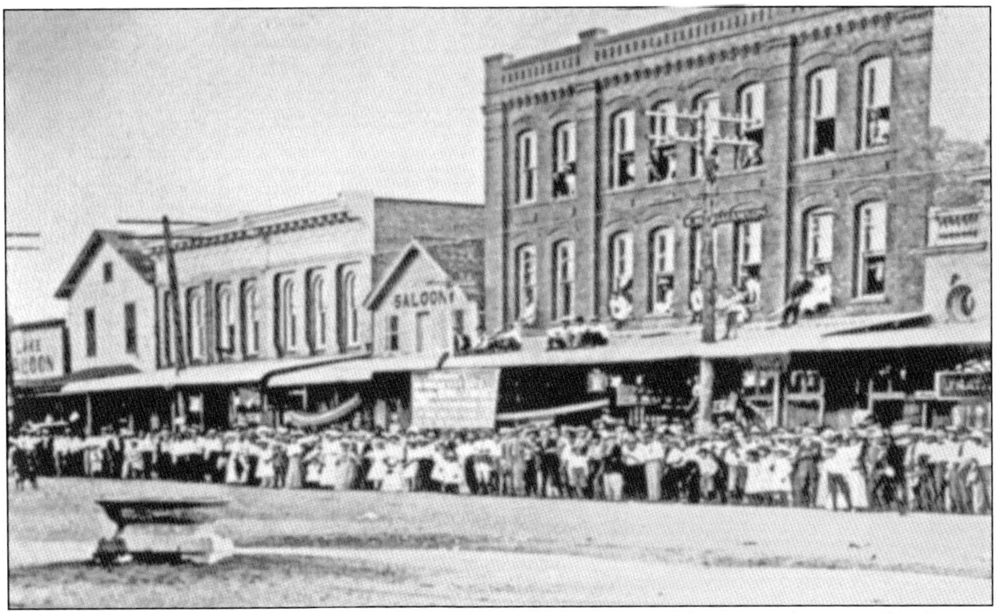

Onlookers and prospective land buyers gather around the square for a parade put on by the city to entice and welcome new residents. This c. 1910 photograph shows a horse trough in the street at left. The Norris Building had opened in 1903. The first floor housed restaurants, a drugstore, and a barbershop; the second story had professional offices, dentists, doctors, lawyers; and the third floor was used as a meeting hall, which was later home to Club Montezuma.

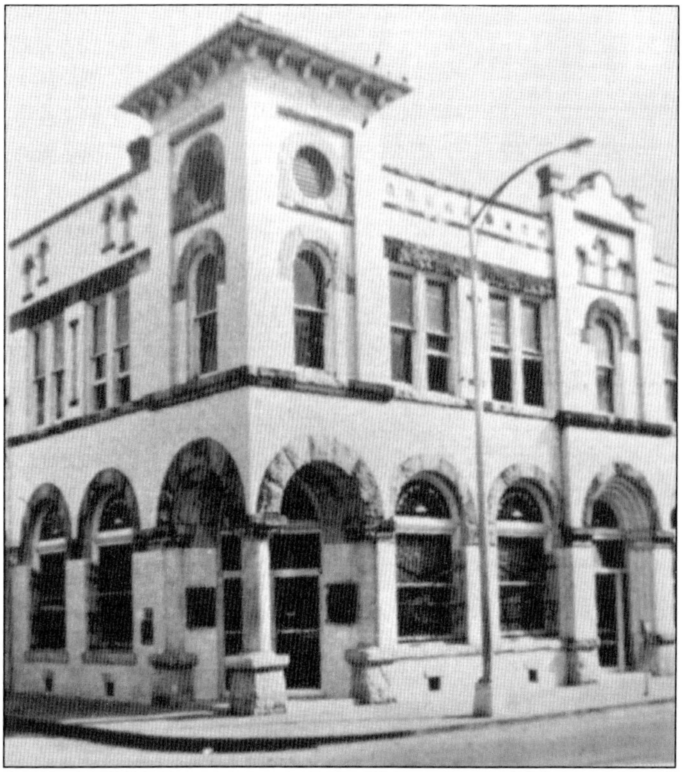

The beautiful two-story First National Bank building, pictured in 1920, was covered in white enameled brick, with stone trim and marble columns. It opened on January 3, 1905, and was located at Main and Commerce Streets, across from the city square. William T. Eldridge, B.L. Vineyard, A.M. Waugh, Charles Davis, and G.W. Deaton founded the bank. It opened with capital of $25,000. In 1958, efforts began to replace, modernize, and expand the bank, and this historic bank was replaced with a modern, brick building.

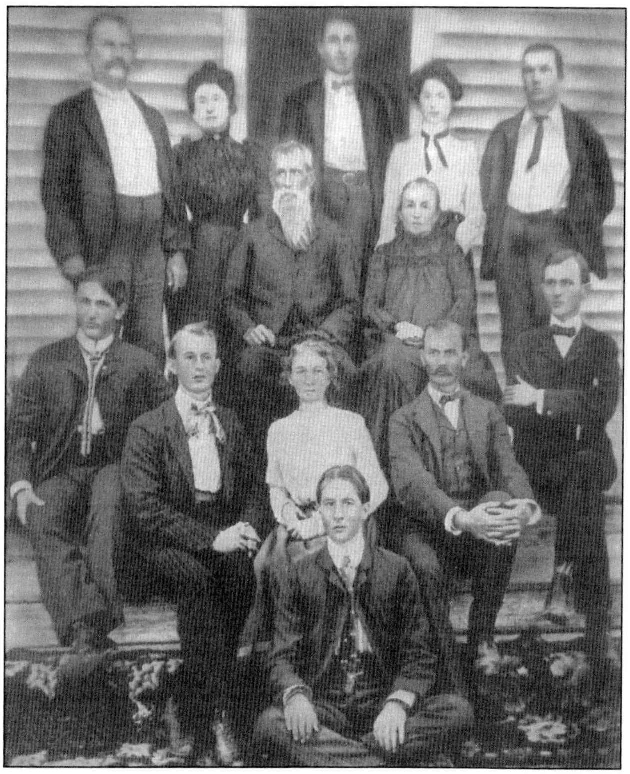

John Thompson and Nancy Guynn Westmoreland pose with their 11 children. All were important to the development of the community; at one time, there were 18 Westmoreland family members working in various businesses throughout Eagle Lake. Pictured here are (first row) Earl Simmons Westmoreland; and, from left to right, (second row) Oliver Wilkins Westmoreland, Ella Guynn Westmoreland, and John Wilburn Westmoreland; (third row) James Chapin Westmoreland and Reid Thompson Westmoreland; (fourth row) John and Nancy; (fifth row) Joseph R. Westmoreland, Mary Elizabeth Westmoreland (Mrs. J.D. Odom), Robert W. Westmoreland, Kitty Lena (Westmoreland) Smith, and William Yancy Westmoreland.

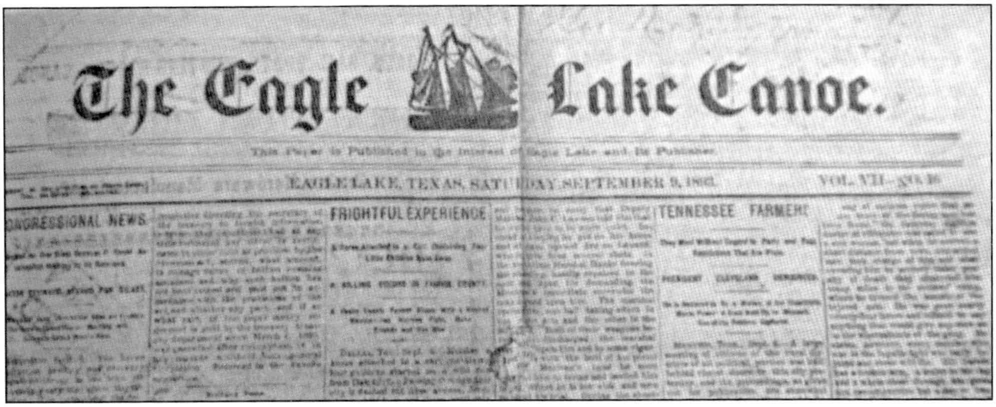

The Eagle Lake Canoe.

This Paper is Published in the Interest of Eagle Lake and Its Publisher

EAGLE LAKE, TEXAS, SATURDAY, SEPTEMBER 9,

CONGRESSIONAL NEWS

FRIGHTFUL EXPERIENCE

TENNESSEE FARMERS

The *Eagle Lake Canoe* newspaper was founded in 1887, with Joseph Jefferson Mansfield serving as editor. In 1895, it was followed by the *Eagle Lake Headlight*, which began as a two-column, four-page paper. After three years, the *Headlight* was discontinued, but Bruce McCarty and "S.O." (full name unknown) reestablished the *Headlight* in 1903. (Courtesy of Prairie Edge Museum.)

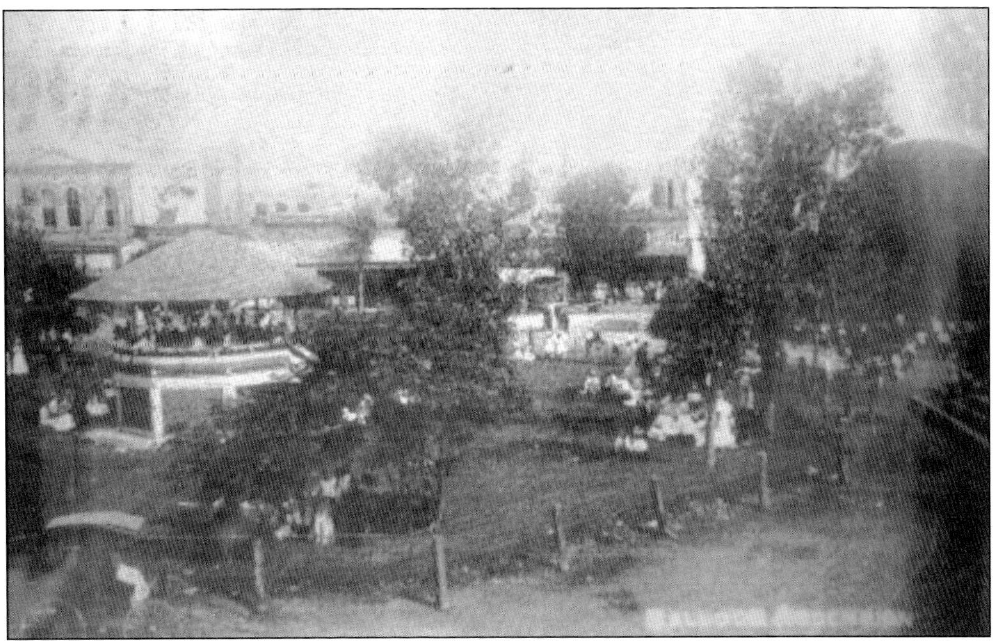

The first hot air balloon ascension in Eagle Lake was a festive occasion, and the community came out to see this unusual wonder. The street fair and balloon ascension were sponsored by the Eagle Lake Cornet Band, with arrangements by the Brownie Balloon Company. The band made $200, which enabled it to participate in the San Antonio International Fair and Band Competition on October 23, 1905; the Eagle Lake Cornet Band won second place, behind the National Band of Mexico.

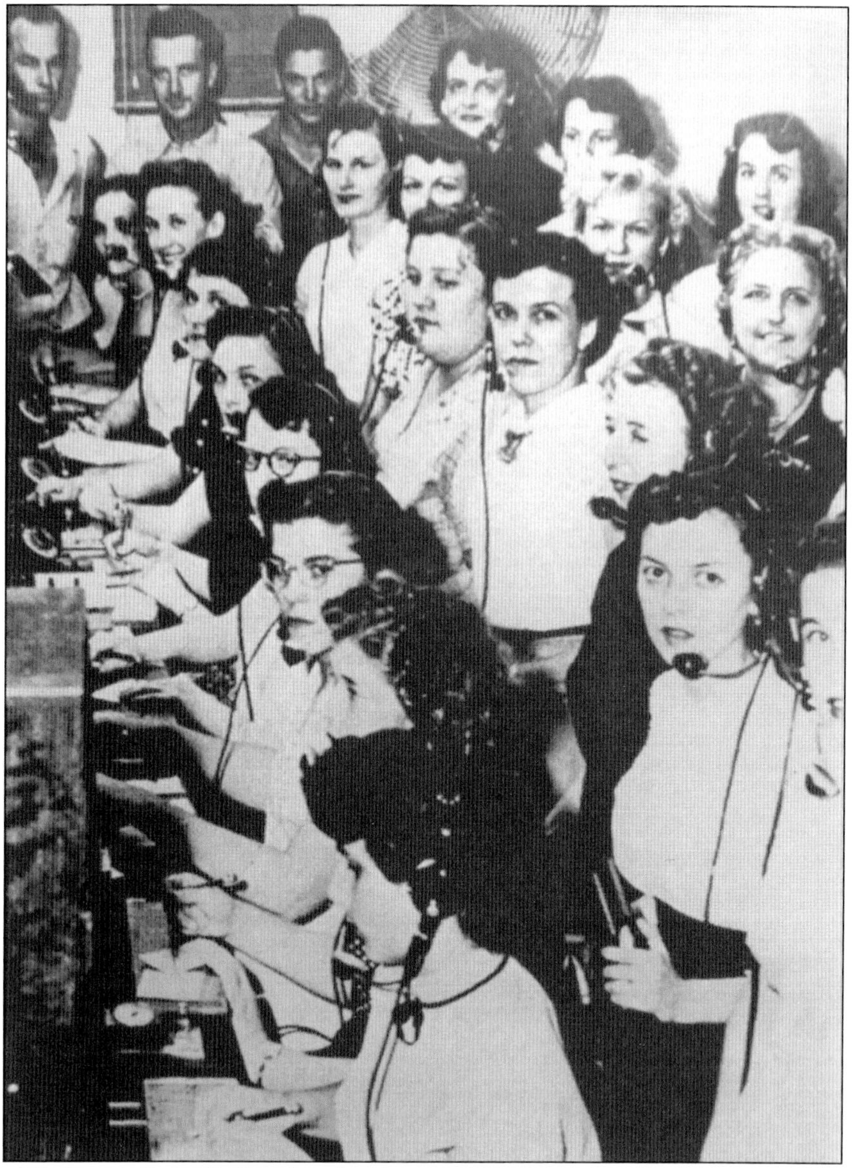

In 1922, H.J. Campbell installed Eagle Lake's first wireless receiving station for telephone, telegraph, and radio transmissions. The communications system, operated by Southwestern Bell Telephone, was staffed by Eagle Lake's finest and friendliest personnel. The telephone office was located on the second floor of the Hughes Building at 101 McCarty Avenue. Operators would answer by saying "number, please." They were helpful in emergencies and with providing information to callers. In 1955, the telephone system was changed to a direct-dial system. Pictured here are, from left to right, (first row) Helen Canaris Wilson, Emily Drymalla Waddell, Mildred Walker McGehee, Melba New Craft, Dortha Lilley Kingsley, Alice M. Dutcher, Betty Dennis, and Bernice Gertson Kochwelp; (second row) Eunice Goode Frnka, Rose Marie Beane Perry, Sophie Hodde Zoeller, Ruby Walker Braden, Carolyn Hollas Rosprim Noska, Alyne Wink Morgan, and Ruth Winzenreid Goode; (third row) Cecil Bookman Gerstenberg, Sue Guthman Walker, chief operator Ella Ziegler, Pat Green, and evening chief Lena Gus Wink Crenwelge; (fourth row, standing in rear) servicemen Leon Steinbeck, E.H. Steinke (also the plant manager), and August Jones.

This railroad signal tower, located on the east side of town, served the Southern Pacific–San Antonio & Aransas Pass crossing. It was an operations hub that gave train operators information about switches, speed, and track condition ahead, enabling trains to continue through an area without having to come to a complete stop, which saved time and money. The tower remained standing as an icon of railroad history until 1996 or 1997.

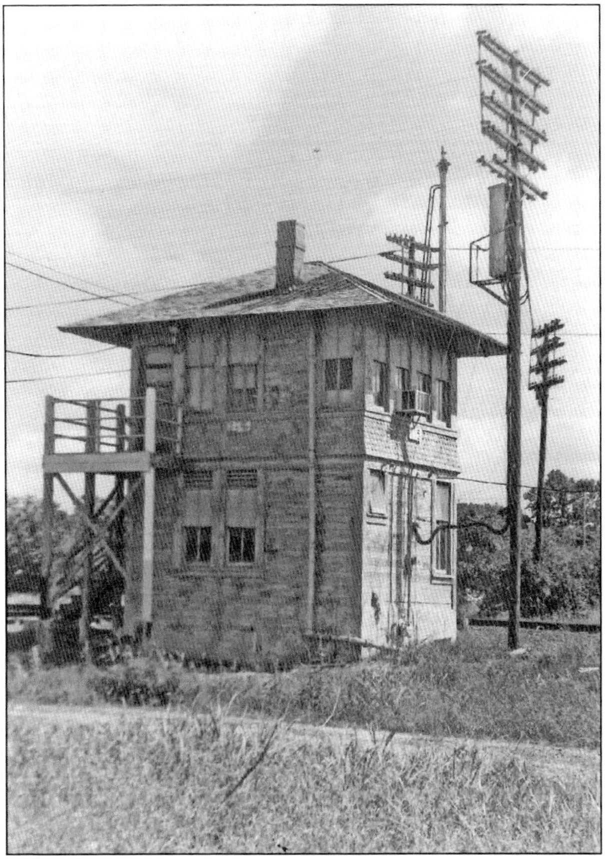

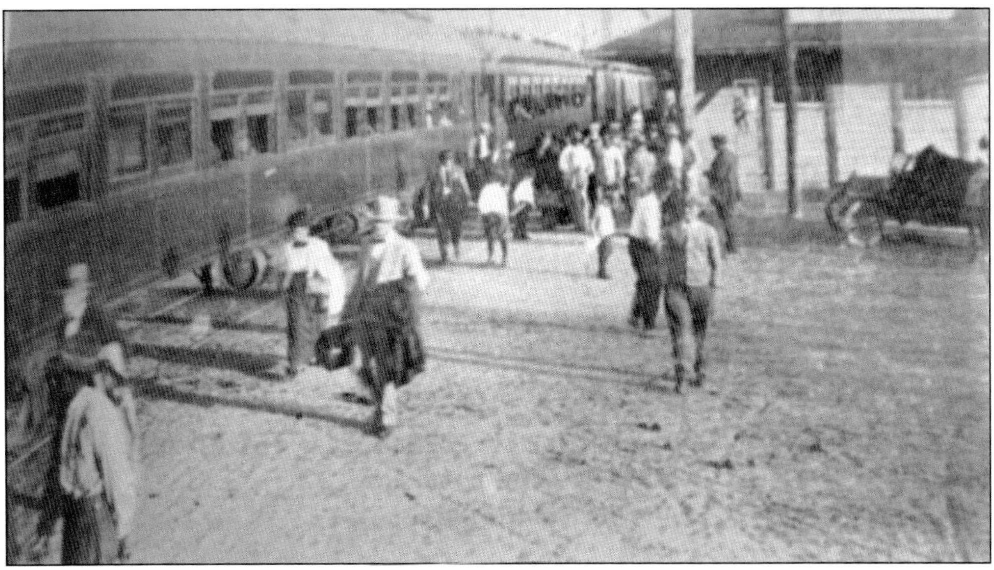

In 1915, passengers and onlookers come and go while the train is stopped at the Eagle Lake Southern Pacific train depot. Young boys would sell bags of fresh figs and fresh lilies from the lake to passengers through the train windows, and many people would come to town just to watch the trains. In 1907, as many as 12 passenger trains traveled in and out of Eagle Lake each day.

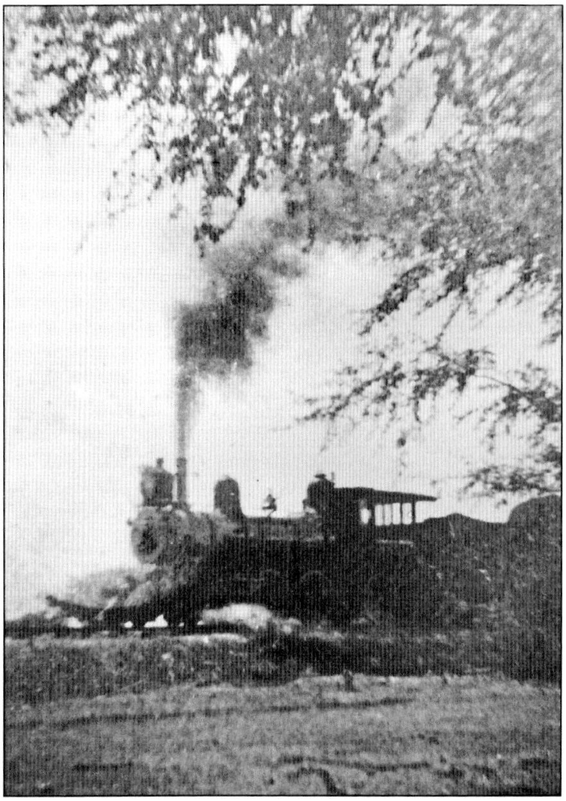

The *General Sherman* was the first locomotive in Texas. Built in the Northeast and shipped to Galveston in 1852, the locomotive was named for Gen. Sidney Sherman, a hero at the Battle of San Jacinto. It went into service on the Buffalo Bayou, Brazos, and Colorado Railway—the first operating railroad in Texas, which was cofounded by Sherman. Gamaliel Good and D.W.C. Harris platted the town of Eagle Lake around the first railroad tracks. The building of the railroad continued on to Alleyton, where it arrived in 1860.

The *General Sherman* reached Eagle Lake in the fall of 1859. The rails extended on to Alleyton, but expansion ended in 1860 because of the Civil War. After the war, the railroad company was renamed the Galveston, Harrisburg, and San Antonio Railway Company. Due to its small size, the *General Sherman* locomotive was retired in 1870 and demolished in 1899.

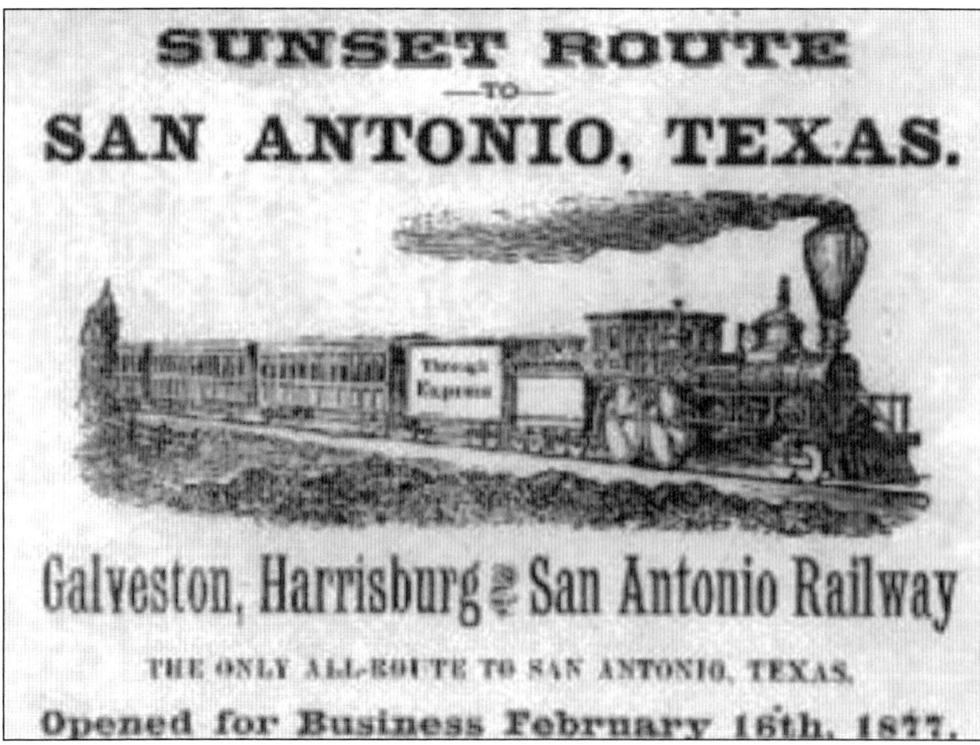

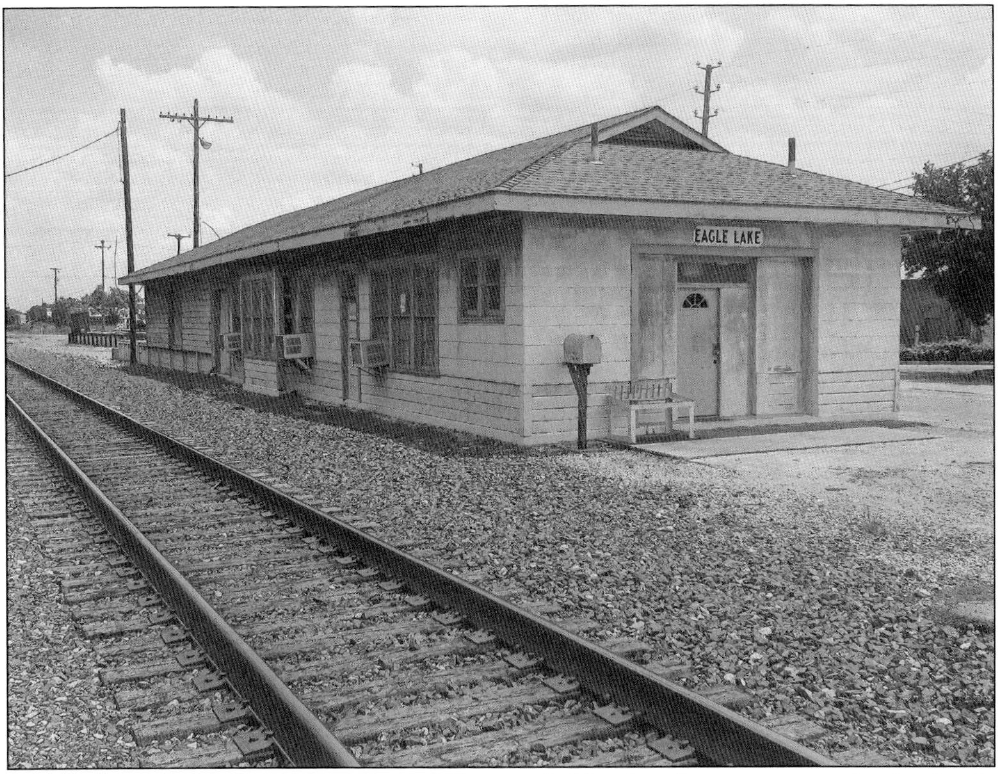

The original train pulled by the *General Sherman* held only a few passengers, plus freight. In the late 1800s, the track extended to Lakeside, and the small station was busy with passengers and freight. The Galveston, Harrisburg, & San Antonio Railway was purchased in 1905 by the Southern Pacific Line, and Eagle Lake became a shipping center between San Francisco and New Orleans.

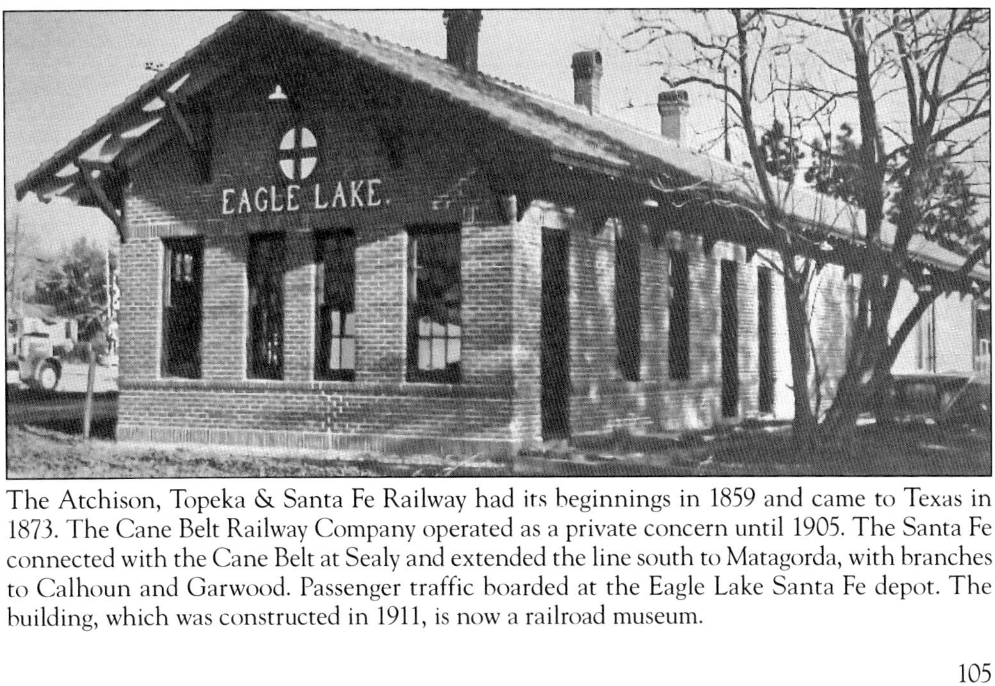

The Atchison, Topeka & Santa Fe Railway had its beginnings in 1859 and came to Texas in 1873. The Cane Belt Railway Company operated as a private concern until 1905. The Santa Fe connected with the Cane Belt at Sealy and extended the line south to Matagorda, with branches to Calhoun and Garwood. Passenger traffic boarded at the Eagle Lake Santa Fe depot. The building, which was constructed in 1911, is now a railroad museum.

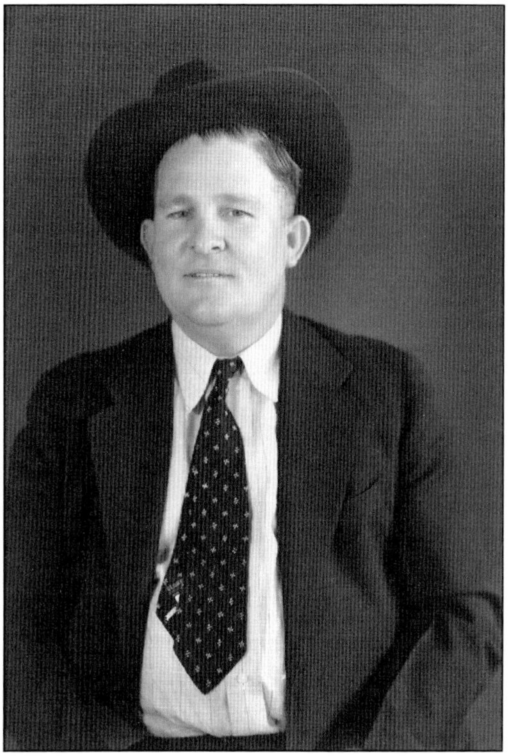

Texas Ranger Zeno Smith was known as "the last of the Black Hat Rangers." He became a Texas Ranger in Eagle Lake in 1934 and oversaw the area from Lubbock to the Rio Grande border for many years. Eagle Lake had at least four Texas Rangers: Smith; Capt. George Albert Wheatley; Joseph Osaba, also a city marshal; and Thomas Hurd, who was the last city marshal. He retired in 1969 as an honored Texan and Ranger.

A crowd gathered in front of the J. Nathan and Son store on Main Street as the Eagle Lake Cornet Band played in front of the opera house, as it did on many festive occasions. People crowded onto the galleries to listen to a speaker and to help raise money for new band uniforms in the early 1900s.

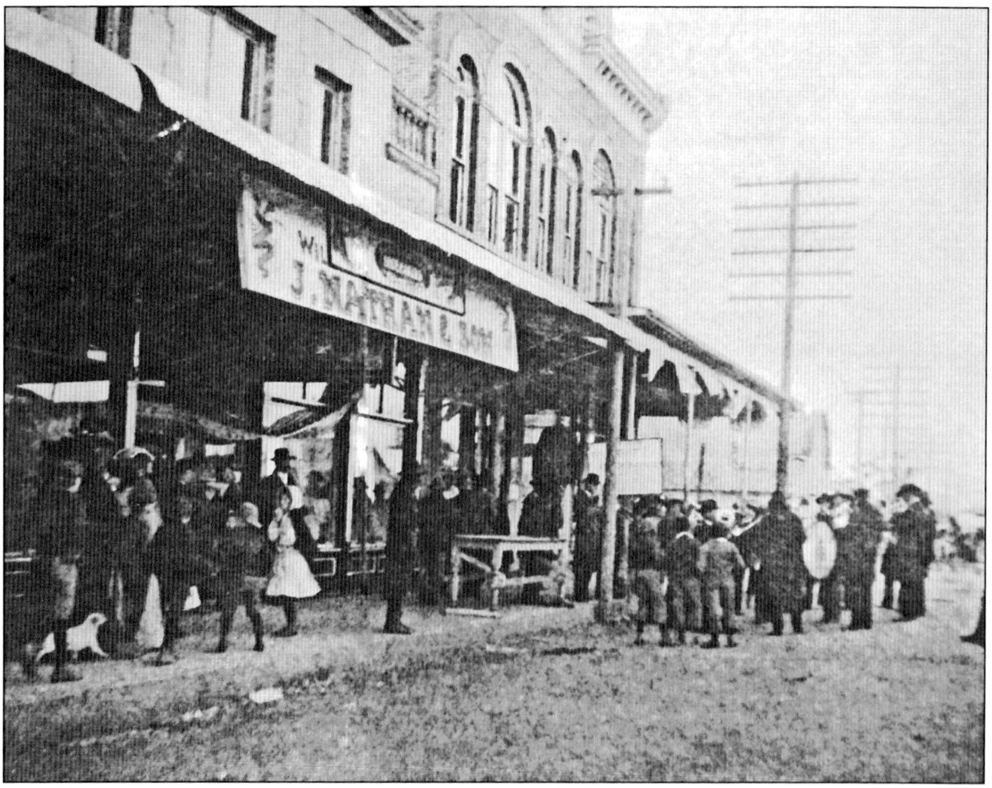

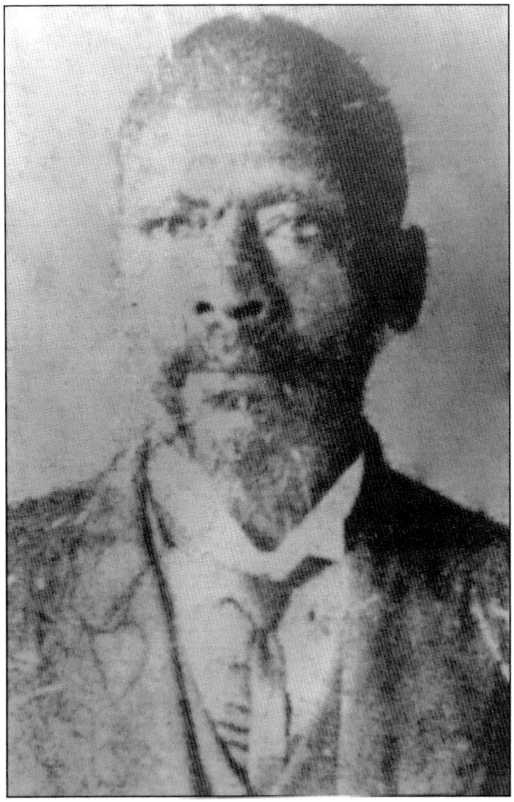

Rev. Daniel L. Whitley (1850–1908) was the youngest son of Nelson Whitley, who came to Texas before the Battle of San Jacinto. Daniel, Nelson's youngest son, was born a slave on the plantation of James S. Montgomery and taught himself to read and write. He farmed cotton and corn, believed strongly in education, and organized the Greater Mount Olive Baptist Church in 1886. He was a respected and recognized citizen and pastor in Colorado County. He married Millie Pillows, daughter of Jerry and Melvina Pillows of Eagle Lake, and they had eight children.

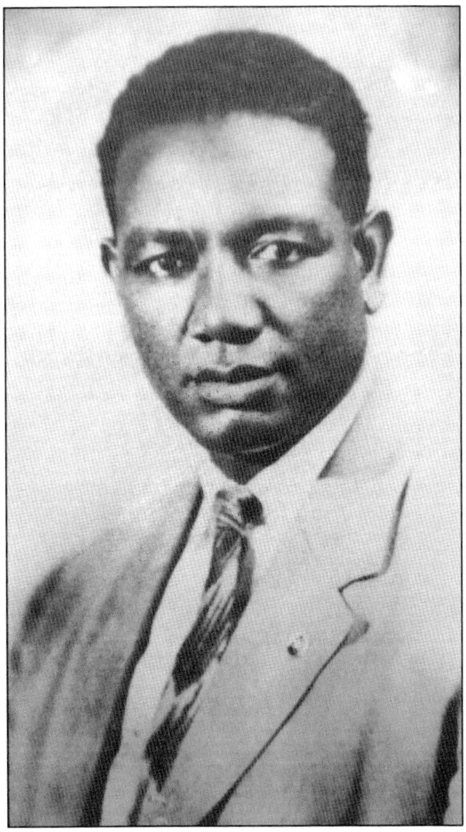

John Whitley (1888–1981) attended Tuskegee Normal and Industrial Institute (now Tuskegee University) in Alabama and knew George Washington Carver and Booker T. Washington, who became his mentors. Whitley was an expert in art restoration, restoring vintage artwork in Austin in the Texas State Capitol, the Driskill Hotel, and the Texas Governor's Mansion, as well as for J. Frank Dobie. Whitley was a founder of the Olivet Baptist Church in Austin and became a minister. He set up a repair shop in Austin called the "Ten Talent Shop," where he taught skills in mechanical training to boys from Huston-Tillotson University. He was raised in Eagle Lake by Cicero and Cornelia Whitley Howard, who had no children; John was the youngest son of Cornelia's brother, Daniel L. Whitley (pictured above).

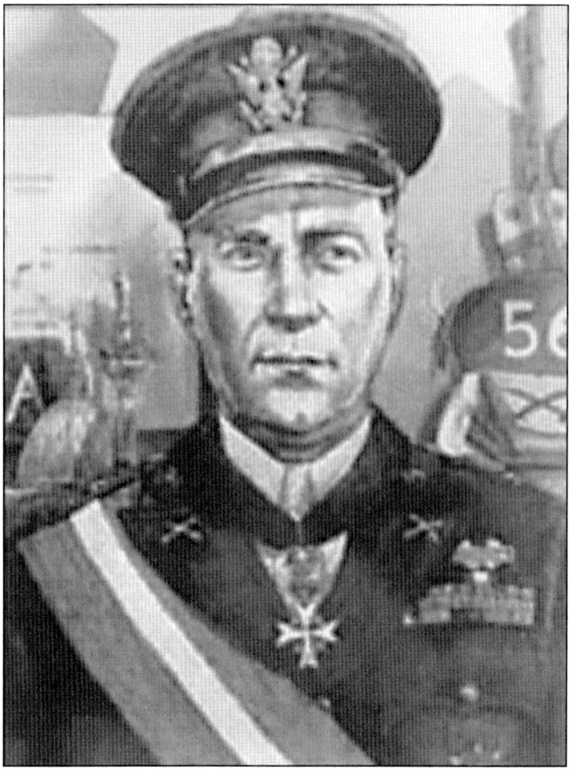

On June 5, 1944, Maj. Gen. Harry Hubbard Johnson was appointed military governor of Rome by Pres. Franklin D. Roosevelt. Major General Johnson was decorated in Rome with the American Legion of Merit and the Grand Cross of the Order of the Crown of Italy. In 1945, Johnson was assigned as a division commander of the 93rd Infantry during the New Guinea campaign. He also served in World War I, in the Infantry Division, and was commander of the 7th and 8th Cavalry Regiments in 1942. Johnson, who lived and went to school in Eagle Lake and attended both Texas A&M and Tyler Community College, is in the Texas Military Forces Hall of Honor.

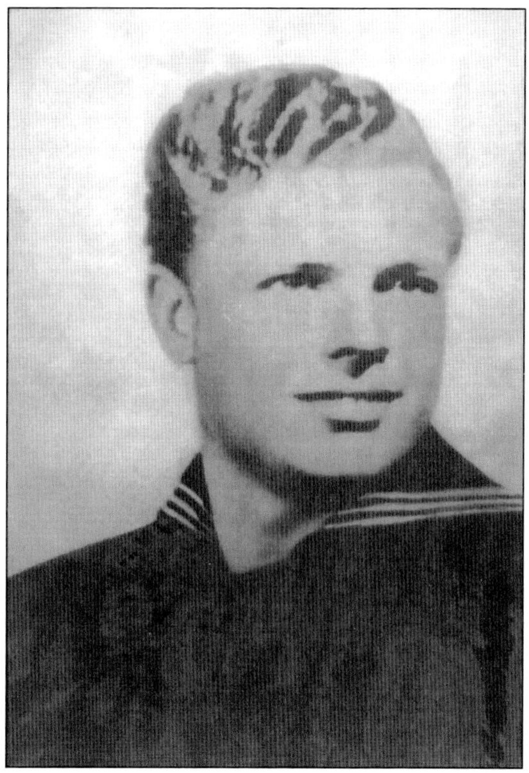

Johnnie David Hutchins, the son of a Lissie farmer, was awarded the Congressional Medal of Honor in World War II. He died on September 4, 1943, during an assault on Lae, New Guinea, while landing a ship during an explosion. His act of heroism—steering his vessel away from advancing forces while wounded—saved many of his shipmates' lives. A destroyer escort named for him, the USS *Johnnie Hutchins*, launched in May 1944.

Six

Schools, Homes, and Churches

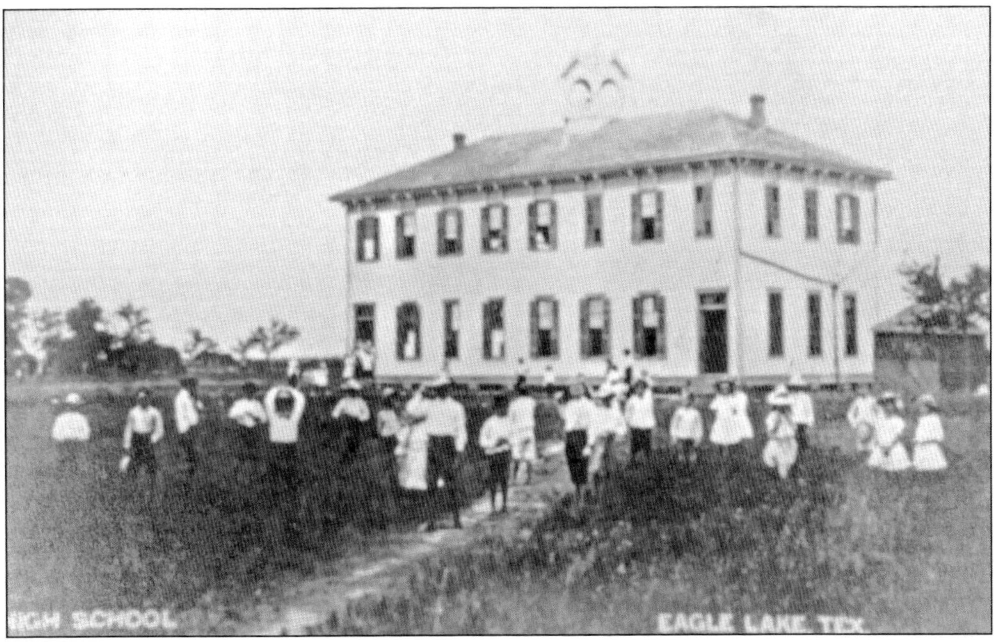

The first full-term public school, Eagle Lake School, was built and opened in 1891. It was a white, clapboard, two-story frame structure with shutters and two large rooms on each floor. In 1892, the first two graduates were Mary Gilmer and Mollie Davidson, and 125 students were enrolled in 1895. Prof. George Wright was the principal. The school was moved to 101 East Prairie Street in 1911, after Eagle Lake's first brick public school was built alongside it. Three private schools operated from 1864 until the public school opened.

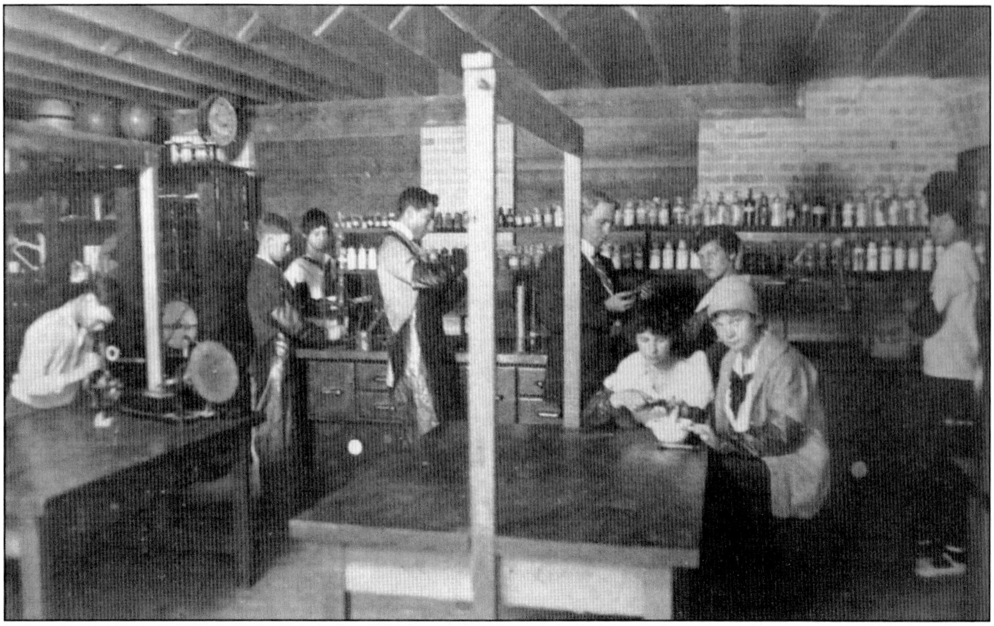

Supervised by Prof. J.H. Morgan, students are hard at work in a chemistry and physics lab at the Eagle Lake School in 1916. Pictured here are, from left to right, Paul Chew, W. Malcolm Williamson, Gladys Willard, Hervin Nussbaum, Professor Morgan, Alice Putney, Netty Hayman, Jewell Vineyard, and Ernest Faber.

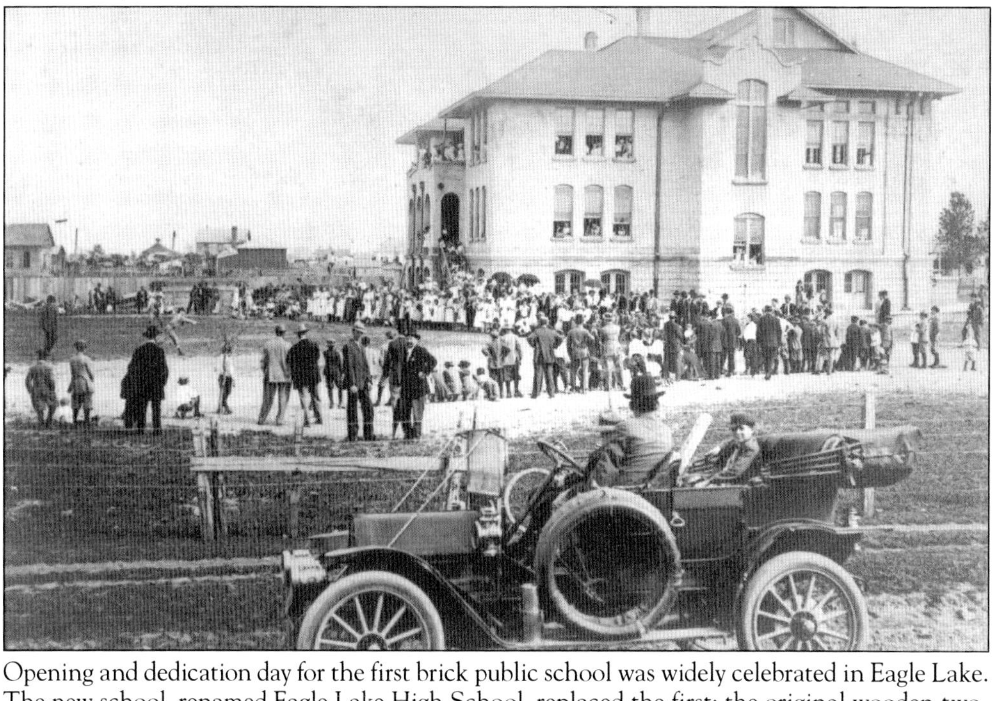

Opening and dedication day for the first brick public school was widely celebrated in Eagle Lake. The new school, renamed Eagle Lake High School, replaced the first; the original wooden two-story frame building was moved down the street. Basketball, football, and baseball teams played on the school grounds, a popular venue for sports and community activities. The original public school on this site was a one-room schoolhouse.

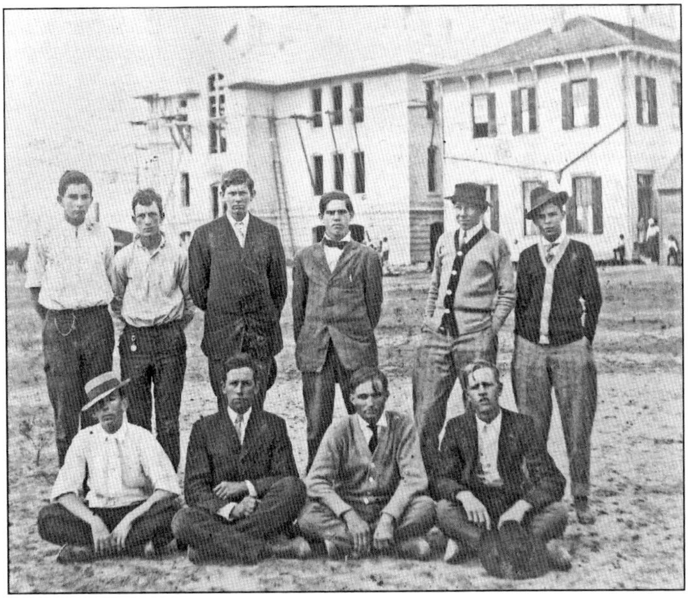

Friends gather in 1911 in front of the new school as it is being finished. The first and second public schools stand side by side. The first school (at right) was moved down the street to 101 East Prairie Street. Pictured here are, from left to right, (first row) Ben Faber, Jim Douglass, Andy Harrington, and George Hayman; (second row) Curtis Dewberry, Preston Wicker, Dwyer Holms, Frank Walker, Loren Abby, and Joe Renshaw. A third public school was built on this same site in 1924–1925.

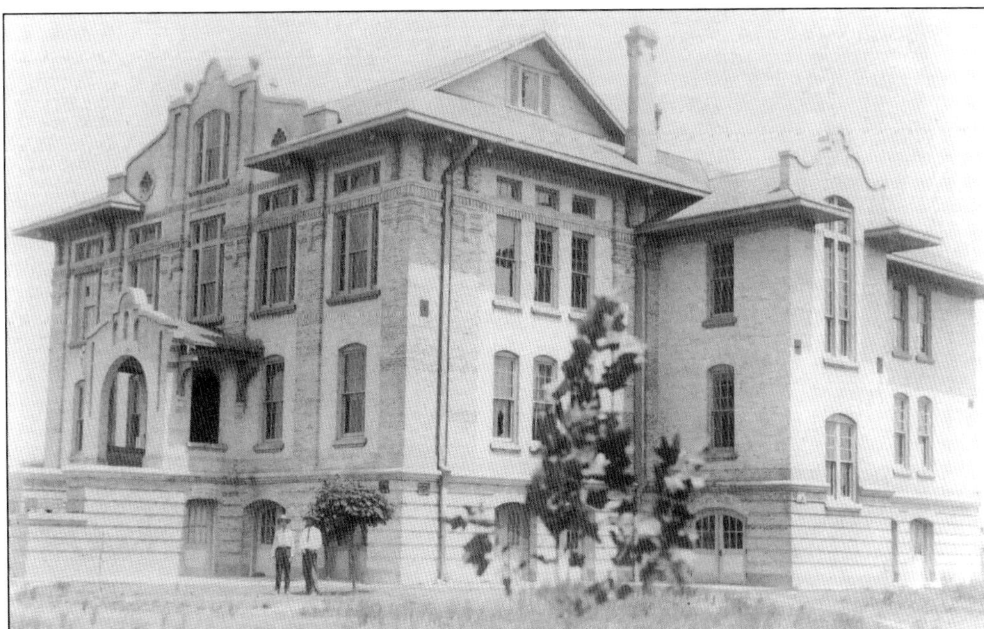

The beautiful public school building pictured here was damaged by a heavy ice storm in February 1923 and deemed unsafe for occupancy. Children had to attend classes in other spaces around town, such as the Shumacher Building, the third floor of the Norris Building, in the hall over the Nathan Building, and upstairs in the old opera house. After the storm, work swiftly began on a new school at the same location.

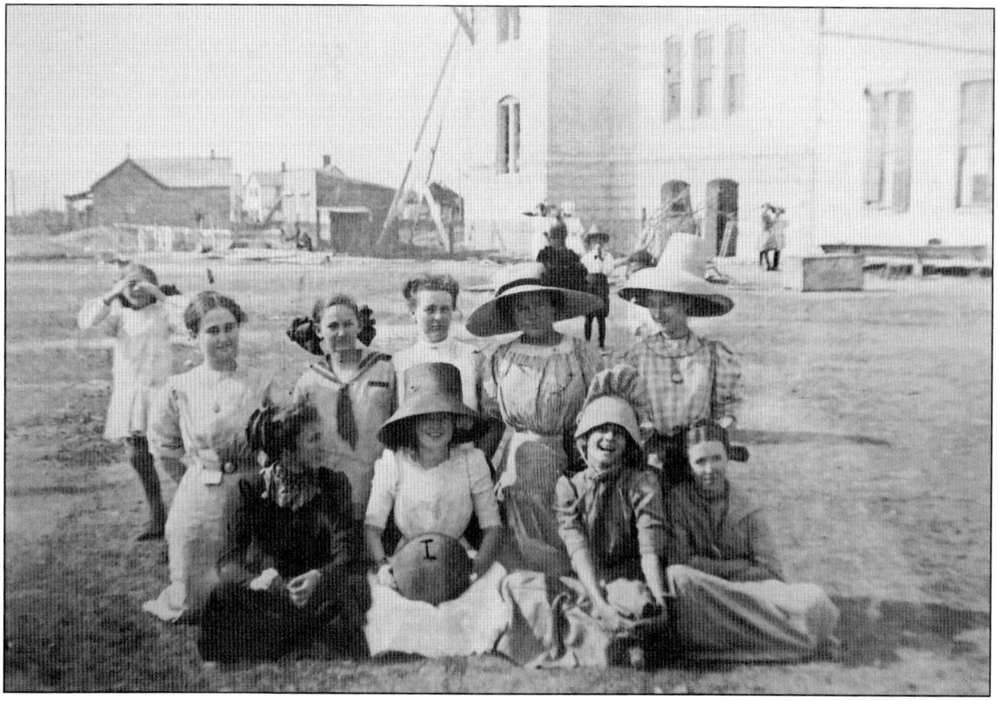

With construction of the first brick school completed, this happy group of schoolgirls is all smiles in 1911. Pictured here are, from left to right, (first row) unidentified, unidentified, Louise Waddell (later Mrs. Justin Smith), and teacher Miss Harrington; (second row) unidentified, Sue Webb, Nora Barrow, Pansy Green, Ray Wilson, Fleta Williamson.

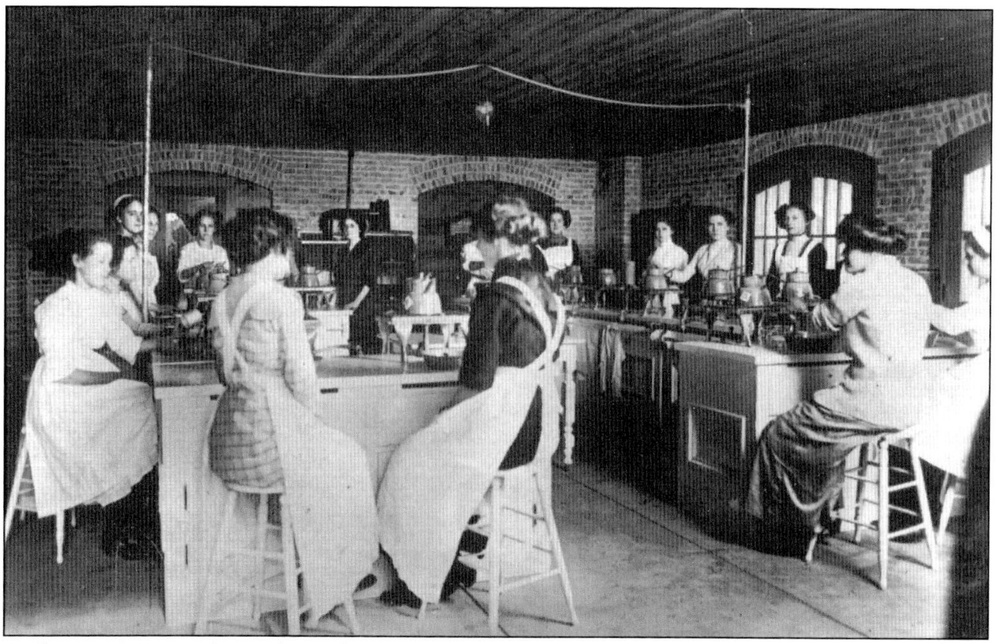

In this 1915 image, the cooking class at Eagle Lake High School is working hard to learn how to cook, sew, and to care for a home. Among the students are Ora Larey (McCreary), Agnes Chew, Mable Seaholm, Mildred Davis (Harbert), Ruth Hayman, and teacher Miss Kahn.

The Eagle Lake girls' basketball team poses in front of the school in 1916. The players are (in no specific order) Lucy Ceene Carney, Sophie Hintz, Martha Fitzgerald, Ernest Faber, Alice Putney, and Helen Chew; their teacher (at left in the third row) is unidentified. The team played in bloomer-type uniforms.

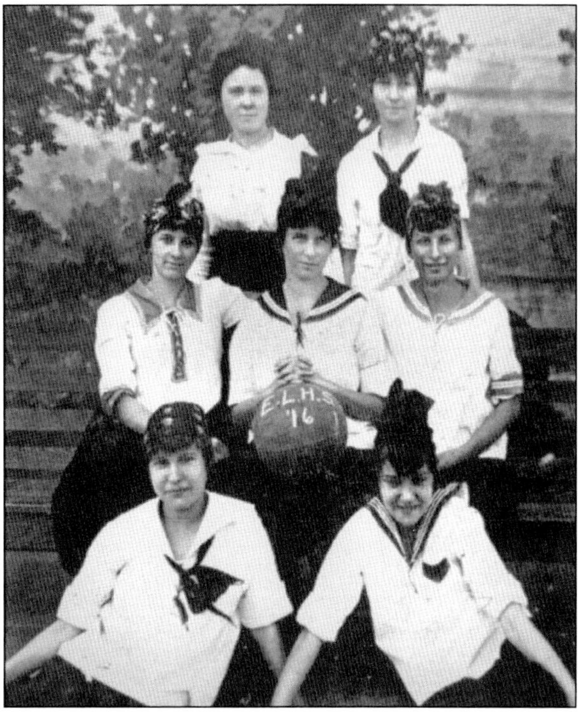

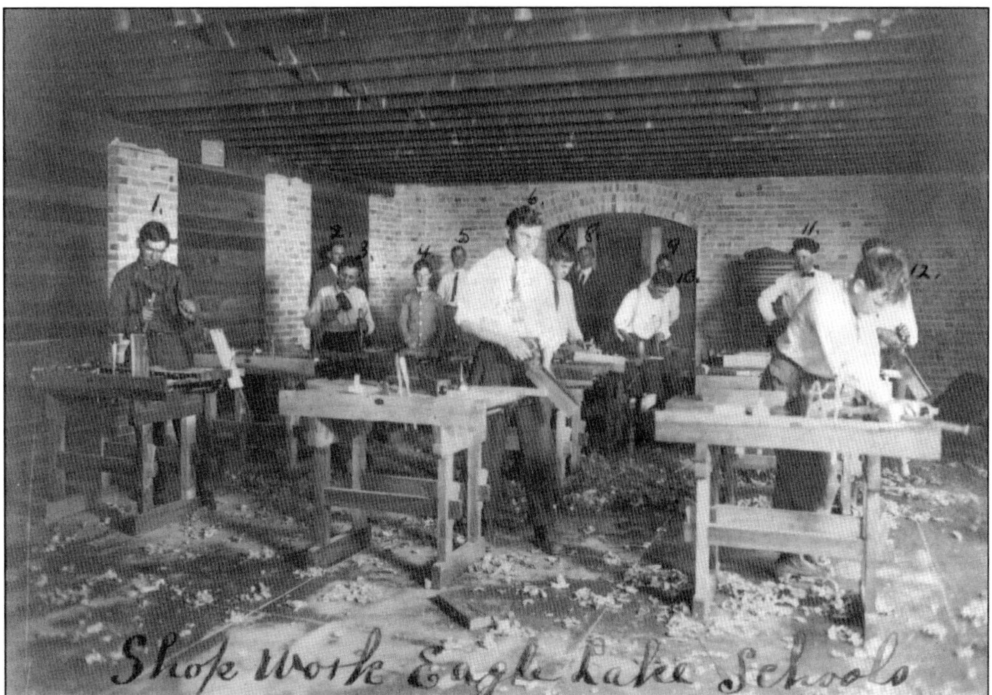

In 1911, Eagle Lake High School was given a state grant to set up a manual education program, which offered students the chance to learn about wood- and metalworking. Harry Hubbard Johnson is pictured in the center of the front row; Prof. J.H. Morgan (in a jacket) stands in the back; and the man in a bow tie in the right background is Curtis Dewberry.

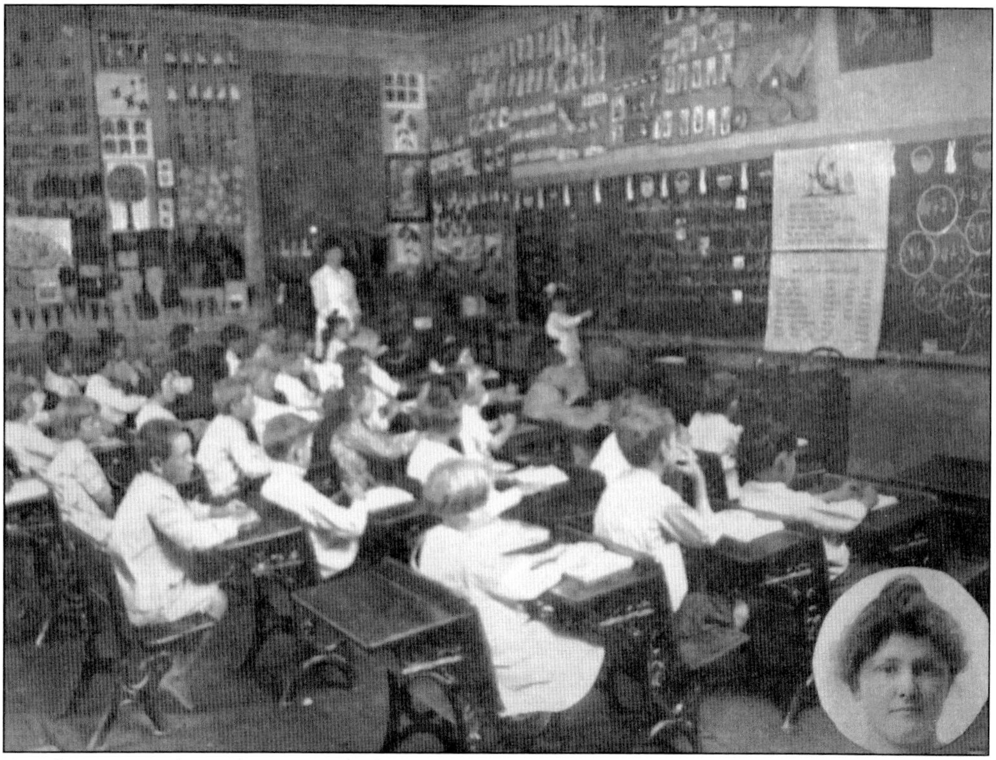

An elementary class is being taught by Lucy Hart (inset) in 1915. The room at the public school displays colorful student exhibits and projects. These desks were used for several generations.

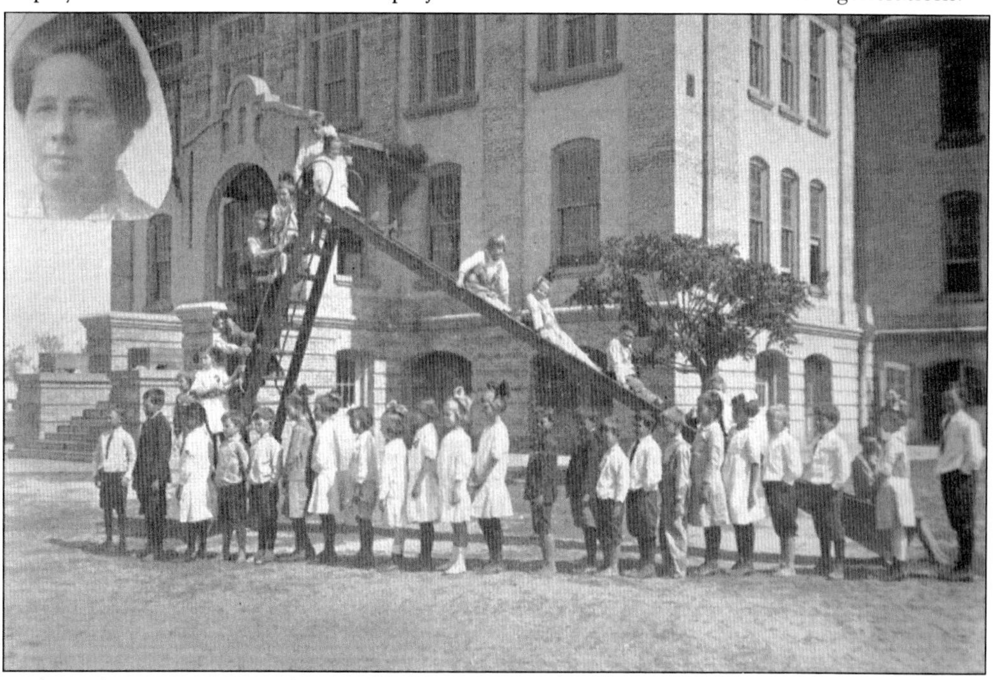

In the early 1920s, a group of second-grade children enjoys recess on the sliding board in front of the first brick public school in Eagle Lake. The teacher (pictured in inset) is Mattie Nerselder.

As more consolidation occurred within the Eagle Lake Public School, additional students came from the countryside and from one-room schoolhouses, including Ramsey and Prairie Center. Some children stayed with families, and some boarded in town to attend school, returning to their homes on weekends. A school bus was authorized for the Chesterville children in 1927. In 1938, the bus was sent to Altair Road and, around 1947, to Matthews and Calhoun, as the rural schools became displaced by the public school.

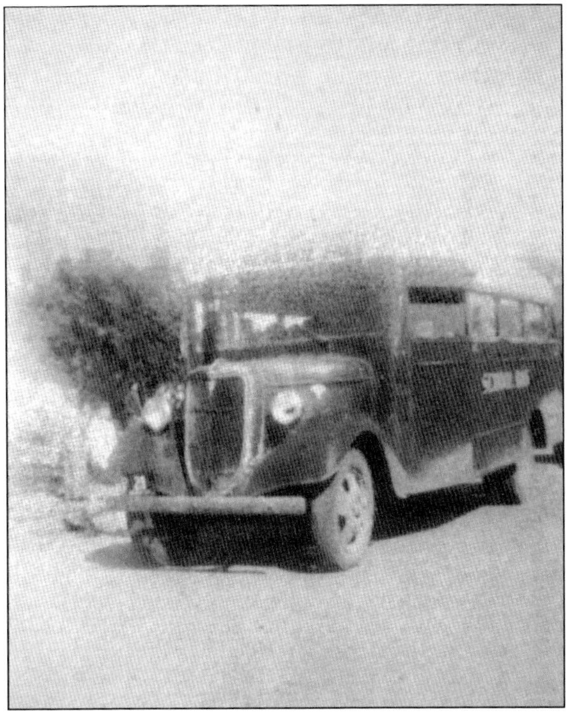

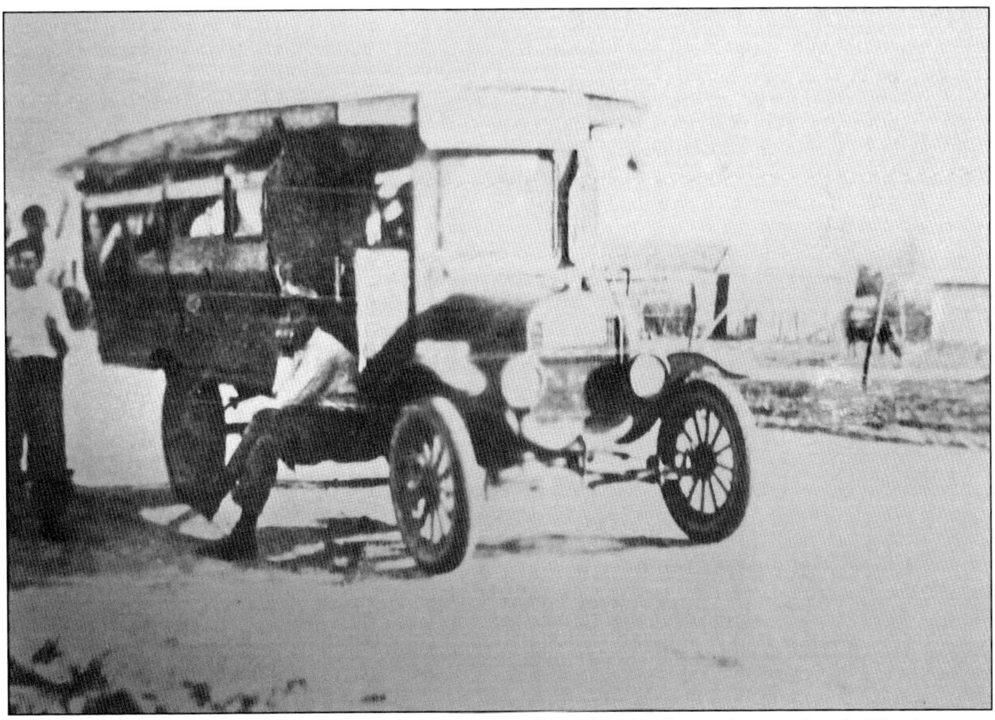

Max Conner (driver) and several students await others for the bus ride to school. The bus was important transportation for students on the outskirts of town and in rural areas, especially during inclement weather. A bus was later sent for children in Chesterville, Ramsey, Matthews, and Lissie.

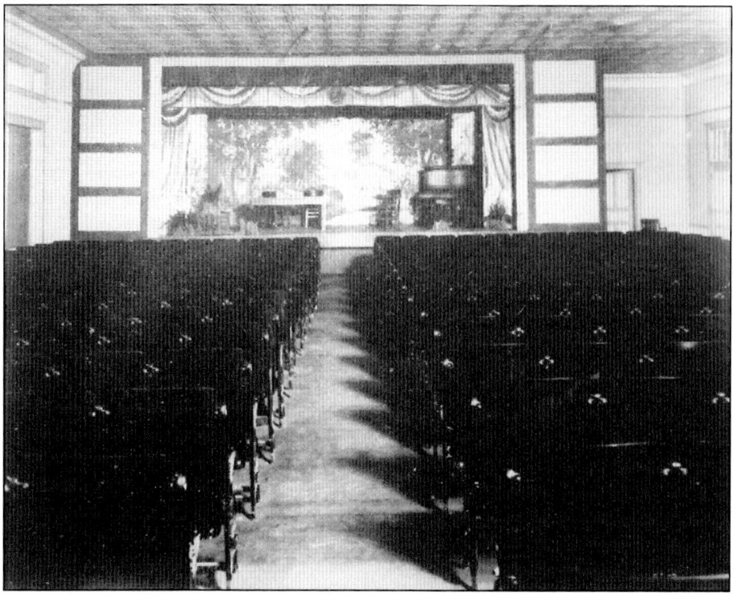

The school auditorium was used for assemblies, concerts, plays, and community events. The school orchestra performed here on many occasions, and the choral group, with almost 50 singers, produced concerts and musical events. Dance recitals, lectures, visiting programs, and public events were also held in the auditorium, which became a community cultural center.

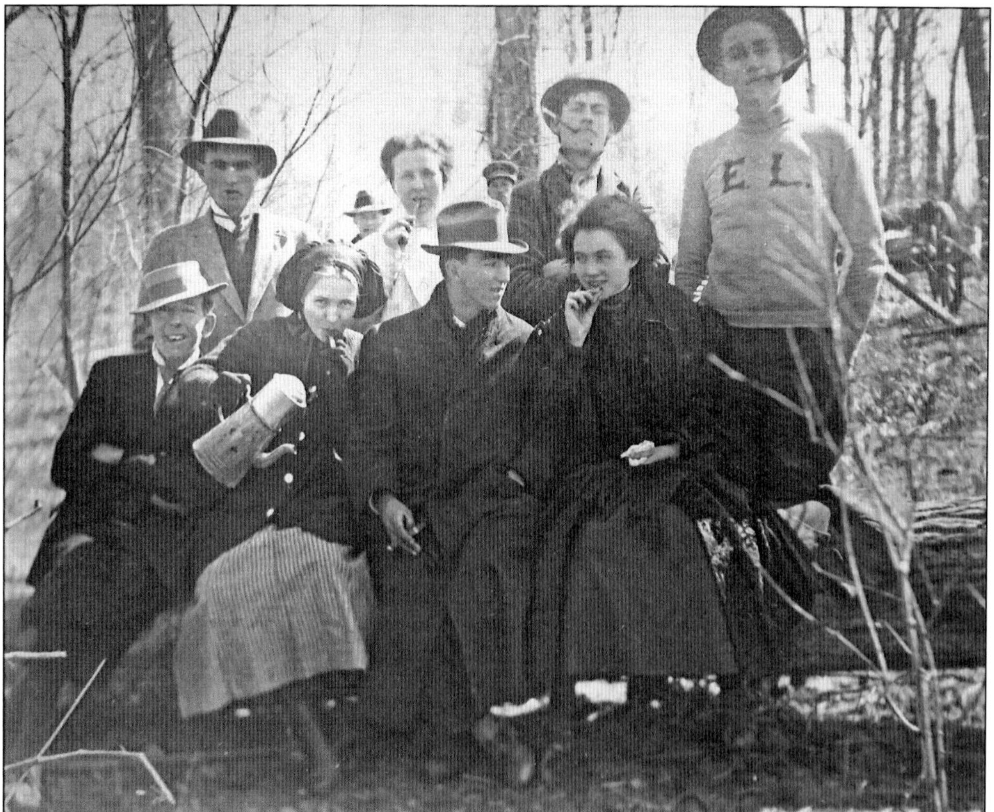

Eagle Lake students, along with their teacher, enjoy a wintertime country outing as a respite from their classroom studies. In this photograph are, from left to right, (first row) Dyer Holmes, Josephine Thatcher, Carl Pross, and Ruth Welch; (second row) L. Abbey, Miss Harrington, Ben Faber, and Ernest Salwig.

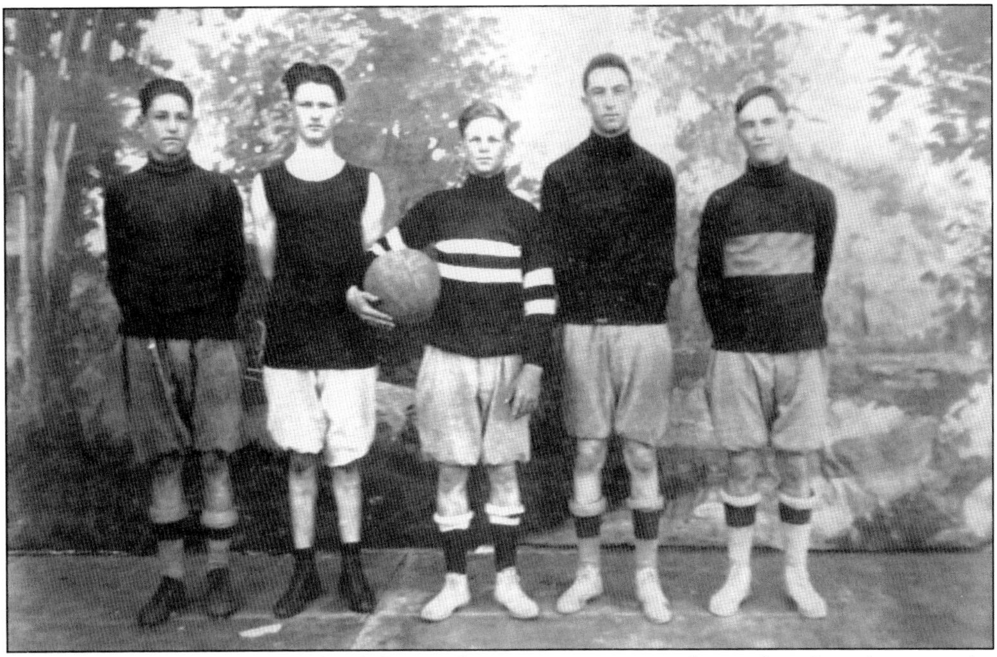

Sports were popular at the school, but with no gymnasium, students played outdoors on the campus grounds. The 1916 boys' basketball team included, from left to right, Arch Cearnal, W. Malcolm Williamson, Hervin W. Nussbaum, Howard Fitzgerald, and Ben Hanly. Verner Matthews is not pictured.

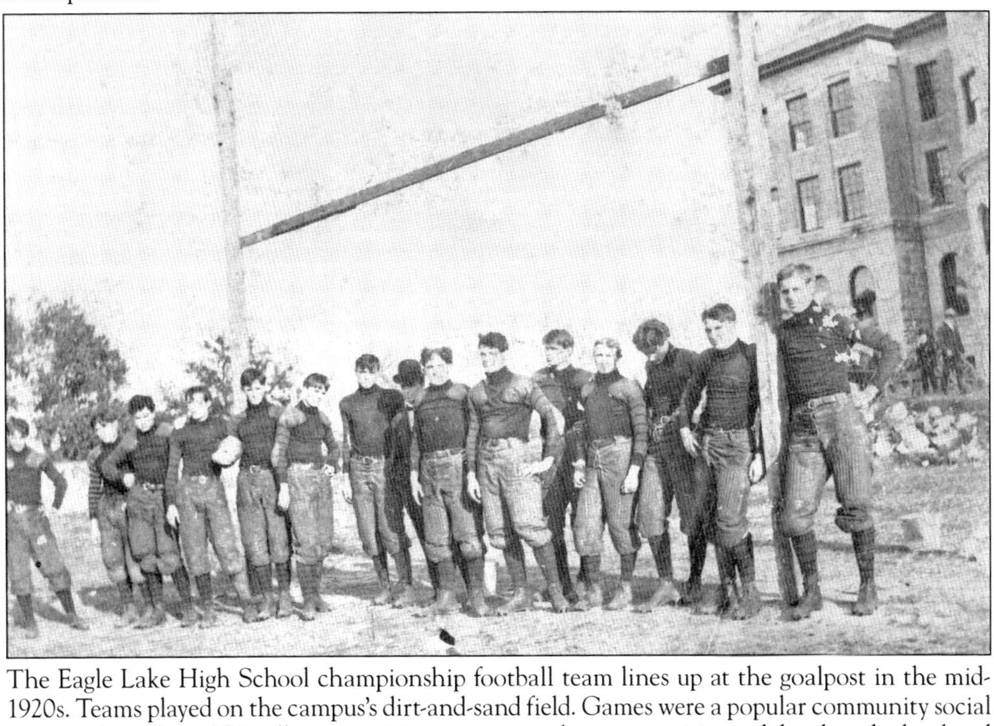

The Eagle Lake High School championship football team lines up at the goalpost in the mid-1920s. Teams played on the campus's dirt-and-sand field. Games were a popular community social activity that allowed friendly competition among nearby communities and developed school and town pride. Eagle Lake's first football team was organized in 1914.

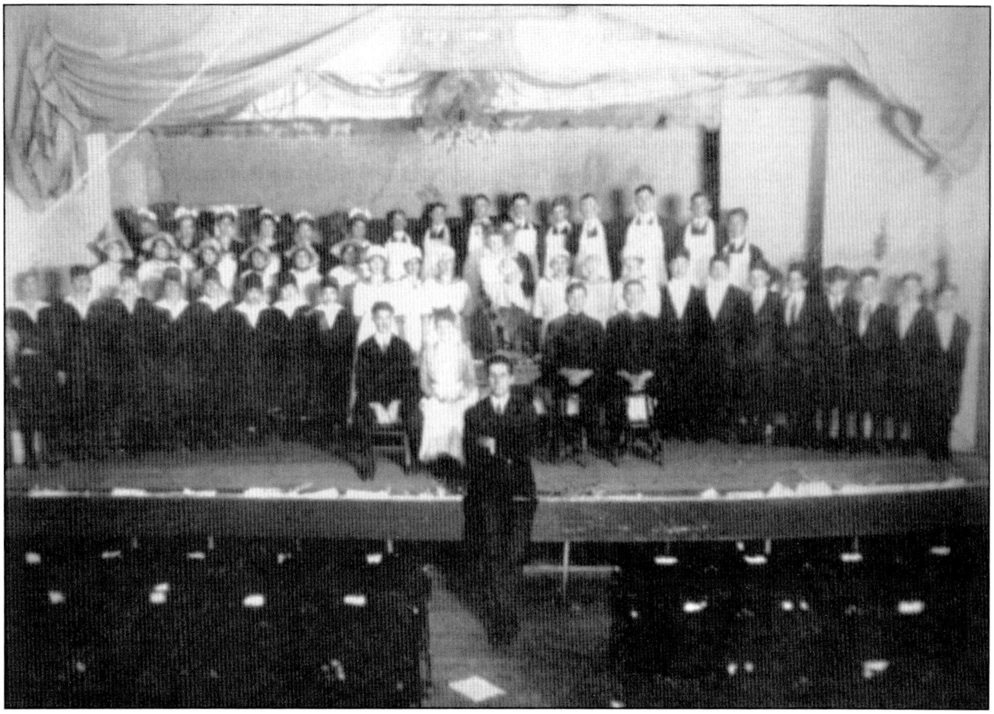

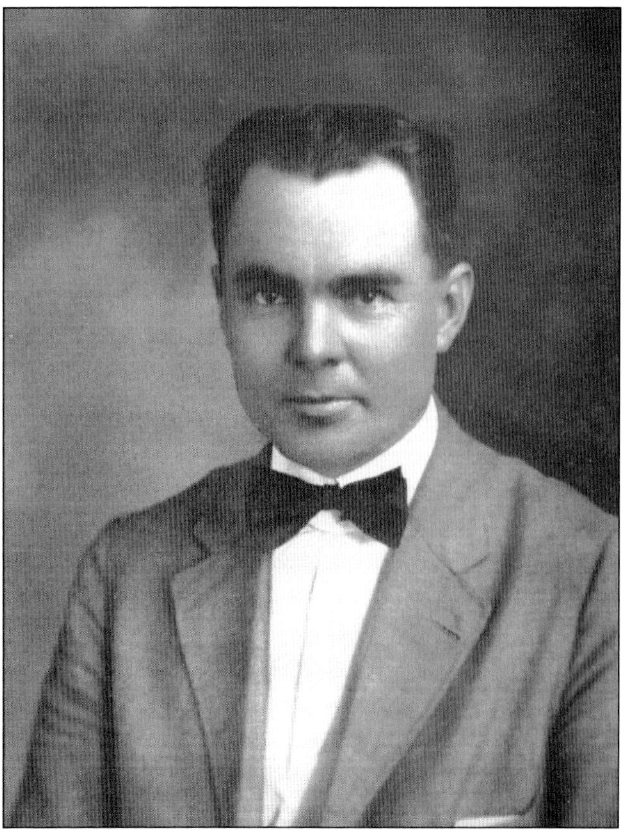

In June 1911, Prof. J.H. Morgan came from Falfurrias, Texas, to become superintendent of the Eagle Lake Public School, where he served until 1926, when he became superintendent of schools in Cisco, Texas. His wife was an assistant teacher, and Morgan taught many classes himself. He oversaw the building of the new redbrick school—which was equipped with large classrooms, science labs, and a modern auditorium (pictured above)—in 1924–1925.

Prof. W.C. Reed came to Eagle Lake in the fall of 1926 to replace J.H. Morgan as superintendent, a job he kept for 25 years. He was affectionately known as "Professor Bear Reed." His wife, Olive, was a teacher. Professor Reed, an active citizen, educational leader, and Rotarian, oversaw many new developments at the school.

Prof. E.H. Henry was an outstanding educator and community leader who served the Eagle Lake School System for 26 years. He led fundraising for the purchase of the school's 3.5-acre site and acquired a $7,000 grant from the Julius Rosenwald Fund in 1930 for building the E.H. Henry High School, Eagle Lake's first African American high school, which began as a five-room brick building. Henry was born in Flatonia in 1894, was a second lieutenant in the US Army in World War I, and attended Prairie View State Normal & Industrial College (now Prairie View A&M University) and Howard University. He retired in Elm Grove, where he lived until his death in 1983.

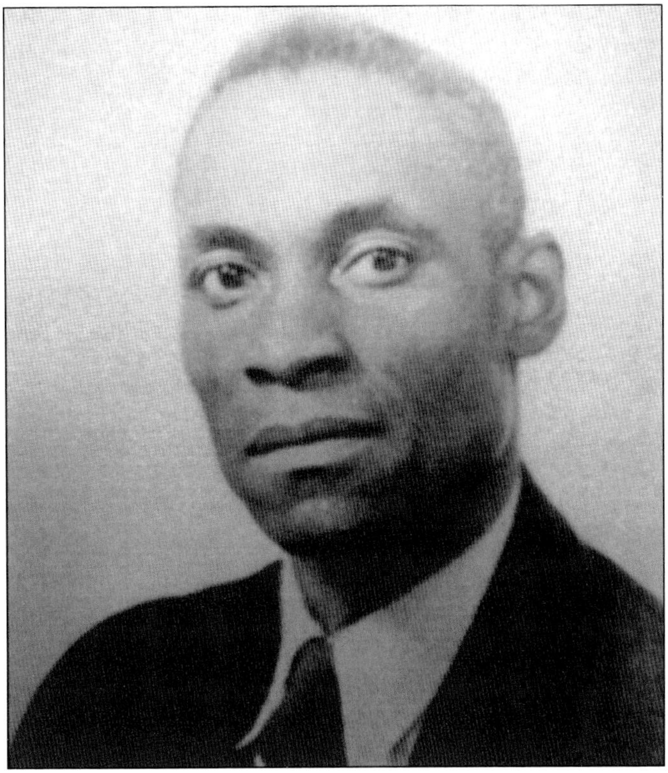

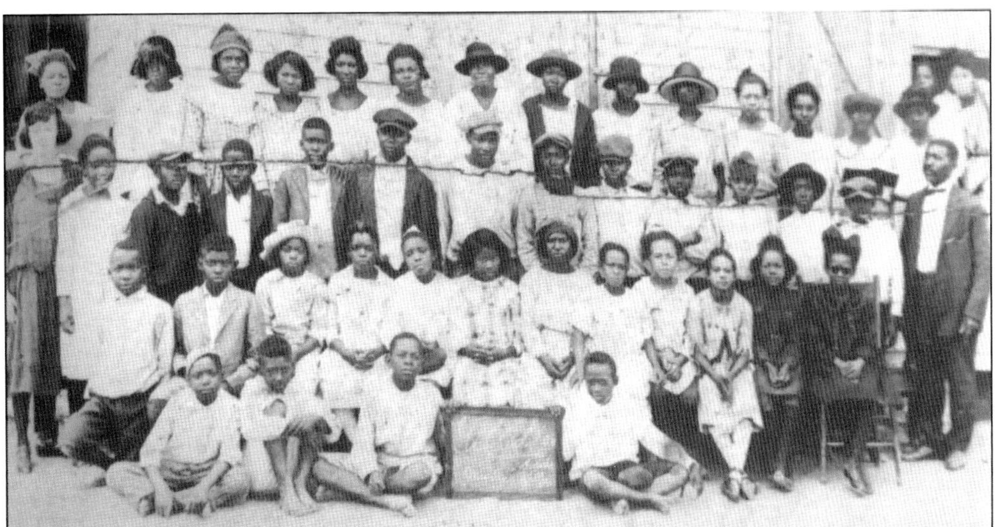

The first school for African American children was located on Main Street in a room on the first floor of the old United Brotherhood of Friendship (UBF) Hall. The school was later relocated to C Street, in "the flat." Will Spencer Chavis was a trustee of the school, and G.J. Perrino (far right, in coat and tie) was a teacher and principal; Perrino's wife was also a teacher.

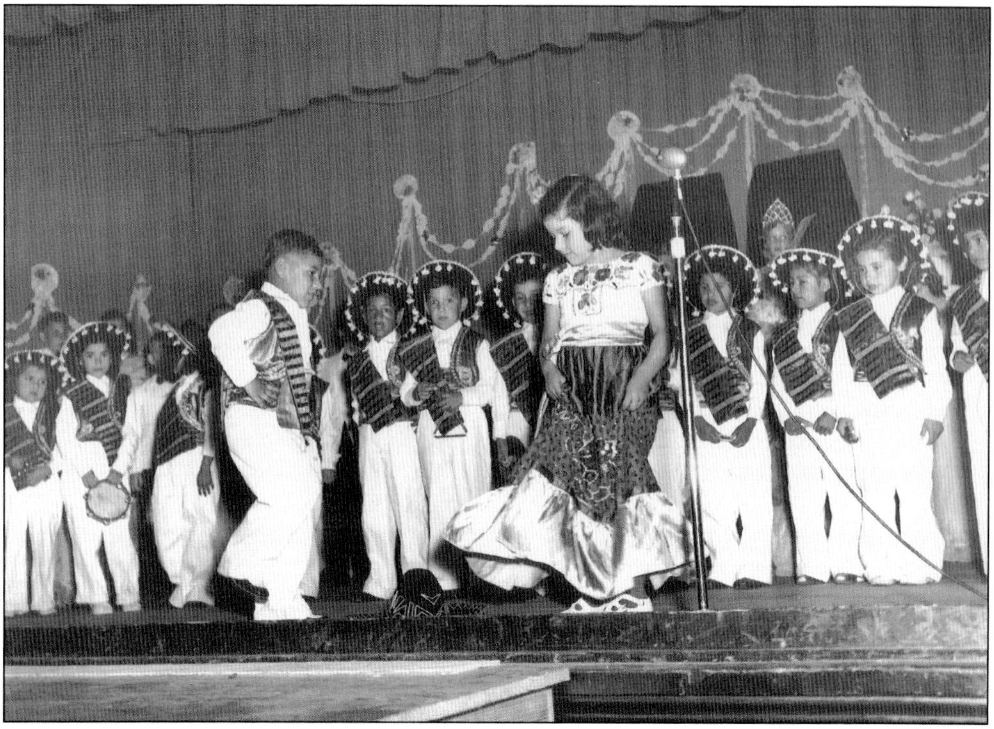

In the 1920s, there were about 50 Hispanic families in Eagle Lake. The first local Mexican Independence celebration was held on September 15 and 16 in 1924. In 1925, a special teacher was hired to teach English to Mexican children, and a school for Hispanic children was maintained on E Street from 1928 until 1948, when Mexican students began to enroll in the Eagle Lake Public School. Here, Mexican students perform at the PTA Country Fair in 1948.

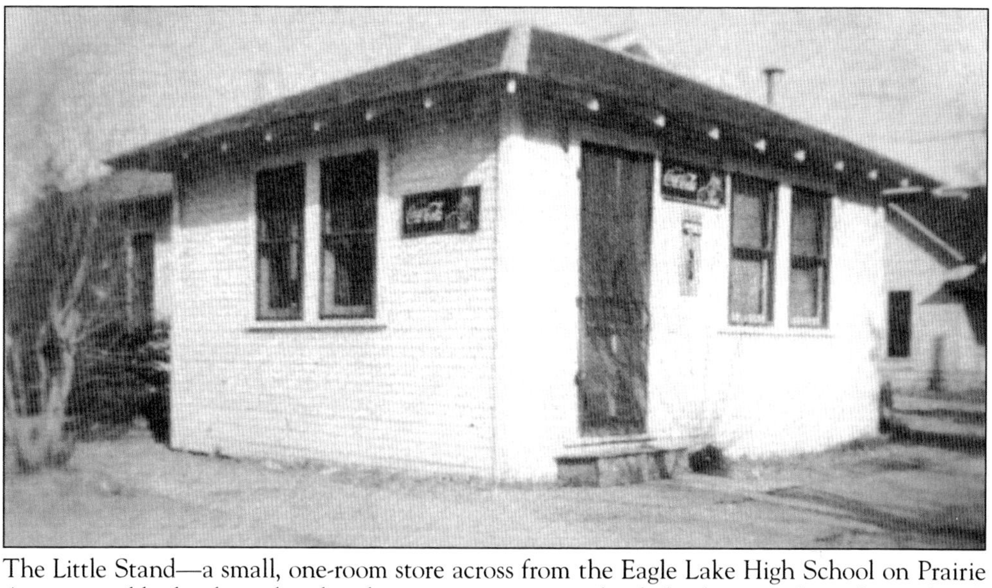

The Little Stand—a small, one-room store across from the Eagle Lake High School on Prairie Avenue—sold school supplies, hamburgers, ice cream, and soft drinks to students during lunch breaks. It was opened by Caroline S. Hart in April 1928 and was known as "Mrs. Hart's Store" until July 1940, when Mrs. H.T. Neiswender bought it; she operated the store until the 1950s.

William "Bill" Wallace (1912–1993) was an outstanding football player at Eagle Lake High School. In 1934, Eagle Lake honored Wallace with a dinner given by the Rotary Club that attracted over 200 people. Wallace was also an acclaimed sprinter and hurdler in track. He was a famed ball-carrier, passer, and punter. He played at Rice Institute from 1932 to 1935 and was included in Rice Institute's initial All-American selection. Wallace was inducted into the College Football Hall of Fame in 1978 and the Texas Sports Hall of Fame in 1985.

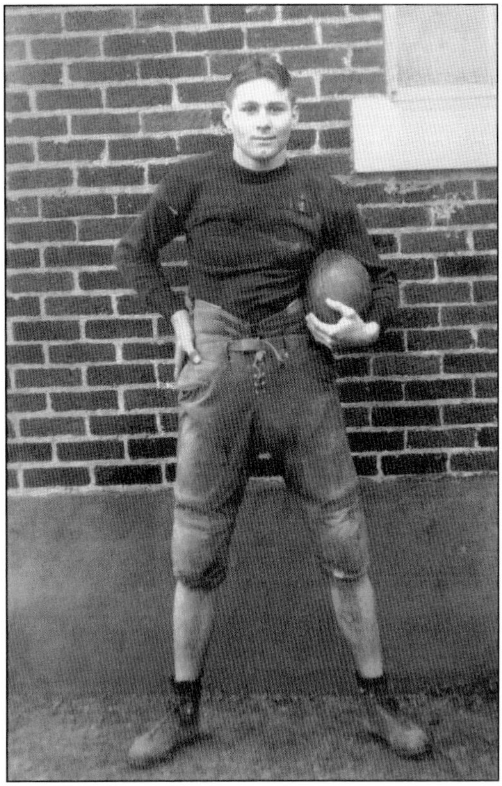

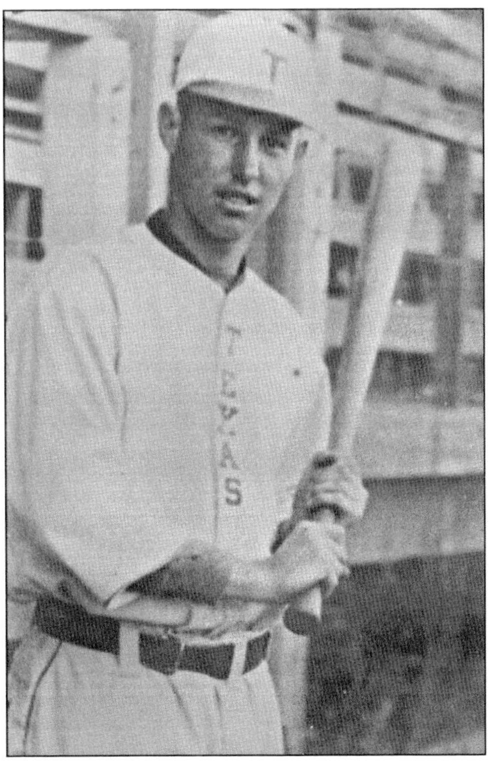

Howard Chumney Fitzgerald (1902–1959), the son of Dr. Howard and Ruby Fitzgerald, was an outstanding baseball player in Eagle Lake and at the University of Texas and played in the major and minor leagues. He was an outfielder for the Chicago Cubs from 1922 to 1924, and played with the Boston Red Sox from 1924 to 1926. Fitzgerald batted and threw left-handed. His baseball career ended in 1939. He returned to Eagle Lake, set up a business, and had farming interests in Matthews.

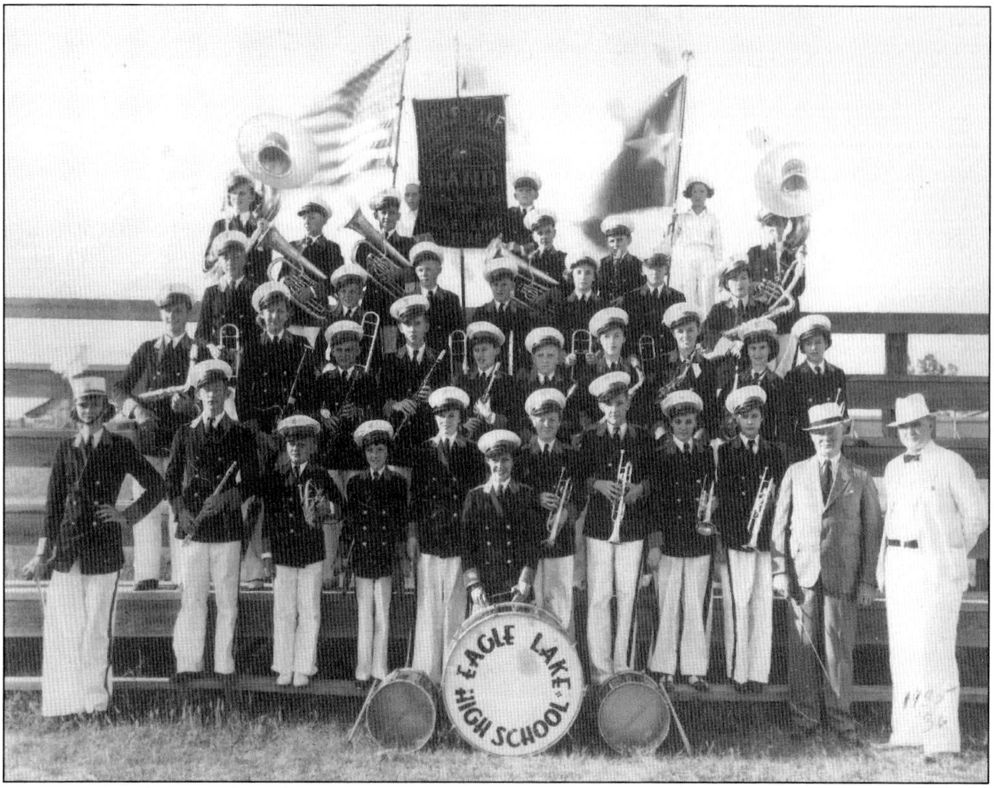

In 1935, the first Eagle Lake High School Band, organized with 25 members, made its first appearance with director A.L. Lundgren. This photograph shows the band in 1937, with Lundgren and superintendent W.C. Reed (in white suit) at right. The band played at school, sports, and community events.

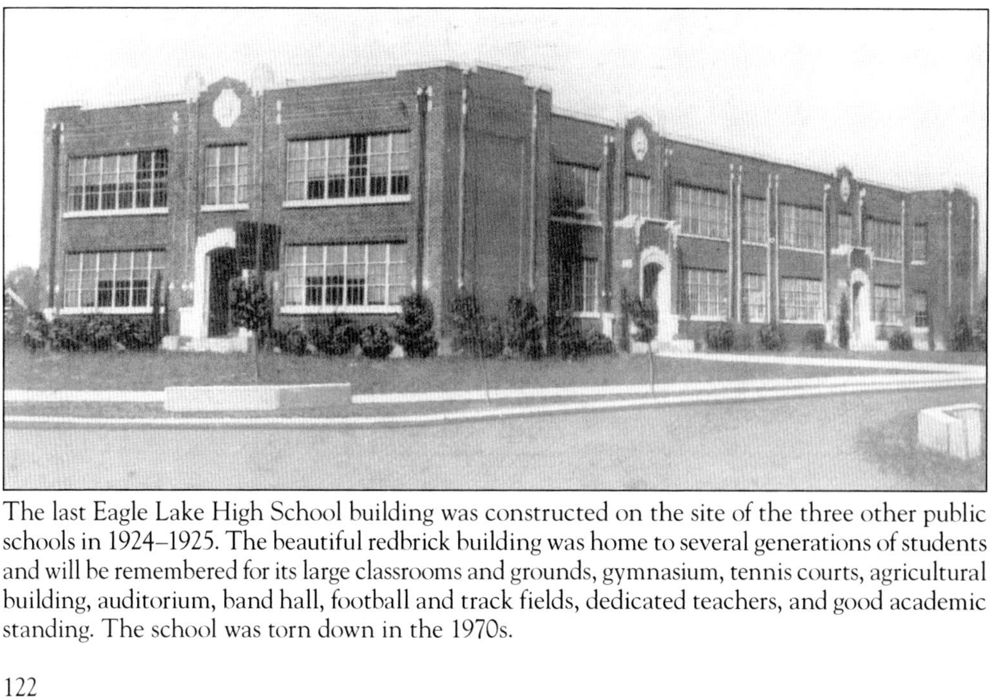

The last Eagle Lake High School building was constructed on the site of the three other public schools in 1924–1925. The beautiful redbrick building was home to several generations of students and will be remembered for its large classrooms and grounds, gymnasium, tennis courts, agricultural building, auditorium, band hall, football and track fields, dedicated teachers, and good academic standing. The school was torn down in the 1970s.

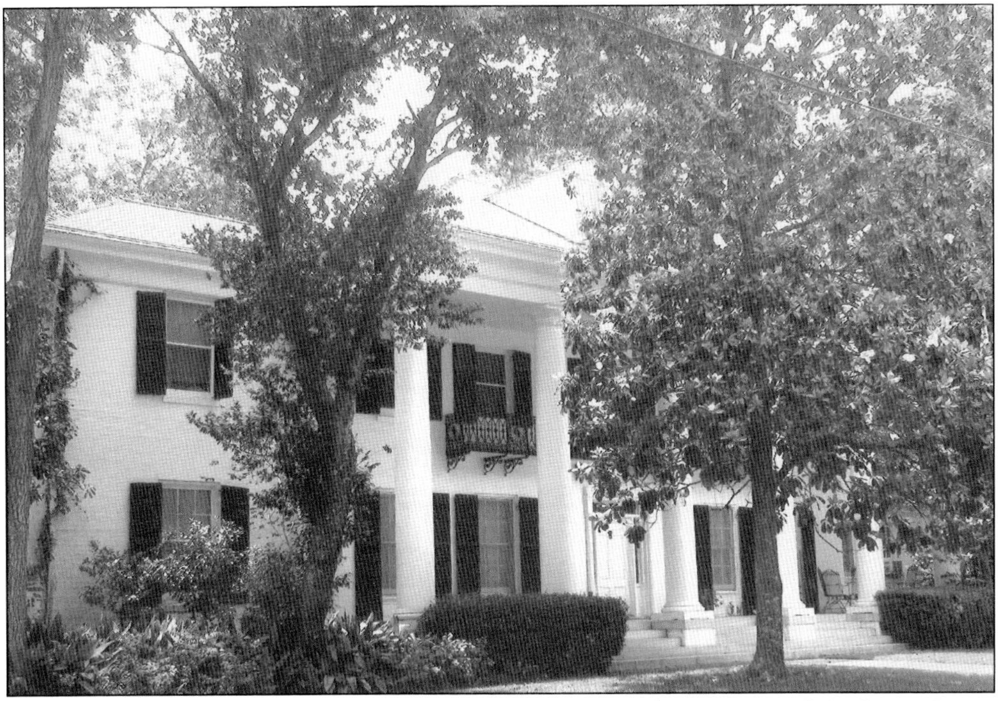

The Hayes Stephens home on State Street was built in 1937 by contractor R.H. Reese. It was among the most beautiful homes in the state.

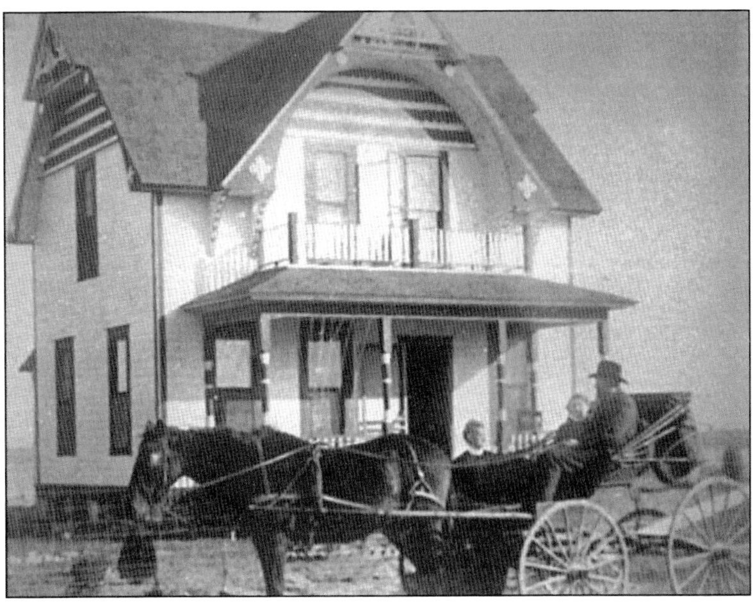

Built in 1908, the Isenhower residence was a Sears, Roebuck Home—one of three in Lissie—ordered by catalog and shipped for assembly. Between 1908 and 1940, Sears, Roebuck issued a catalog to sell home kits that included materials and plans, which were usually shipped by rail. The materials for this house arrived at the Lissie train station in 1908.

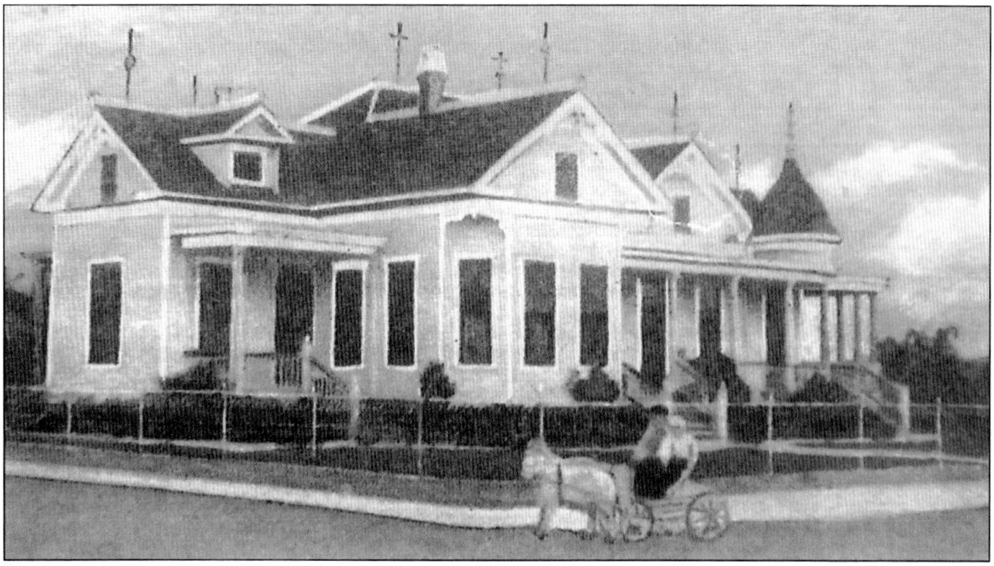

The large A.C. McClanahan home on Prairie Avenue was built in 1912. McClanahan was a prominent businessman, president of the McClanahan Lumber Company, and a director of the Eagle Lake State Bank. The original one-story house (pictured), built in 1907, was moved to a lot next door so that his new two-story home could be constructed on the corner lot.

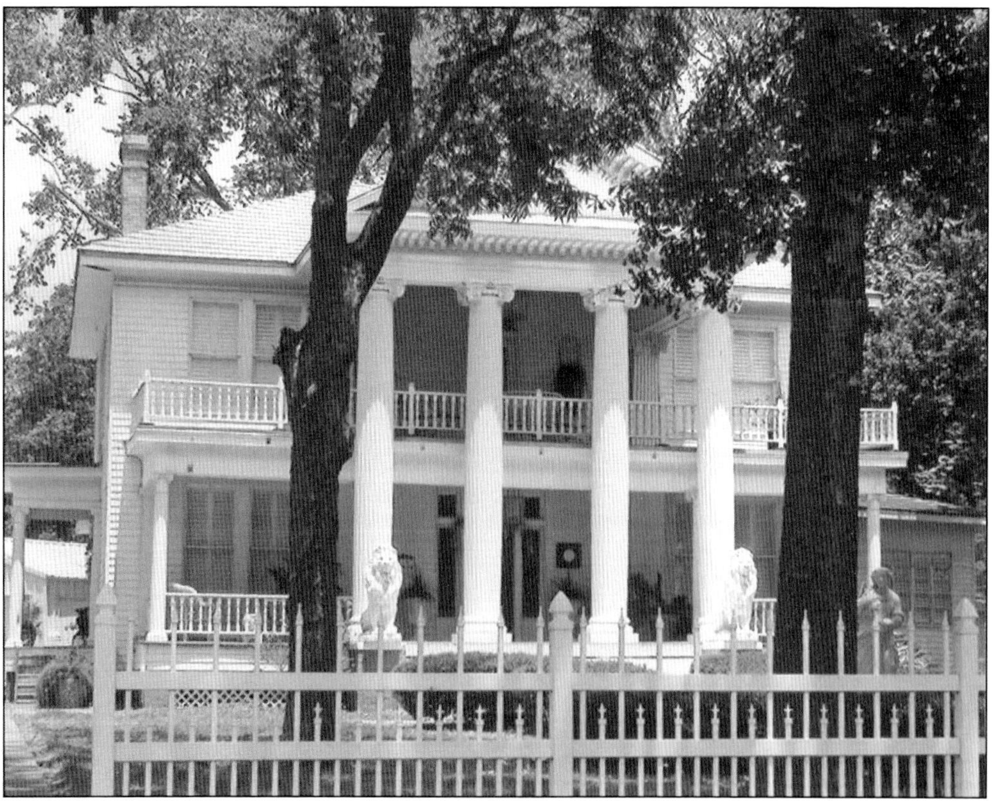

The McCarty home on Stockbridge Street was built in 1911 by Capt. James William McCarty, the first mayor of Eagle Lake.

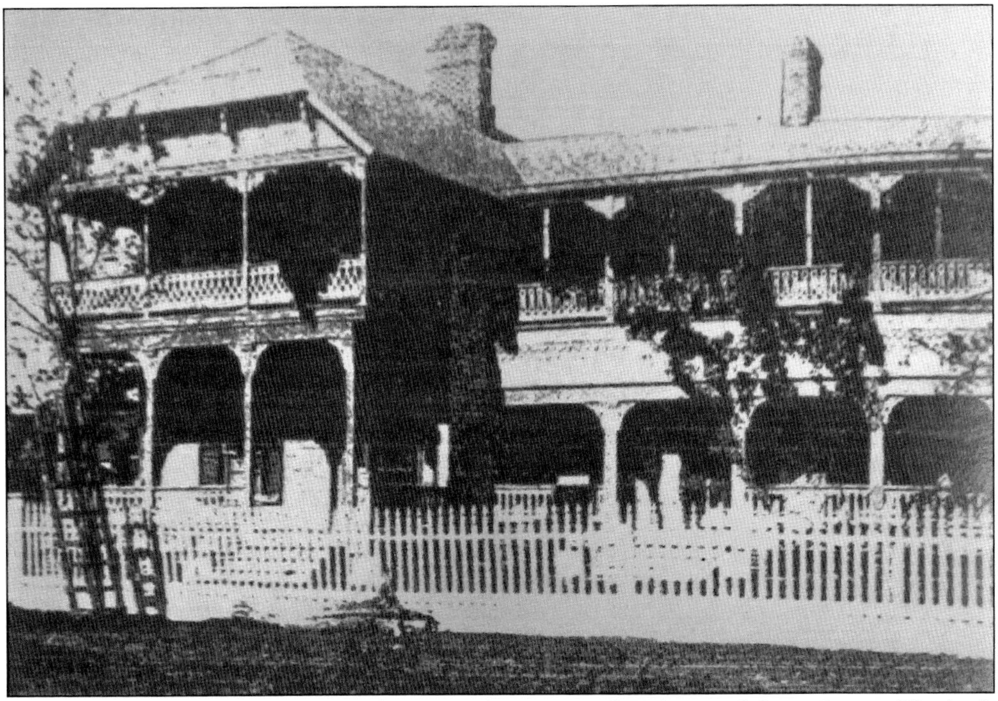

The Frazar sisters owned this large home on the corner of Walnut and State Streets. Elizabeth (1840–1923) and Julia (1850–1912) were two of seven children of lawyer/farmer Micajah Frazar. The sisters lived in the house until they died. It was built around the beginning of the 20th century and was torn down in the 1920s.

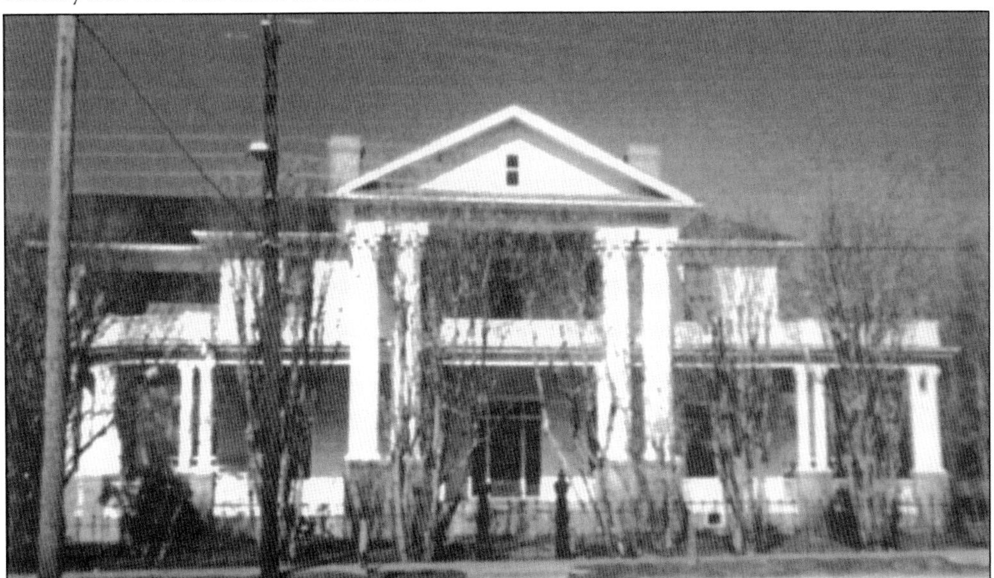

The Haynie Matthews home is an imposing structure. The Matthewses were among the earliest settlers in the area. They ran a mercantile store and shipped abundant cotton from the large plantation, located near the community of Matthews, where they lived until 1913, when they moved into this home on North Walnut Street in Eagle Lake.

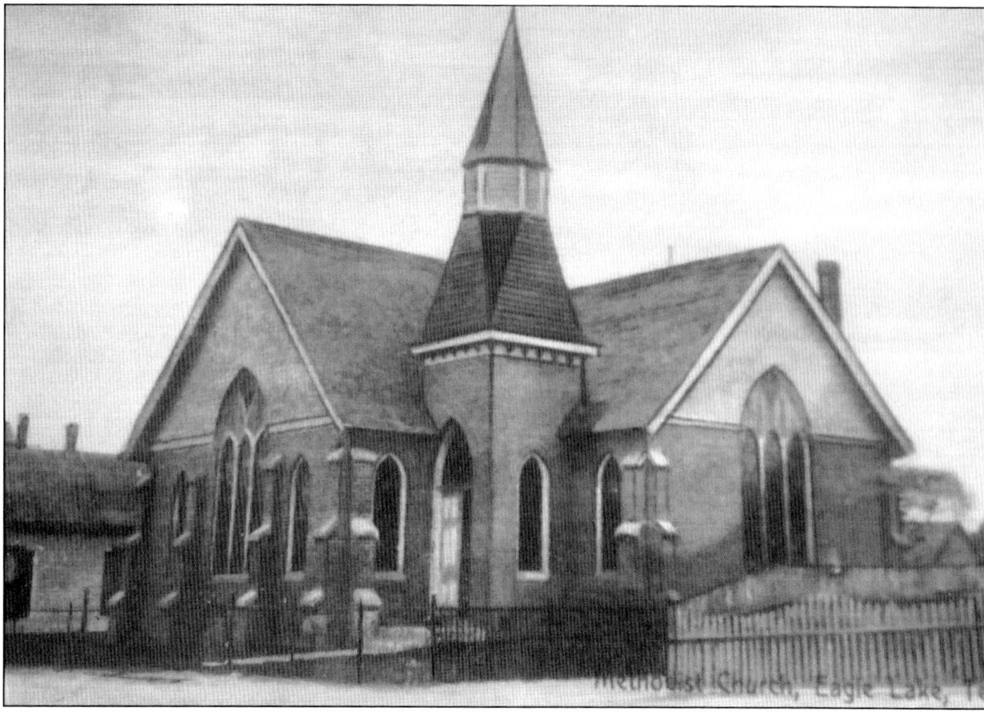

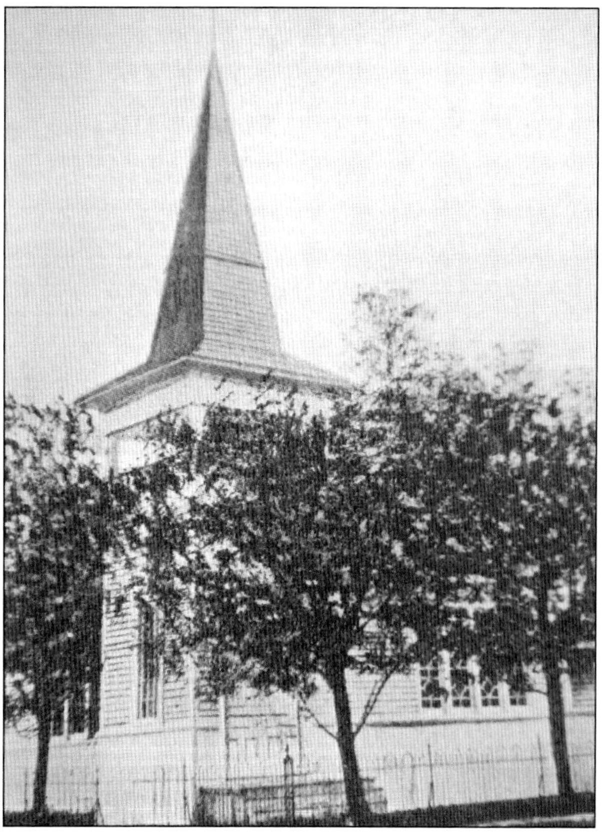

In 1872, a one-room schoolhouse served as the first church meetinghouse. The Methodists, the oldest Protestant congregation in the community, met there until 1880, when Union Church was constructed to house the Methodist, Baptist, Episcopal, and Christian congregations. In 1899, the brick Methodist Episcopal Church South was built by the Methodist congregation on Lake Street, near the Episcopal church and behind the Hayes Stephens home.

The Christian church was constructed in 1888 and later became an Assembly of God church. It first held meetings in the old Union Church along with the Methodists, Baptists, and Episcopalians and held its Sunday school in the afternoons. Capt. James W. McCarty was an early church superintendent. The original church is still standing.

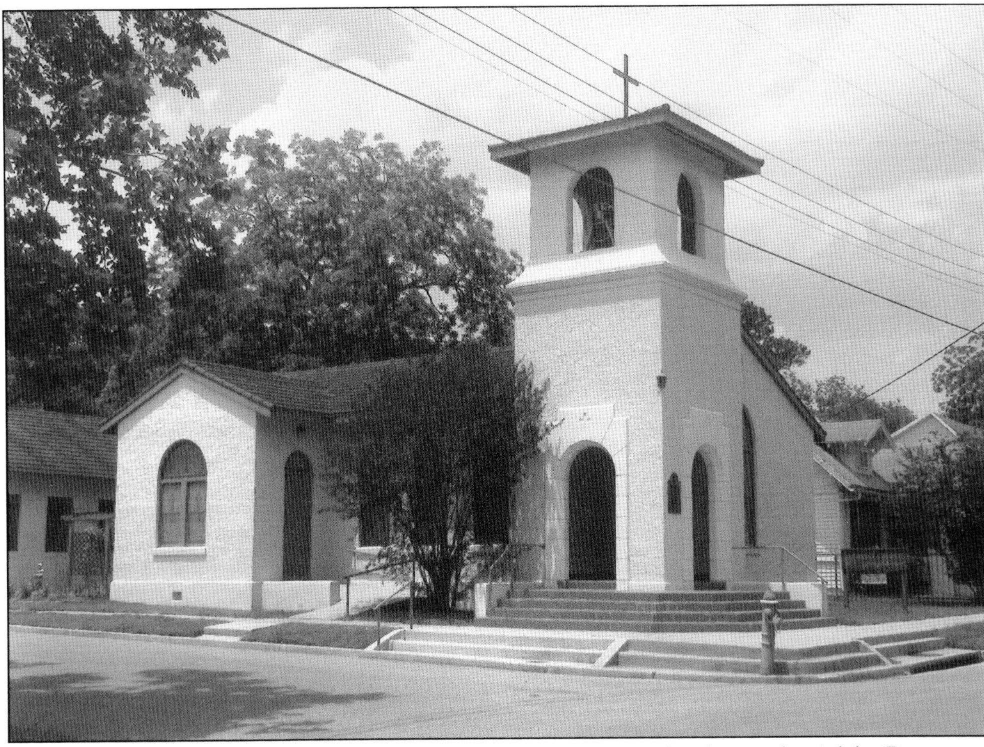

The first Episcopal church was built in 1885 on Main Street on land given by Adelia Dunovant, sister of Capt. William Dunovant. It was rebuilt in 1903 at its current location—at Lake and Stockbridge Streets—but was destroyed by fire in 1925. The current Spanish Mission–style building was completed in 1926.

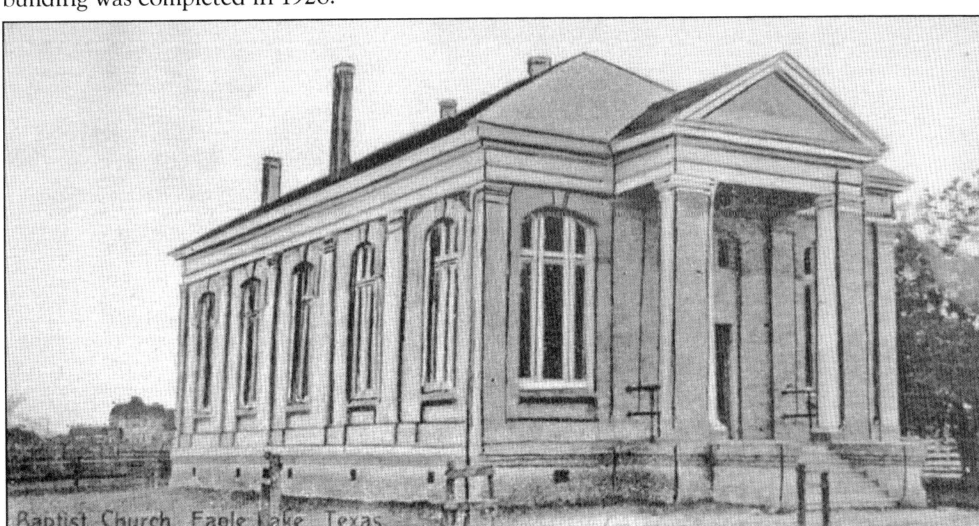

The Baptist church was organized in 1875 and held services in various buildings until 1888, when the congregation erected its first building on Church Street for $1,500; the frame structure was blown down by the Great Storm of 1900. A brick building (shown here) was constructed in 1907. It was replaced in 1927 by a larger church, which was used for 29 years. In 1956, a new building was dedicated on Prairie Street.